The Theology of Dracula

The Theology of Dracula

Reading the Book of Stoker as Sacred Text

Noël Montague-Étienne Rarignac

McFarland & Company, Inc., Publishers
Jefferson, North Carolina, and London

Library of Congress Cataloguing-in-Publication Data

Rarignac, Noël Montague-Étienne.
The theology of Dracula : reading the book of Stoker as sacred text / Noël Montague-Étienne Rarignac.
p. cm.
Includes bibliographical references and index.

ISBN 978-0-7864-6499-9
softcover : acid free paper ∞

1. Stoker, Bram, 1847–1912. Dracula. 2. Christianity in literature. 3. Horror tales, English — History and criticism. 4. Dracula, Count (Fictitious character) 5. Vampires in literature. I. Title.
PR6037.T617D7864 2012
823'.8 — dc23 2011051316

British Library cataloguing data are available

Front cover design by David K. Landis (Shake It Loose Graphics)

Manufactured in the United States of America

McFarland & Company, Inc., Publishers
Box 611, Jefferson, North Carolina 28640
www.mcfarlandpub.com

Table of Contents

Acknowledgments

This is to recognize the generous contribution made to this project by Professor Mark M. Hennelly, Jr., who took time to read and comment on four or five first draft chapters of someone he has never met. Having come across his essay "*Dracula*: The Gnostic Quest and Victorian Wasteland," I sought Mark out as the only critic to have approached Stoker's text in ways that were familiar to me. Certain paragraphs of the book were written in direct answer to his probing questions ("What do you mean by sacred?") regarding my own conclusions. Thanks is also due to Dr. Massimo Introvigne of the Centre for the Study of New Religions (CENSUR) in Turin for his willingness to read and comment on sections of a book being written by an absolute stranger. The generosity of these scholars deserves acknowledgment and this expression of my gratitude.

I am also grateful for the assistance of many dedicated librarians, particularly the staff of the Bibliothèque Gaston Baty, Paris, the Bibliothèque de l'Arsenal, Paris; the Bibliothèque de Chalons-sur-Marne, Chalons-sur-Marne, and the special collections department of the John Rylands Library, Manchester, England. I would like to thank my old friend Jacques Aumont for his belief in what analysis can accomplish and his embrace of the descriptive act; M. le Comte d'Haussonville and Esther Duran, administrative director of the Château de Coppet; the Frères et Soeurs de Jerusalem au Mont-Saint-Michel; Isabelle Grasswill and the staff of the Monuments nationaux de France; and Lizzie Calligas and her band of friends at the Cyceon in Elefsina who were so kind and helpful to me as I walked the Sacred Way.

Preface

Largely drafted during the late spring and early summer of 2010, the chapters of this book quickly followed each other into existence. While some sustained hard thinking went into the effort, an unstanchable flow sourced in Stoker's novel carried the project forward, new chapters appearing every second or third week. An informed belief that *Dracula* might be a sacred text, derived from a study of earlier iterations of the Vampire Tale, provided irresistible impetus; the ways in which the novel *is* a spiritual meditation carried the project forward to completion, leaving its author awed by the depth of the work Stoker bequeathed to posterity and by its cleverness and conceptual beauty.

While medical researchers doggedly pursue the study of deadly pathologies without ever being suspected of being enthusiasts of disease, within the domains of letters, arts, and humanities there is an assumption that some kind of pre-existing passion for a subject must be present to drive the researcher, that scholars pursue only those subjects for which they feel a particular affinity, that somehow the researcher's leisure interests and professional activities align. This is not necessarily true, since it is not the case here. No inexplicable attraction to the sanguine, no predilection for superstition, no dedication to the Vampire as a Romantic figure nor fervent fan's love of fantasy and horror motivated this exercise.

My initial interest in the Vampire is attributable to a disquieted curiosity about the increasing prevalence of deliberately grotesque cultural objects that slowly but surely are filling the world, objects that seem to emanate from some cultural plasma out of which forgotten totems, gods, and mythologies recombine into icons of virtual beliefs seemingly handed down to us by ancestors not our own. At a time when practices of self-mutilation, fetishism, and degradation flourish, fantasy is given precedent over practical and prudent behavior, and the virtual interpenetrates the real, the grotesque is our lingua franca. Through fiction, film, video games, pixilated avatars, and extruded-resin statuettes the grotesque exists to challenge our evolving global community and its predicates, expressing itself primarily as an often-reiterated question: If the aesthetic object presupposes and projects its natural receptor — from materials and production techniques to symbolic language and encoded discourse — is contemporary cultural production suggesting that, subordinated to a tradition-displacing, commercial cult of the grotesque, humanity has become horrifying to itself?

If no pathology, the grotesque constitutes a phenomenon worthy of examination. Following Edmund Burke's mid–eighteenth century codification of our ideas on the beautiful and the sublime as complementarily charged elements of a dynamic system, a modern poetics has emerged in which the grotesque vies with beauty as art's object. Congealing through emergent genres, forms, and media concurrent to a period of successive and interrelated transformations so intense as to be termed "revolutions" — rapid demographic shift (urbanization), equally radical changes in prevailing modes of production/distribution of goods (industrialization, development of transportation and communication networks) and social organization (democratization, secularization) — the anti–beauty paradigm transported the West from the agrarianism that had endured since the late Neolithic era to the mechanized mercantile societies that began to take form over the eighteenth and nineteenth centuries. In this dawn of the industrial, twilight of the agrarian, the grotesque attained the increasingly dominant position it has maintained ever since, to begin extending its influence beyond the decorative or peripheral to permeate — from underlying structures to overarching themes — entire artworks and modes of creation. The grotesque became its own subject, object, and creative process.

Parallel to technological, political, and aesthetic displacements, the processes through which cultural objects became socially enfranchised underwent a polar shift as well: Instead of integrating alien symbols through transformative accommodation and recontextualization as traditional cultures had, our post-revolutionary hegemonic culture began to appropriate symbols through assimilative desacralization, decontextualization, and fragmentation, the grotesque often being produced through the promiscuous mating of the sacred and the vulgar, the archaic and the modern, the mythic and the commercial. If this tendency began by a Romantic turn towards orientalism, familiar titles *Tomb Raiders, Dungeons and Dragons, Harry Potter, Indiana Jones: Raiders of the Lost Ark*, and *Forsaken Gods* suggest the penetration of the cultural mainstream this creative process of sacrilegious coupling has more recently enjoyed.

The English Gothic and related "paraliteratures," unwearying carriers of the grotesque's poetic virus, helped found what Victor Hugo termed "The Third Epoch of Poetry" — our own era — during which the grotesque has become coequal to and dominant over beauty as art's subject and object. A lively, worldly aesthetic, no longer subservient to notions of the sacred and classic, the grotesque's premier iconoclastic, confrontational, and enduring genre was Horror; its primordial emblematic antihero, the Vampire. Yet if horror arose with and out of the death of the sacred, it seems that its continuation could not have been assured without the sacred's ghost, for, surprisingly, horror as perpetuated by the Vampire repeatedly serves to reframe myth.

In my book *Dionysus Unmasked*, being prepared for publication, I maintain that within the Vampire Tale dwells a Neoplatonist allegory, developed from Thomas Taylor's understanding of Eleusinian rites, whose Neolithic roots entwine a mythological nexus focused on an agrarian order's preoccupation: the tension between light and dark. The cyclical interplay between those opposing values drives all the great vampire texts to be produced over the succeeding centuries. The Vampire appears as a refugee from earlier ages and revisits the rise of the dying-god, a corollary to the development of metallic tools and agriculture, and his cosmetic attainment of supremacy over bloodthirsty fertility goddesses in order to inform cosmic rites of renewal. Contrasting markedly with other creations of Gothic horror, the Vampire permits, indeed propounds and perpetuates, a sacred discourse. Although the lessons that can be abstracted from the Vampire to inform the grotesque are not the topic of this book, it does seem that the Vampire suggests that the grotesque speaks to a spiritual unease and general alienation from society and ourselves. Remarkably, the Vampire prescribes a spiritual remedy, and it is within this context that *Dracula*—as aesthetic emblem and synthesizing paragon of earlier vampire texts—was approached.

Upon its creation, the English-speaking world critically dismissed the Vampire Tale as abhorrent, grotesque, even as its genius was being hailed on the Continent by the likes of Johann Goethe and Charles Nodier. Continental romantics welcomed the Vampire and rapidly assimilated it into new and evolving forms. The internationalization of the grotesque gained great impetus through Nodier's insertion of the Vampire into the still developing form of melodrama—creating a radical variant that not only placed a Manichean universe in suspenseful imbalance, but plunged its divided protagonist into a metaphysical conflict pitting body against soul. In transforming melodrama, the Vampire's content projected form. The Vampire has since proved to be a peerless generator of grotesque formal developments and a singular motor for producing modernity and unique ability to spawn new poetic vehicles has not yet been exhausted.

Stoker's Victorian novel, though separated from the literary Gothic by any close historic standard, insists on allying itself in subject matter and style with the Gothic—echoes of Emily St. Aubert's coach ride to Udolpho being heard at once in Jonathan Harker's journal—and most closely with its horror phase. As with earlier vampire texts, *Dracula* was for a long period deplored or ignored by academics, until, that is, the critical establishment actively came to embrace the grotesque. During the latter decades of the twentieth century, after a long winter of critical dormancy, *Dracula* became a cherished object and subject of intense interest. Unsurprisingly, the literature to coalesce around the novel tended to reflect the concerns of contemporary cultural theory. While I have used the Norton Critical Edition of *Dracula* and its pagination for my references principally due to its inclusion of excerpts from Emily Gerard's *Transylvania Superstitions*, a text that Stoker cites as influential to his own, its fine sampling of influential essays also recommends the edition. Other publishers offer the novel similarly framed — Bedford/St. Martin's for example, follows *Dracula* with seminal essays from four contemporary critical perspectives. The best-crafted critical pieces — nearly always discovering that Stoker has drafted a sociological text lending credence to the critic's given stance — concur that *Dracula*'s core interest is rooted in its excesses, transgressions, and subversive nature. Should this more or less align with the critics' general view of the Vampire over the past two centuries, there is an important difference: Today the grotesque is celebrated.

My previous work on the Vampire led me to suspect that contemporary criticism was missing something of the Vampire's quintessence, hence the profound sense of Stoker's masterwork. I felt compelled to take a closer look at this apogee of the Vampire Tale, suspecting that it was no coincidence that *Dracula*, rich in latent religious symbolism, was produced at a time of mounting interest in folklore, Neolithic fertility rites, archaeological and anthropological exploration, Christian symbolism, theosophical sycretism, and the Frazer-elaborated sacral king/dying-god mythologem. Critics have also largely ignored the extent to which, beyond *Varney the Vampire*, *Dracula* depends upon and subsumes within itself the work of earlier authors; it is not easily or happily separated from its antecedents. My feeling is that the novel should be read within the context of its creation. Although both pre–and post–Romantic vampire literature is known through Continental anthologies, it has resisted determined consideration by Anglo-American commentators, no doubt due to its origin in "foreign" cultural traditions. Yet the passage leading to *Dracula*'s sacred sense twists through symbols that link it to *le Vampire* as it served a mystical discourse in France. While French innovations were unfailingly assimilated at the behest of British entrepreneurs, their projects were always accompanied by a certain fundamental distortion due to the adapting hirelings' blind lack of understanding of or interest in the symbolic discourse involved. In my efforts to correct this shortfall, I consider several of these little studied texts, using when possible existing translations (referenced), but imposing my own when necessary (not referenced).

The approach taken here to *Dracula* as a signifying work of art eschews all identity-driven readings in favor of textual and structural analyses (informed by analytic techniques borrowed from musical, visual, and cinematic arts) that uncover extensive and coherently intertwining classical-era references. Intended for academic readership but written to be accessible to a general public, *The Theology of Dracula* is conceived as a useful companion to the student of a widely taught novel. The book's value comes not merely from its findings, but from the analytic methods used, cultural intersections mapped, and a sustained focus on how to identify and read symbolic systems. This approach differs from "critical" approaches in that it directly extracts meaning from the text rather than importing an alien critical structure through which to mediate the artwork.

Ultimately, the literary vampire is quite removed from the creature that dominates the popular imagination, as this, the first and only book-length, in-depth exegesis of Stoker's text will show. *Dracula*, both profoundly Christian and one of the more misunderstood literary works in the canon, advances a complex and nuanced theology. While numerous authors — Bruno D. Starr, Mark M. Hennelly, Jr., Lloyd Worley, and others — have considered the use of religious symbols and symbolism in the fiction through articles and conference papers, this book is likely unique in considering *Dracula* wholly as a hermetic sacred text.

The Sealed Receptacle

"'Now we wish to get into the house, but we have no key; is it not so?'" [256]

Abraham Stoker's best remembered work repeatedly evokes a hermetic space—a coffin, chamber, house, vault, castle, chapel, or other formidably material structure—seemingly containing unique insight into some sublime mystery of death and life, but whose desperately needed penetration requires a key that simply cannot be found. This frequently encountered situation inscribes *Dracula*'s fundamental premise. The text constitutes itself as a partially encrypted manuscript secured in an asylum and locked in its safe, a document containing miraculous tidings, yet whose meaning is destined to remain inaccessible until the proper combination or key is discovered. Stoker encloses within his text successive instructions on how to find the key, though he deliberately makes them difficult to discern, hypnotically materializing Un-Dead getting in the way, continually distracting readers and protagonists alike.

A report secreted in a bottle by the captain of *The Demeter* as he bravely awaited his mortal ends concludes with a plea: "God and the Blessed Virgin and the saints help a poor ignorant soul trying to do his duty" (84). He had put the bottle "in his pocket ... carefully corked, empty save for a little roll of paper, which proved to be the addendum to the log" (79). The captain was discovered alone, two days dead, lashed to the wheel of his schooner. A reporter with access to the authorities who boarded the vessel, driven aground at Whitby before an unnaturally savage storm, filed a report on the state of the body: "Between the inner hand and the wood was a crucifix, the set of beads on which it was fastened being around both wrists and wheel, and all kept fast by the binding cords" (79). This deposition stands in need of some minor amendment: The crucifix and beads should rightly be termed a rosary, a necklace-like object whose beads offer a decadal system of counting off a prayer cycle through which petitioning sinners beseech the intercession of the Holy Mother with her divine Son on their behalf. The occulted paper would be more precisely called a scroll; its status more an apocryphal account than an official addendum to the ship's log. Although discussed in admiralty court, the prayerful message contains no information relevant to the affairs of nautical authorities, insurers, or customs officials, no evidence admissible before their tribunals, only solemn witness absolutely essential to The Book of Abraham Stoker.

Like much else in *Dracula*, the dead captain's statement seems to demand a *lectio divina*, a sacred reading, both to expose its true significance and to reveal the full reach of its parabolic relation to the novel as a whole. The captain's message in a bottle signals the importance of addenda, the rosary, and the Holy Mother; of death, our preparations for it, and the hazardous nature of our journey across life; it emphasizes the watery element, the shifting tides, the ancient port of Whitby, and the intersection of all mothers, pagan and Christian, divine and mortal. This message and the greater text that contains it require a sacred reading because they are offered as a unified holy writ. Yet the Neoplatonic, Gnostic-influenced meditation on the soul that is The Book of Stoker remains one of the more misunderstood texts of all those ever written across the span of human history. The images of blood, incestuous, cannibalistic relationships, sexualized, seductive lamiae, blood-lusting vampires, and the gleeful joys of immortality that have so captivated and frenzied the popular imagination are not the essence of the book, but its detritus. As Stoker warns his reader: "This is no jest, but life and death, perhaps more" (107). He also strives to reassure and to educate: "There is something of a guiding purpose manifest throughout, which is comforting" (274). The Vampire Count, his victims and pursuing hunters were created to work in concert in the belief that they will perhaps become "the instruments of ultimate good" (275).

Envisioning stories a bit like schooners — always impossible to know before setting out if and when "the story should get wind" (89) and make headway — Stoker loudly launches *Dracula* before the Furies to assure the eventual attainment of its destination, but assuming a surprisingly monkish posture he also invests in penning delicate marginalia evocative of scriptorium calm and a prayerful hush. As Jonathan Harker's coach flies over the road towards his St. George's Eve rendezvous at "Borgo Prund" (14), peasants are seen genuflected, praying at shrines constructed along the way of the rude road, displaced Sacred Way — *Iera Odos*. The worshippers, engrossed in meditation, seemingly insensible to the moving world, do not so much as turn when the rattling vehicle and its charging horses thunder by.

On St. George's Eve, tradition dictates the saying of the Little Office of the Virgin Mary, also known as The Hours of the Virgin, an ensemble of psalms and prayers derived from the medieval Book of Hours. *Dracula* offers the era of modernity a richly illuminated Book of Hours — Stoker's vellums contain many elements of the *Sarum Primer*, the standard lay prayer book of Roman Catholicism. The similarly-constituted Anglican Common Book of Prayers translates the Sarum's Latin contents (*Laud*, *Vespers*, etc.) into Morning Prayer, Evening Prayer, Litany, Holy Communion, Services for Baptism, Confirmation, Marriage, Prayers to Accompany the Sick, and Office of the Dead. These essentially form the kernel of the waking activities that animate *Dracula*'s protagonists: the routines of meditation at dawn and dusk — the listening by the living through the ears of the dead, the caring for the afflicted, the Office of the Dead said for Lucy, Mr. Hawkins, and Mina, the shared communion and joining of hands, and the marriage, baptism and confirmation rites that the Harkers undergo. These define and structure the relationships established between the novel's various actors, including those engaging the Count Dracula.

The Professor's use of the sacred Eucharist dogmatically imposes Roman Catholic associations on all these sacramental activities. Anglican discomfort with Catholic paraphernalia and iconography is found expressed throughout the plot, a discomfort only begrudgingly surmounted, Thomas-like, by miracle-engendered faith. It may be significant that across the Victorian period Ritualism became a contentious movement within the Anglican Church, a movement striving to effect a liturgical rapprochement between Church of England practices and those of a unified "Western Church," a euphemism contrasting Rome with manifold "Eastern" and "Orthodox Churches." Ritualism was quickly opposed by an Anglican hierarchy determined to maintain its own ritualistically-expressed theology. Contentious Roman practices included the use of an unleavened Eucharistic wafer, having the celebrant of the mass face East — towards Jerusalem — with his congregants at the moment of transubstantiation, the ringing of bells at the moment of miracle, the making of the Sign of the Cross, the mixing of water and wine, the organization of liturgical processions, and, most particularly, the veneration of the Virgin Mary. All these sacred acts, rites, and activities are prominent features of The Book of Abraham Stoker; without them, the book could not exist.

The great question behind the Ritualism polemic turned on the nature of the schism separating Rome and Canterbury: Was it merely an expression of nationalism or should it be more rightly seen as a fundamental act of the Reformation? Was the rift political or theological? Although Anglican authorities maintain it was both, initially nationalistic, then after the fact reformist and theologically justified, the Church of England has more demonstrably and triumphantly served the national cause and marked the British Commonwealth materially. It is given credit for spurring the popularity of the neo-Gothic in English architecture, a style adopted or rather perpetuated to disassociate the Anglican from counter-Reformation discourse implicit in the Italian and Spanish baroque and French and Austrian rococo styles. Similarly, resistance to "Ritualism" has been projected as being potentially stimulating to the various 19th-century Gothic revivals that impacted British culture in all its manifestations. As *Dracula* is habitually offered as a revived Gothic text par excellence, Stoker's pro-Ritualism stance is just one more indication of the weakness of the generic attribution.

While far more than Ritualism is at work in *Dracula*, the role of Roman Catholic theology and the Sarum Missal provide important clues to locating the novel's key, as Seward sensing the "mighty power" (267) of the sacred wafer and Cross shoot along his arm, Mina requesting to have "the Burial Service" (288) read over her, and countless other details persistently indicate. In this context it is also notable that the Holy See only established ecclesiastical authority in England through a 7th-century synod held in the impressive buildings that later became the Whitby Abbey. The Abbey's consecrated grounds figure rather prominently in *Dracula* as a ruin, counterpoint to Castle Dracula, and place of mystery about which Mina had heard tales of a ghostly Lady in White, embodying a haunting Catholic presence. The oracular Swales dismisses her tales of the White Lady and of mysterious Abbey bells that sound as drowning sailors give up their souls as "all wore out. 'Mind, I don't say that they never was, but I do say that they wasn't in my time'" (64). Swales, whose bark-like skin figures him as the tree of life, is a centenarian.

As with vampire superstitions, tales like that of the White Lady perpetuate sacred knowledge while insulating the secular from serious reflection on shrouded mysteries. "It is something like the way Dame Nature gathers round a foreign body an envelope of some insensitive tissue which can protect from evil that which it would otherwise harm by contact" (112), but in reverse, being about taboo and contact with the sacred. There comes a time, nevertheless, when it is right that the sacred should be exposed to the light of day—superstitions cast aside.

What precisely is meant here by the term "sacred"? Could any defensible notion of "sacred" be applicable to so seemingly profane a work? Is it related to Rudolf Otto's *Idea of the Holy*, a sentiment of awareness of the potently chilling awfulness of a burgeoning numinous presence? Or to the ghostly sensation of Devendra Varma's flickering *Gothic Flame*, that terrifyingly "'dim religious light' ... sensations of awe, and ... ingrained primitive element of natural and superstitious fear" (22) that still clings within the nearly abandoned edifices of ancient beliefs discarded since grown quaintly exotic? That is, is this some type of Gothick intuition, indulgence, or feeling?

Dracula seems little concerned with the numinous, intuitions of terrifying powers beyond human comprehension, morbid thralldom to some dim primal recollection of forgotten beliefs; the weird and uncanny are on occasion accorded a place in the work as passing atmospherics only to be vigorously dismissed as distracting and debilitating to the protagonists' mission. Gothickness is consigned to the same pragmatically-defined refuse pile, discarded in favor of the actionable. *Dracula* is sacred like a temple—from its conception to the materials employed, to its intended function. It is constructed in the world as a monument to things beyond this world and takes as its subject the construction of itself; it writes itself, actively, prayerfully piling Word upon Word, enriching the profane with the sacred and making the sacred the subject of the profane's busy-ness. The *mysterium tremendum* that is so resonant with the Old Testament's jealous God is antithetical to the ends of *Dracula*: The establishment of a new sacred order and a more divine humanity, the proof "that there is a heaven where we can enter, and that its light can be here on earth" (*Dracula* 168–69) and that the mighty power (267) of God can move through human agency. The operative understanding of the "sacred" here proudly and happily basks in the broad light of day and resides in a trinity of sharp, clear, bright manifestations that are interdependent.

First, "sacred" concerns the activity and artifact of a practice of artistic representation. "Sacred" refers to a respectful stance towards that which Hegel termed the "spiritual," the cathartic essence of art, or, at any rate, of true art, a quality binding primitive representations to classical traditions to the arts of the Gothic, the Renaissance and mannerism to the baroque to the Romantic—that movement of the scientific age that refused to surrender spirituality to materialism—to Eastern art to Western art to Northern art to Southern art in a piacular chain of sacredness. It reflects an investment in the tangible of a belief in that which is intangible. As life is the ecological condition *sine qua non* that permits life's perpetuation, art makes spirit manifest to affect the spiritual, a quality that flows in part from the fact that art serves to mediate time.

Promulgated in recent decades by atomic clocks that, in infinitely adding successive pulses, expand temporality with space, time has only recently been figured primarily as a linear construct. Sacred Time was understood as elliptical, cyclic, a turning thing, reflected in the movement of heavenly bodies, contained within the round face of timepieces, illustrated by sunlight's penetration of oculi in temples, measured as shadow through the careful positioning of obelisks and calibrated by megalithic runes and dolmens. Light chased shadow in circles. Each of time's divisions—days, months, years—was understood as a fractal element of a universal geometry and geometric universe; a period of 40 days and one of 40 years could somehow be equivalent. In time's fullness, each moment returned. To sustain beliefs beyond the collective memory of an intergenerational lifetime—grandparent, parent, child—was the realm and mission of art. Art was thus the practice of preserving ideas and ideals, beliefs and values, distilled into a system of symbolization that constituted the discursive sacred that, projecting the symbolic sacred order forward, created futurity by externalizing and making visible the obscure, immaterial, and the spiritual, thereby effecting our renewal by returning ends and finalities to beginnings.

Committed to perpetuating the presence of ancestors and projecting generations towards futurity's exhaustion and beyond—beyond limitations of beginnings and ends to the state of unbegottenness—art's vocation, sacred, is forcibly religious. Edmund Leach, very much considering means of representation, states: "The central doctrine of all religion is the denial that death implies the automatic annihilation of the individual self.... But ... to survive after death as some sort of 'other being,' then this 'other being' must be located in some 'other world' in some 'other time.' The most fundamental characteristic of such 'otherness' is that it is the reverse of ordinary experience" (71). Emile Durkheim divides the social sphere "into two domains, the one containing all that is sacred, the other all that is profane," and that "division is the distinctive trait of religious thought; the beliefs, myths, dogmas, and legends are either representations or systems of representations which express the nature of sacred things, the virtues and powers which are attributed to them, or their relations with each other and with profane things" (37). Few books are as self-consciously sacred as *Dracula*.

"Sacred" also applies to the *represented*, the showing of things known, not intuited, through faith, worshipful things, as clear as daylight, as ordinary and exceptional as life itself, that provide constant motivation and inspiration. This is embodied, for example, in the praying peasants that Stoker has Jonathan observe, and whose devotional concentration contrasts with the facile superstitions of the many; also in the dutiful sea captain still at watch, still at the helm, though now drifting beyond the tides of life. The clearly outlined storybook illustration, tending slightly more towards the Pre-Raphaelite than the Symbolist, more Rossetti than Moreau, is *Dracula*'s privileged vehicle of representation. To characterize his representational ideal Stoker observes: "Sometimes we saw little towns or castles on the top of steep hills such as we see in old missals" (11). Still, occasionally—

> as the road was cut through the pine woods that seemed in the darkness to be closing down upon us, great masses of greyness, which here and there bestrewed the trees, produced a peculiarly weird and solemn effect, which carried on the thoughts and grim fancies engendered earlier in the evening, when the falling sunset threw into strange relief the ghost-like clouds which amongst the Carpathians seem to wind ceaselessly through the valleys (15–6)

— *Dracula* is visited by the shadow of the sublime. Yet even when "grim fancies" of the numinous seem to imbue occasionally visited Gothic spaces with an awesome presence that inflicts "some nervousness growing on" (222) fearful protagonists, unleashed natural animal energies are all that is required to banish the numinous and "any symptom of uneasiness" (223), as Art's terriers demonstrate with a few vigorous shakes of their heads. This is not to discount the role of anamnesis in the fiction, it is the light of day and the love of God and the self that calls us to awake, not dread. The power of God, whether felt coursing along the arm as an invigorating and empowering divine electrical charge, or as a warming and comforting familial presence of Mother and Son in a rosary, is brilliantly illuminating.

Finally "sacred" centers on the representer, the storyteller, he who engages the practice of representation to represent the represented: Abraham Stoker. "The storyteller is the figure in which the righteous man encounters himself" is the apt formula of Walter Benjamin, and here the interest is in the righteous figure of Abraham Stoker's encounter with himself. This text seeks to track his sacred journey within his novel, and therefore accepts the definitions he suggests or provides and the limitations inherent in the times in which he lived. Stoker's symbol system appears deeply consonant, for example, with Carl Jung's Gnostic and alchemical meditations — a striking linkage exists between Stoker and Jung. The specific symbols that Stoker brings to his book and the transformational forces they are exposed to through the rites that are imbricated in plot seem to find further resolution in Jung's work. No doubt they were working on similar, if not the very same philosophic and theologic problems. The nature of these linkages, however, remain beyond the scope of a work which simply sets out to examine The Book of Stoker.

Each of the chapters to follow considers one aspect of *Dracula* or its antecedents that marks it as a sacred text. First, the foundation provided by earlier iterations of the Vampire Tale is reviewed in two lengthy chapters: "Genesis," treating the Neoplatonic parables and Ossianic atheism of primitive recountings, and "Revelation," dealing with the alchemical Christianization imposed by Alexandre Dumas. Temporal ordering and chronological aspects aligning *Dracula*'s plot events with pagan religious festivities and a Neolithic agricultural calendar are examined in "Revolution." The theological groundings of the text in *The Book of Enoch* is taken up in "The Syzygy." The opening of a mythical portal to the dreamlike universe of Mythic Time facilitated by Morpheus, Thanatos, Hypnos and other "Children of Night" is considered in a chapter of that name. The triumph of the Holy Mother who leads petitioning sinners to Our Father forms the subject of "Kingdom Come." "The Overturned Lamp" examines the role of blood and communion as a missing commodity, and strives to illuminate the feminine duality of Lucy and Mina. Finally,

"*Coniunctio Oppositorium*" gazes past the glare of day to peer deeply into the dark celestial drama of *Dracula* as it is distilled and funneled into a microcosm of late Victorian society as the essence of a sacred discourse of ancient origin.

Much has been made of and whole industries developed around the historical foundation that McNally and Florescu elucidate in *Dracula: Prince of Many Faces*, their book on Vlad Tepes, knight of the Order of the Dragon. *Dracula*'s sacred aspects easily accommodate, and transcend, the historic. All these elements join in concert to construct a conceptual cathedral built under the alchemistic hand of a master architect. *Dracula*'s deserved status as a masterwork is due to the fact that it is the product of an author striving to be a worthy servant to an idea and to his expansive Christian ideals.

The saga of *The Demeter*, wherein all hands were lost, was reported insofar as it concerned the living. The derelict ship, herself a sealed chamber containing a mysterious cargo, presented a legal conundrum: how to locate her ill-defined key. It had "one young law student ... loudly asserting that the rights of the owner are already completely sacrificed, his property being held in contravention of the statutes of mortmain, since the tiller, as emblemship, if not proof, of delegated possession, is held in a dead hand" (79).

This type of obscure detail is typical of Stoker's own handiwork. The 13th-century Statutes of Mortmain were enacted to deny the English landholder the ability to cede his property to the Church while, by dint of the terms of transfer, he and his heirs continued to enjoy the benefits of the donated property, a type of agreement frequently entered into to deny the crown revenue, fealty, and arms. Such arrangements benefited the interested parties eternally by enriching the Church upon the depletion of the family's earthly stock while increasing the family's heavenly stock through the ecclesiastical *backsheesh* (81) of temporal indulgences. The dead hand is that of the engaging landholder whose signature on the contract endures beyond his lifetime and across generations, for the Church, imbued with perpetual life, is always possessed of a *main vive* and *vivante*. The Holy See's hand was nonetheless stayed by Henry VIII's confiscation of Church properties, annulment of Catholic liturgy, and founding of the Anglican Church, which thereby eliminated, once and for all, the problem of Church holdings.

Through the emblemship of *The Demeter*, the tack that Stoker took in setting sail is confirmed: He habitually harnesses tensions existing between the temporal and the sacred, being particularly interested in religious conflict, the role of property, the corrupting and corruptible nature of the material, and the ultimate disposition of the contents of derelict vessels.

Extant notes, now published as *Bram Stoker's Notes for "Dracula,"* show Stoker initially breaking up his testament into four books: "Transylvania to London," "Tragedy," "Discovery," "Punishment" (*Notes* 26–8). Despite intervening changes, even as insistence on "Punishment" gave way to belief in "Forgiveness," the four-part structure was maintained. In constructing his fictional world, Stoker brings together Nordic mythology, pagan initiatic rites, Christian symbology and sacramental ordering, diverse Classical era references, and post–Renaissance mysticism, each contributing layer-thickening meaning and reinforcing lamina previously fashioned and fixed in place. Curious Mysteries elements persist throughout, as do comments on gnosis and the Gnostic: "'So you shall keep knowledge in its place, where it may rest—where it may gather and breed. You and I shall keep as yet what we know here, and here.' He touched me on the heart and on the forehead, and then touched himself the same way" (111).

Stoker lightheartedly inscribes his new theology and its construction within plot through frequent discussions of angels, awareness, a new era of salvation and the suppression of Hell: "One of these suggested that there was being erected at Cross Angel Street a new 'cold storage' building; and as this suited the condition of a 'new-fangled ware'us,' I at once drove to it" (231). Stoker then renders an unflattering portrait of Catholicism's rock, St. Peter, describing "An interview with a surly gatekeeper and a surlier foreman, both of whom were appeased with coin of the realm" (231). Stoker's attitude softens, however, when his gaze falls on the unhappy faces of his fellow sinners; these he universally liberates from their earthly confines—that ultimate enclosed space, the human body—dispatching them to join the angels. "'Instead of working wickedness by night and growing more debased in the assimilating of it by day, she shall take her place with the other Angels. So that, my friend, it will be a blessed hand for her that shall strike the blow that sets her free'" (191).

The visages of those to be released from the imprisoning confines of the corporeal register felicity, similar to the regard of Mina when assured that she will not be allowed to become subservient to Evil, "and if there be indeed a Recording Angel that look noted to her everlasting honour" (284). Stoker particularly celebrates the feminine, maintaining that "good women tell all their lives, and by day and by hour and by minute, such things that angels can read. And we men who wish to know have in us something of angels' eyes" (165). For the divine and those in pursuit of gnosis, good women embody a living Book of Hours. Seward, not to be excluded from angelic thoughts, and perhaps in retrospective reference to the curious blue flames that Jonathan will soon encounter on his destined way towards Borgo Prund, obscurely proclaims: "'Transcendentalism is a beacon to the angels, even if it be a will-o'-the-wisp to man.' ... Van Helsing raised his hand over his head for a moment, as though in remonstrance with the Almighty" (293). Perhaps the voice of the distinguished Dutch medical, legal, and theological scholar was joined to those of the humble peasants in petitioning The Mother Mary.

My soul proclaims the greatness of the Lord, my spirit rejoices in God my Saviour; for he has looked with favour on his lowly servant.

From this day all generations will call me blessed: the Almighty has done great things for me, and holy is his Name.

He has mercy on those who fear him in every generation.

He has shown the strength of his arm, he has scattered the proud in their conceit.

He has cast down the mighty from their thrones, and has lifted up the lowly.

He has filled the hungry with good things, and the rich he has sent away empty.

He has come to the help of his servant Israel, for he has remembered his promise of mercy,

The promise he made to our fathers, to Abraham and his children for ever.

[*The Magnifcat*, or *Canticle of Mary*, from Luke 1:46–55]

Genesis

> "Believe me, it is no idle curiosity. I have a motive of which, be sure, she would have approved. I have them all here. I took them before we knew that all was yours, so that no strange hand might touch them — no strange eye look through words into her soul. I shall keep them, if I may; even you may not see them yet, but I shall keep them safe. No word shall be lost; and in the good time I shall give them to you. It is a hard thing I ask, but you will do it, will you not, for Lucy's sake?" [154].

Bram Stoker's Notes for "Dracula" transcribes and annotates a sheaf of hand- and typewritten notes that, after long decades of passing from hand to hand, found a home in the collections of Philadelphia's Rosenbach Museum and Library. In part 1, "Handwritten Notes on the Plot," a single-page document, labeled Rosenbach #38c, records the following:

> The dinner party at the
> Mad doctor's
> Thirteen — each has a number
> Each asked to tell something
> strange — order of numbers
> makes the story complete — at
> the end the Count comes in —
>
> ---
>
> The divisional surgeon being sick the
> doctor is asked to see man in coffin
> restores him to life [22].

Footnote 50 asserts that what is to be heard in this outline is an echo of the "celebrated literary gathering at the Villa Diodati," apparently predicated on figuring Dr. Polidori as "the mad doctor" and Percy Shelley as "the man in the coffin." Eschewing Polidori's contemporaneous journal, the authors elaborate their thought by quoting the 1818 "preface" to *Frankenstein*— a dubious account written by Percy posing as Mary — which describes the stormy 16

June 1816 Cologny soirée that led to Mary's celebrated novel, Polidori's *Ernestus Brechtold* and *The Vampyre*, Byron's *Fragment* and, ultimately, *Manfred*. Rosenbach #38's footnote 52 claims that *Dracula*'s "early drafts include a parody of the Last Supper, with the Count fulfilling the role of the anti–Christ." The editors further remark that "*Bram Stoker's Original Foundation Notes & Dates for His 'Dracula'* list many of his research documents but, surprisingly, they do not mention any of his literary inspirations" (309).

Stoker spent nearly a decade on his version of the Vampire Tale. The *Notes* likely reflect but a small portion of his research, their preservation seeming largely due to sheer good fortune. But they, and the editors' comment on literary inspiration, raise the interesting question of whether anyone would recognize a reference to Stoker's literary guiding lights should they come upon it. Could Stoker's influences go undetected even where he largely points them out because — like the golden treasure of Transylvania — they stem from sources secreted in unfamiliar terrain?

The Vampire Tale in all its concatenated manifestations springs from a vine-like structure — with grasping tendrils and racing underground roots — whose ostentatiously colored fruits break through the sheltering soil to appear and reappear here and there, less a mottled whole than a multiplicity of coherent fragments. Like Russian dolls, each further iteration contains and subsumes all earlier instantiations. The problem for researchers stems from what Miller and Eighteen-Bisang term "the myth of *Dracula*" (291), something regularly posited by writers ranging from Maud Ellman (viii) to William Patrick Day (143–49) to James B. Twitchell (124). It would be more reasonable to assume, based on all evidence, that Stoker inherited ancient myths reworked to accommodate modernity to an unchanging subject — the mysteries of life that embrace those of death — and was led by them. Building upon foundations laid long ago, and working within the Vampire Tale ethos, Stoker furthered ancient myth and belief, forging a robust syncretic amalgam of startling depth and relevance.

In many respects Stoker's notes *are* but what they seem. Stoker — trying to keep track of focused research on narrow detail necessary to lend his narration verisimilitude, and to keep up with the undoubtedly shifting calendrical plotting that furnishes his project its hinge — felt no need to record the grand lines and themes that motivated him, nor to list those that preceded and influenced him; these he knew intimately. Still, between the lines, the notes — Rosenbach #38c in particular — reveal more than has so far been discerned.

Much of what forms the body of *Dracula*, a novel frankly purporting to be a cento, are earlier vampire texts recycled, both in the surface incidents of plot and the rigidity of a skeletal structure in whose marrow is implanted the Vampire Tale's Logos. It is this Logos that has gone unseen even when laid bare. As Heraclitus observes: "Although this account holds forever men fail to comprehend it, both before they hear it and when they first hear. Even though all happenings are in accordance with this account, people behave like the unlearned when they experience works and words" (Fr. 1). The way forward is lengthy, but it is very possible to elucidate a literary reference being made in the excerpt from Rosenbach #38c which will help illuminate the sacred nature of *Dracula* and its meaning. It requires sifting through three generations of the Vampire Tale, particularly as it developed in France. Considering that the ritual-encoding initiatic plots to most of these now ancient works are obscure, interpretative summaries of the principal markers are needed. Plot summary, held in contempt by literary critics, constitutes, for the analyst, the descriptive act, a primordial — critical and interpretative — step upon which meanings depend. By the end of the next chapter, after a forced march through these forgotten first drafts of Stoker's magnum opus, the sense of Rosenbach #38c should be clearer and certain literary influences revealed.

The Corinthian Bride

The unlikely region of Lac Léman, near Geneva, is the birthplace of the prose vampire, with Germaine de Staël's French-language recounting of the conceit of Goethe's 1797 "Die Braut von Korinth" being instrumental to its establishment. Her account converts the *récit* of Goethe's ballad, itself an embellishment of "Philinnion's story" in Phlegon of Tralles' *Book of Wonders*, into prose. Goethe's reworking of the classical-era supernatural tale, blazing the path for the Vampire Tale to come, superposes a theological gloss that pits Christian against pagan, as Staël's French *résumé* makes clear.

Betrothed as children by their fathers, two young people matured as in their hearts grew a love which, sewn in the knowledge that they were promised one to the other, possessed them though they had never met. Over this period of maturation, the Gospel of Christ was carried to Corinth and the bride's family converted to the new religion, while the young man's Athenian family remained faithful to the ancient gods. Stricken by a serious illness, the mother of the bride prayed to Jesus to spare her life, pledging her eldest daughter to a religious life in exchange for her recovery. When her prayers were answered, it was determined that a younger sister would replace her elder in fulfilling the marriage contract, the elder being given instead to Jesus.

Late one evening, the groom, now a fine young man, arrives in Corinth unannounced to claim his bride. Welcomed by the mother, he is placed in the best room of the house. Servants appear with wine and food with which he can refresh himself and he is provided a bed on which to retire. He has just settled in when a veiled maiden clad in white, a black and gold ribbon banding her forehead, enters. Seemingly taken aback by the stranger, she begins to withdraw as if in perplexed embarrassment. The young man, discovering she is his promised one, begs her to stay and share with him the gifts of Ceres and Bacchus, honoring the gods by indulging in their pleasures. She replies that she no longer belongs to joy, that the only gods left to the house were an invisible being in the heavens and a dying-god on the cross; no longer were bulls or lambs offered in sacrifice but in their stead her own youth and humanity. She warns the young man off, but he persists in his courtship. The midnight hour arrives to comfort and set her at ease; she avidly drinks the bloodred wine — similar, says Staël, to that *The Odyssey*'s shades take to retrace their memories — but she obstinately refuses to partake of a crumb of bread. She gives a gold chain to her would-be husband, asking for a lock of his hair. The exchange made, the young man, enchanted by the beauteous maiden, takes her in his arms, but feels neither the beating of her heart nor the warmth of her limbs. It doesn't matter, he exclaims, I'll know how to revive you with the heat of my love even when it is the tomb itself that sends you to me. So begins, enthuses Staël, the most extraordinary scene delirium or imagination could devise, blending love and fright, a redoubtable union of death and life.

The sound of their lovemaking breaks the night's solemn silence. The mother, thinking a brash, lusting slave has penetrated the stranger's room, enters, ready to give vent to her just wrath; but the maiden rises off the couch and swells like a shadow till she reaches the ceiling's vault, and reproaches her mother for having caused her death by making her take the veil. She asks:

> Why do you trouble me on this wedding night? Isn't it enough that in my youth you had me covered in a shroud and carried to the tomb? A wretched curse has forced me from my cold dwelling place; the chants of your priests have not relieved my heart; the salt and the water have not appeased my youth: Ah! Earth herself cannot cool love. This young man was promised me when Venus's serene temple was still not overthrown. My mother, should you fail to keep your word in order to honour your mad vows? No god received your oath when you refused the marriage of your daughter. And you, handsome youth, can no longer live; you will linger within this place where you have taken my chain and I a lock of your hair: Tomorrow your hair will whiten and you will only find your youth in the Empire of Shades. Listen at least, my mother, to the last prayer I would make to you. Order a pyre lit; open the narrow shroud that encloses me; send us lovers to rest through the flames; and when the sparks flare and ashes are aglow, we will hurry off together to join our ancient gods.

The bride, revenant and devotee of the ancient gods, is a romanticized version of the Assyrian Vampire and Levantine Ghoul: a female daemon emergent from remotely ancient traditions. Ceres and Bacchus, Roman gods of bread and wine, authentically Demeter and Dionysus, are central to Goethe's composition. On one hand, these are gods of pleasure, terrestrial life, and sexual reproduction; on the other, chthonic masters of death and resurrection. They rule and are ruled by cyclic forces of dark and light. The only gods left to the house of Corinth, in contrast, are depicted as effete and ineffective: an invisible being in the heavens, and a dying-god on a cross.

In the new dying-god that has displaced Dionysus, the mystery of resurrection mingles bread with wine as flesh and blood, combining the masculine and feminine, but it is the ancient gods that triumph in returning the bride to earth. For the bride, Jesus is a god of renunciation, far paler and less potent than orgiastic Dionysus. The bride accepts the bloodred wine but rejects the flesh that the gift of Ceres represents. Her rejection of Demeter's bread reflects her own bitter anger with her Christian mother. She resides buried in the sheltering earth so nearby the Bay of Eleusis, insensitive to the salted waters of its nourishing sacred spring. In the salt and water, the Christian rites of Extreme Unction are confounded with the initiative, purifying rites of the Eleusinian Mysteries, just as matrimony and holy orders are conflated through the symbol of the veil, and the rites of marriage and of the dead are entwined in the bride's black and gold headband. The forehead wreathed with black and gold figures the maiden as bride, corpse, Hekate: Persephone.

Staël's French-language recounting of Goethe's ballad's *récit* was translated into English in 1813, six years prior to the translation of Goethe's poem into English. The French-English give-and-take establishes a cross-Channel intellectual commerce critical to the Vampire Tale's development. Staël's is but the first of many French-to-English exchanges concerning the sacred wedding of the living and the dead.

Byron and Polidori

Across the lake from Staël's Chateau de Coppet, in spring 1816, Lord Byron began a "ghost-tale" in which he invested but a single evening. He later had his story fragment published to distance himself from *The Vampyre* by John William Polidori, Byron's one-time personal physician. Polidori's novella initially appeared in an unauthorized publication with the ironic subtitle "A Tale by the Honourable Lord Byron," which goes far to explain Byron's insistence on publishing his own incomplete draft. Byron's prose fragment recounts the incidents of a voyage whose itinerary noticeably mirrors the coming of age tour he undertook in the company of John Cam Hobhouse. Polidori's father, Gaetano, in an 1818 letter to his brother Luigi, contends that, despite his best efforts to discourage John William from accepting Byron's offer of employment, Hobhouse's published record of his tour with Byron, *A Journey Through Albania and Provinces of Turkey*, convinced John William to put aside his paternal counsel and accompany Byron to the Continent.*

Over the summer months of 1816, Polidori, goaded by a lady encountered at Madame de Staël's Coppet into illustrating how Byron's tale might have concluded, scribbled out *The Vampyre* over the few love-drenched mornings he passed at her side. By the time it was completed, Hobhouse had rejoined Byron, and Polidori was dismissed from service. Polidori went his own way, and though his path crisscrossed with Byron's on several occasions in Italy over the autumn and winter months of 1816, his story remained in Geneva with his shrewd inamorata. Three years later it reached the hands of Byron tormentor publisher Henry Colburn, apparently supplied by the lady or a confederate, and Colburn published it along with appended extraneous material as Byron's in the 1 April 1819 edition of *New Monthly Magazine*, causing Byron to order his own publisher, John Murray, to publish his only prose work in its unfinished state. Murray tacked it on to the end of *Mazeppa*, much to Byron's consternation. One hundred and fifty years later, E. F. Bleiler had the good sense to publish both texts, Bryon's and Polidori's, in his influential *Three Gothic Novels*.

Byron's reflexive tale breaks off with its dying protagonist, Darvell, charging his companion, the tale's narrator, to complete a mission in his stead, and to bear a ring on his behalf. The journey begun was one whose destination was enlightenment. The ring, symbol of continuity, suggests that such a voyage shall have no end. Yet by the morning after Byron began work on it, the journey was definitely ruptured, Byron retiring his pen and ceasing work on his "ghost-story." Curiously, however, the fictional incident neatly describes what occurred in the world when Polidori is charged with driving Byron's spirit to its destined conclusion. While the Byron-Polidori relationship has been much discussed through *The Vampyre*, what remains obscure is that through their fiction(s) they collectively retrace the ancient Sacred Way of classical-era Athens, *Iera Odos*.

Byron's tale opens with its anonymous narrator reaching into cobwebbed memories to a day whose sublime events remained crystalline. The narrator, who boasts, "I was yet young in life, which I had begun early" (287), carries half the fiction; Augustus Darvell, "man of considerable fortune and ancient family," having "a power of giving to one passion the appearance of another" (287), sustains the other. They form a dichotomy, the narrator confessing that Darvell "had been deeply initiated into what is called the world ... I was yet in my novitiate" (287). Contrast between knowledge and ignorance, mystagogue and myste threads their paths on the labyrinthine Way. The narrator consciously ingratiates himself with Darvell in order to undertake this journey: "It was my secret wish

*See McDonald, *Poor Polidori*, pp. 55–56.

that he might be prevailed upon to accompany me; it was also a probable hope, founded upon the shadowy restlessness which I observed in him ... and his apparent indifference to all by which he was more immediately surrounded" (288).

Dispatched upon an "intended journey" become journey-of-intent, the narrator soon remarks that, having wound their way through southern Europe, their "attention was turned towards the East" (288). The phrase's passive construction reads as if their turning were involuntary, but we are soon reassured their "intent" had always been thus. In Western Christendom, to turn towards the East is to embrace the sacred: The faithful ranged in Gothic churches prayed towards altars situated at the eastern extreme of cruciform structures, the architecture serving to point assembled worshippers as a unique crucified body, *corpus mysticus*, towards Jerusalem, resurrecting God, rising sun: the Levant. Yet given Byron's tale's geography, being "turned toward the East" is, more narrowly, to turn against both Roman "Mother" and her Protestant churches, for finding themselves on the schismatic fault dividing East from West, our protagonists irrevocably turn East.

Tradition tells us that cardinal points East and West symbolize birth and death, sunrise and sunset, Jerusalem and the Western Isle; aberrantly, Darvell suffers from an affliction whose debilitating effects become increasingly acute relative to his eastward position. Despite Darvell's condition, our protagonists determine to undertake "an excursion to the ruins of Ephesus" (289). From Smyrna, they push through "that wild and tenantless tract through the marshes and defiles which lead to the few huts yet lingering over the broken columns of Diana — the roofless walls of expelled Christianity, and the still more recent but complete desolation of abandoned mosques" (289). Intentionality leads to a disputed, then abandoned crossroad of civilizations, sites of the huntress's temples and haunted realm, a land from which Christianity has been exorcised and in which the more recent enveloping faith of the Turk has failed to take root. Geography and pathology working in tandem, Darvell's incapacitation forces a stop at a "Turkish cemetery, the turbaned tombstones of which were the only indication that human life had ever been a sojourner in this vastness" (289). Reclining upon a grave, Darvell sends for water, describing to his janissary a hidden desert fountain from which it might be procured. Observing his companion's stupefaction at this prescience, Darvell reveals that he had passed that way before. Having drunk from the occult source, Darvell declares his life over, exhorting his companion to indulge his final request and swear to not reveal his death to anyone. The oath taken, Darvell removes a ring from his finger, presents it to his companion with instructions: "'On the ninth day of the month at noon, fling the ring into the salt springs which run into the Bay of Eleusis, the day after, the tenth day ... repair to the ruins of the temple of Ceres and wait one hour'" (290).

When, just then, a stork "perched upon a tombstone near" (291), a snake clamped in its beak, the narrator compulsively tries to chase the bird off. After circling overhead, the stork, with its writhing cargo, returns to the same spot. Darvell instructs his companion to bury him where the bird has lighted. Our narrator wonders at this unnatural spectacle. Grinning "in a ghastly manner," Darvell explains the stork has not swallowed the snake because "'it is not yet time'" (291). At Darvell's conclusive observation on temporality, the stork takes flight, drawing the narrator's gaze aloft. Within that nearly imperceptible interval of distraction, Darvell's mass surrendered itself to Earth. Instantly, Darvell's figure became "nearly black" (291). The story cuts off with the tale-bearer recalling how a grave was rapidly prepared, the soil having previously been broken to accommodate "some Mahometan tenant" (291). With the exclamation, "'Between astonishment and grief, I was tearless'" (291), the mystery travelogue ceases to meander.

Darvell has connected the Eleusinian Temple of Demeter (Ceres) to the Ephesian Temple of Artemis (Diana). The latter divinity, both chaste goddess of the hunt and potent fertility deity, embodies one aspect of the Olympian virgin triune, ruling over the moon and subconscious; in her inverted form of black Hekate, she is goddess of shadows, the damned, haunter of crossroads, wearer of serpents. Before having Darvell turn black, Byron insistently emphasizes stork and serpent, symbols expressing the paradox of the goddess, the stork representing purity, chastity; the serpent, evil. Darvell seems to also reference Jeremiah 8:9: "Yea, the stork in the heaven knoweth her appointed times ... but my people know not the judgment of the Lord." The stork and serpent are concerned individually with the spring, birth, and resurrection, collectively with the hieroglyph for light; confounding stork and ibis, the iconography is Isiac. R. E. Witt reconciles the goddess's paradox:

> Artemis is ... a puzzling figure ... young virgin of the chase ... vowed to perpetual chastity and filled with loathing for sex even when it is exercised within the marriage bond.... No less indubitably, however, there stands ... an Artemis ripe for motherhood, a fertility goddess from Asia Minor with her main cult centre at ... Ephesus. The ardent votaries of this Artemis are the Amazons. The Amazons ... indulge, once yearly, in sexual intercourse, but then simply for one reason, to produce girl descendants.... Divine blending of Virgin and Mother contradicts human experience, for bringing forth a child means, for a woman, the loss of maidenhood. How are the two views of Artemis to be reconciled?
>
> —The secret seems to lie in the religious thinking of the Mediterranean world as early as the Mycenaean age. The Great Goddess was revered both as virgin and as mother. [Persephone] the daughter and Demeter the mother were one person looked at under two aspects [141].

Between his July reading of the Henry Colburn–published, Byron-damning *Glenarvon* by Caroline Lamb and his late September Genevan departure, Polidori gallantly dashed off his novella for the lady who had challenged him. Releasing Darvell from his service and appropriating the name "Ruthven" from Lady Lamb's *roman à clef*, Polidori concocted *The Vampyre*. To complete Darvell's voyage, Ruthven begins anew.

Ruthven too envelops contradiction, binding a being "material" to one "astral." Titled "a nobleman" (265), he is "more remarkable for his singularities than his rank" (265). Disdain separates him from life's hubbub; a "dead grey eye" (265) unable to perceive the material, pierces "through to the inward workings of the heart" (265). The more contemptuously Ruthven regards society, the more enthusiastically society regales in his regard. Painted as immune to seduction by the debauched, seemingly without vice, Ruthven's interest is seized by the virginal or virtuous. "In spite of the deadly hue of his face" (265), his magnetic appeal captivates society during London's winter "season."

Aubrey, wealthy orphan, arrives in London having "cultivated more his imagination than his judgement" (266). Disappointed by the world, by modernity, keen on exploring vestiges of earlier ages, the youth, steeped in ruinously romantic notions of "honour and candour" (266), "believed all to sympathise with virtue, and thought that vice was thrown in by Providence merely for the picturesque effect of the scene, as we see in romances" (266). "Handsome, frank, and rich" (266), pursued by mothers and daughters alike, his romance will be more picaresque than picturesque.

A cleavage between the real and imagined furnishes Aubrey with *his* internal contradiction. As he was set to reconcile his mind to the real, fate introduced him to the reality of an image materialized. Noticing at a "drawing-room" Ruthven, "a man entirely absorbed in himself, who gave few other signs of his observation of external objects, than the tacit assent to their existence, implied by the avoidance of their contact" (267), Aubrey transfers his nearly-discarded notions of the hero onto him. Discovering that Ruthven, lacking in funds, is preparing to voyage abroad, Aubrey contrives to "perform the tour, which for many generations has been thought necessary" (267). The verb "perform" invests a ritualistic sense in "the tour" as initiatory ordeal.

The pair traverses Flanders on, on Ruthven's part, a rampage of corruption. Wherever he passes, Ruthven spreads an infectious degeneracy, contact with his corrosive loadstone effecting a moral polar shift. When Ruthven sets to deflower a Roman matron's daughter, Aubrey denounces his hero. Alone, Aubrey reaches Greece. Taking up lodgings with a nameless Athenian family, he passes time "tracing the faded records of ancient glory upon monuments that apparently, ashamed of chronicling the deeds of freemen only before slaves, had hidden themselves beneath the sheltering soil" (270)—"sheltering soil" sounding a phrase that resounds across centuries. His hosts' daughter, Ianthe, replaces Ruthven as Aubrey's guide. This beautiful "conductress" (273) an apparition from Delacroix as rendered by Ingres, is Romanticism itself, a pure spirit steeped in the superstitions of her native soil:

> Her earnestness and apparent belief of what she narrated excited the interest even of Aubrey: and often as she told him the tale of the living vampyre ... forced every year, by feeding upon the life of a lovely female to prolong his existence for the ensuing months, his blood would run cold [271].

Unlike Artemis's Amazons, engaging once yearly in procreative sex, the Vampyre annually feeds on life to animate death on a specific matrimonial day. "*Matrimonium,*" describing the rite of transformation that changes The Maiden into The Mother, becomes, as will be seen, thoroughly perverted by the Vampire.

While dismissing Ianthe's stories as ridiculous, Aubrey "wondered at the many coincidences which had all tended to excite a belief in the supernatural power of Lord Ruthven" (271). Ianthe's presence banished from his mind all thoughts of classical relics, the simple play of light in her hair inflicting forgetfulness on a tour-performing youth become Pausanias-led "antiquary": He fell in love. Polidori's phrase—"her tresses falling, as she flitted around, exhibit in the sun's ray such delicately brilliant and swiftly fading hues" (270)—invests sense in his sole name. Ianthe is portrayed flitting about in the light of Aubrey's regard. In "Aubrey," the notion of *aube*, referencing the rising sun's light, is apposed to "ray," a beam of light, or *rey*, "king," invoking a Dawn King, Eastern Light: the Levant.

One evening, as Aubrey announces his intent to visit a "particular destination" (272) the following day, Ianthe's family, "when they heard the name of the place" (272), insists he reconsider—woods that must be traversed en route are the "resort of vampyres" (272). Should he go, he must return by sunset, "ere night allowed the power of these beings to be put in action" (272). Humouring his hosts, Aubrey dismissively, condescendingly agrees.

> Next morning Aubrey set off ... unattended; he was surprised to observe the melancholy face of his host ... Ianthe came to the side of his horse, and earnestly begged of him to return, ere night.... He was, however, so occupied in his research, that he did not perceive that day-light would soon end, and that in the horizon there was one of those specks which, in the warmer climates, so rapidly gather into a tremendous mass, and pour all their rage upon the devoted country.—He ... mounted his horse, determined to make up by speed for his delay.... Twilight, in these southern climates, is almost unknown; immediately the sun sets, night begins [272–73].

A polarizing land knowing but day and night having tricked him into overstaying his allotted time, Aubrey set off homeward at a gallop. Thunder caused his horse to bolt, charge through an "entangled forest" (273), and stop before a "hovel" (273). Dismounting, Aubrey started as a flash of blue light radiated "at his very feet" (273). Alarmed by a woman's scream that, intermingled with salacious laughter, resonated between thunderclaps, he rushed into the hut to find himself locked in battle against "one whose strength seemed superhuman" (273). Aubrey was "lifted from his feet and hurled with enormous force against the ground:—his enemy threw himself upon him, and kneeling upon his breast, had placed his hands upon his throat—when the glare of many torches penetrating through the hole that gave light in the day, disturbed him" (273). Aubrey's assailant ran crashing into the woods.

> The storm was now still ... Aubrey, incapable of moving, was soon heard by those without. They entered; the light of their torches fell upon nothing but the mud walls, and the thatch loaded on every individual straw with heavy flakes of soot, though at this moment it was apparently untenanted. There was one spot slippery with blood but it was hardly visible [273].

Aubrey, dispatching the party to locate the vanished woman, "was again left in darkness; but what was his horror, when the light of the torches once more burst upon him, to perceive the airy form of his fair conductress brought in a lifeless corpse" (273). He "shut his eyes, hoping that it was but a vision" (273):

> ...no colour upon her cheek, not even upon her lip: yet there was a stillness about her face that seemed almost as attaching as the life that once dwelt there:—upon her neck and breast was blood, and upon her throat were the marks of teeth having opened the vein: to this the men pointed, crying, simultaneously struck with horror, "A Vampyre!" [274].

Aubrey was stretched upon a litter, Ianthe, "who had lately been to him the object of so many bright and fairy visions, now fallen with the flower of life that had died within her," by his side; his hand "held almost unconsciously ... a naked dagger ... found in the hut" (274). They were "met by different parties who had been engaged in the search of her whom a mother had missed. Their lamentable cries, as they approached the city, forewarned the parents of some dreadful catastrophe" (274).

Beholding Ianthe's corpse, her horrified parents expired. Aubrey, fevered, succumbed to tortured visions of himself imploring Ruthven to spare Ianthe's life. Returning to his senses, Aubrey is bewildered to find at his side he whom delirium had confounded with the Un-Dead. Swayed by Ruthven's tender ministries, Aubrey forgives all. Resuming Aubrey's interrupted activities as before, the pair revisits scenes of previous excavation; yet wherever within the "Athenian neighborhood" (275) they roam, Aubrey is haunted by Ianthe, pale-faced, stigmatized, "wandering amidst the underwood, in quest of the humble violet" (275).

One day, beyond Athens, while passing through a "narrow defile" between two hills, the pair falls into an ambuscade, as if set upon by the god of war himself. During the altercation, Ruthven is mortally wounded. To save his companion, Aubrey contracts a ransom if only their assailants convey Ruthven to a nearby hut. There, Ruthven obtains Aubrey's promise to keep secret his demise for a year-and-a-day. On Aubrey's utterance of the oath, Ruthven expires. Aubrey withdraws to rest, but, haunted by his pledge, cannot. At dawn, he starts for "the hovel in which he had left the corpse, when a robber met him, and informed him that it was no longer there, having been conveyed ... to the pinnacle of a neighbouring mount, according to a promise they had given his lordship, that it should be exposed to the first cold ray of the moon that rose after his death" (277). Alarmed, Aubrey hastens to bury the cadaver, but Ruthven's remains have vanished. Robbers, having stripped the corpse, buried it to obscure their crime, Aubrey rationalizes.

As if returning from Ephesus, Aubrey arrives "at Smyrna" (277) with Ruthven's effects. "There were several daggers and ataghans ... examining their curious forms, what was his surprise at finding a sheath apparently ornamented in the same style as the dagger discovered in the fatal hut ... his horror may be imagined, when he discovered that it fitted" (277). Ruthven had plucked his "flower of life" (274). Aubrey returns westward. From Calais, "a breeze, which seemed obedient to his will, soon wafted him to the English shores" (278) where his virgin sister awaited. Neither worldly nor urbane, this "melancholy" (278) maiden lived for fraternal approbation. In his absence, she hadn't debuted in society. Thus "it was ... resolved that the next drawing-room ... should be the epoch of her entry into the 'busy scene'" (278), whose performance constituted a feminine equivalent to "the tour."

Eons had passed since that fateful "drawing-room" where he first beheld Ruthven, but Aubrey was back at another elegant London occasion, now as his sister's protector. Society's hubbub being unchanged, Aubrey retires to a shadowed corner. He is soon startled by a hand upon his back, words murmured into his ear by a voice uncannily familiar: "remember your oath" (279). Afar, he can perceive if not the voice's source, its master. The Vampyre plied the crowd. Clutching the arm of an acquaintance, Aubrey struggles towards transport home. Collecting himself, he returns to recover his sister and verify his senses. Indeed, it was Ruthven. Aubrey "sprang forward, seized his sister's arm, and ... forced her towards the street; at the door he found himself impeded by the crowd ... he again heard that voice close to him—'Remember your oath!'—He dared not turn" (279–80).

Aubrey, much altered by this encounter, is presumed mad. Informed of his sister's betrothal to the Earl of Marsden, he quickly surrenders his blessing, relieved to see her pledged to anyone but Ruthven. Yet perceiving a miniature of the earl in a locket dangling over his sister's heart, his torment is transported beyond limits. Realization of Ruthven's impending triumph speeds Aubrey towards a relapse of delirium, though he is sufficiently lucid to calculate that 365 days have passed since he pledged silence. The nuptials are set for the morrow. Ruthven, citing an obligation to leave for the continent by dawn, strives to hasten a wedding Aubrey struggles to delay. In extremis, Aubrey violates his soul-damning oath. Dismissed as insane, Aubrey bursts an artery and dies. Midnight brings realization that Aubrey's sister has disappeared. Polidori concludes, taunting, she "had glutted the thirst of a Vampyre" (283).

Polidori's uniquely unsatisfying final line hardly justifies a tragedy's heap of cadavers; nothing cathartic is left to retain, but grim spectacle climaxed by surprise. Rather than cleansing and renewing, the ending pollutes. Ianthe dead, Sun–king departed, the Vampire — intoxicated on Miss Aubrey's blood — free to wreak another leap year's havoc on a disbelieving world, *The Vampyre* yields but grotesque comedy with as many deformities as strokes of genius competing for attention. While with Polidori causality does not spur the rationalizing contortions of Ann Radcliffe, the obvious lack of it inevitably leads to the appearance of maladroitness: the crowd that happens by with torches in "a wood, where no Greek would ever remain, after the day had closed" (272); the malleable, amenable robbers always ready to lend a hand whenever the plot is bogged down; Aubrey's weak-willed readiness to forget Ruthven's transgressions. Ruthven's attack on Aubrey's unnamed sister seems aimed at Aubrey, rather that the victim herself. Could not Ruthven have found some other maiden? Somewhere "between astonishment and grief" the reader, like Byron's narrator, is left "tearless."

The limits of Polidori's craftsmanship inevitably cause his tale to fall shy of its mark should that be Coleridgian suspension of disbelief; yet his irreverent pomposity enlivens, his frequent self–conscious touches so amuse that one is tempted to believe he is in command of the aesthetic he defines: Is it not in Gothic fun that the hero awaits a ship to Otranto? In ridicule that, en route for England, he abandons Athens for Smyrna? As diversion that a vampire is offered to a lady? It nevertheless appears that Polidori's genius was accidental, residing in the starkness of fortuitous detail recycled until congealed into canon: the throat punctured by vampiric dentition; the moonlight circumstance and empowerment of evil; the being capable of hurling men about as if babes; the menacing forces of nature which announce the coming of the Vampire (the speck in the air which presages things more ominous, the sudden anaemic dusk, the will-driven winds and tides, the troubled dreams); the empirical, orphaned hero driven to madness; the ascendant villain, that seductive and sophisticated aristocrat run amok in a modern world; the incestuous ties that bind them.

Perchance, Polidori has tersely summarized, catalogued, bequeathed to posterity now familiar attributes, images seemingly torn from delirium and nightmare projected onto a fictional realm representing contemporary bourgeois quotidian experience. Yet in remarking these surface, now familiar elements of a profaning being, we are blinded to the interior sacred contents with which Polidori has invested his story. It is this cleverness that earned *The Vampyre* Goethe's highest praise.* Yes, the facile landscape of huts, roving mobs, and bandits, tormenting secrets and guilty suspicions have been purloined from the likes of Godwin, yet remarkable differences, concordant with the foundation Byron laid in that sketch he could not bring to completion, exist, separating Polidori's *Vampyre* from anything written since Lucius Apuleius. Why has Polidori transposed the setting from Ephesus to Athens? For what is Aubrey searching so unrelentingly? What dangerous road leads him out of Athens on his expedition? Why is he so absorbed by Pausanias? Who are the torch-bearing souls wandering woods in the dead of night? Why can't Ruthven leave Aubrey and those he loves alone? What mother has lost her daughter? What is the significance of Ianthe?

Ianthe, who conducts Aubrey to the Sacred Way he must descend alone, bears a name signifying "Flower of Violet"; this explains much. The Homeric "To Demeter" lists Ianthe as one of the maidens who accompanied Persephone as she went flower-gathering on the day she was abducted and became against her will queen of the underworld. Inspired by Lamb's *Glenarvon,* Polidori's is a novel *roman à clef.* In recalling Darvell's dying imperative to have his ring tossed into "the salt springs which run into the bay at Eleusis," we fathom the depths to which Polidori plunged to retrieve Byron's discarded bauble. The salt springs bubble at the mouth of the Rheitoi, near which "is Erineos, the place where Plouton descended, they say, when he carried off" Persephone and "Eumolpos and the daughters of the Keleus performed the holy rites of the two goddesses" (Pausanias 1971: 107). We can confidently assert Polidori's familiarity with Neoplatonist Thomas Taylor's 1796 translation of Pausanias, an edition Byron used when trekking Eleusis and Ephesus with Hobhouse in 1809 to 1810: In a letter written just after the Darvell fiction was begun, Byron invites Hobhouse to Geneva, requesting that he bring "some of Waite's red tooth powder and toothbrushes, Taylor's *Pausanias*, and I forget the other things" (23 June 1816).

Pausanias and a Neolithic myth, relating the story of mothers and daughters, fathers and sons, gods who represent our complex natures and Nature's

*See Butler, *Goethe and Byron*, p. 55.

complexities, who become lost in and emergent from one another, provide a template for enlightenment. At the myth's darkest depths, two figures appear, one recognizably feminine, another generally, if intermittently, masculine: a "gentle" man, effeminate in his courtly nature, who reveals himself to be a savage hunter who periodically becomes the hunted, and whose double nature expresses ancient dualities. Its canonical rendition concerns Demeter, her brothers Zeus and Plouton, and daughter. Aware that Zeus had promised their daughter Persephone to brother Plouton, Demeter hid her before leaving to worship her mother Rhea. Discovering Persephone's whereabouts, Zeus sped Aphrodite, Athena, and Artemis to lure the maiden to a place where she might be ambushed and abducted. The goddesses, finding the girl embroidering a scarf for her mother that incorporated the sacred symbol of the initial chaos, the primordial void, into its fabric, entreated her to come flower-gathering with the daughters of Okeanus. Persephone consented.

In a meadow lying by the briny sea, the divine Maiden spied a magnificent Narcissus and went to pluck it. As she pulled on its stem, the earth "gaped" as if the plant's roots burrowed into Hades. When the many-named lord of the underworld burst through, Persephone let out a piercing cry. None but "Hekate of the shining headband ... from her cave" ("To Demeter" ¶25) and distant Demeter admitted to hearing it. According to Taylor's translation of *Discourse on the Mysteries*, Persephone, "in the new spring, was ravished ... and being carried from thence through thick woods, and over a length of sea, was brought by Plouton into a cavern, the residence of departed spirits, over whom she afterward ruled" (87). "The place where this happened was pointed out by the river Kephisos near Eleusis" (Kerényi 35).

Alerted by the scream, Demeter descended, tearfully wandering for nine days, unbathed, taking neither food nor drink, combing the world "with bright torches in her hand" ("To Demeter" ¶48). The "nine days" reference suggests that Demeter bears torches by night and day in order to apperceive one who has become darkness, earning her "the name of *Pheraia,* the torch-bearing goddess seated on a running horse" (Jung, Kerényi 198). On Demeter's passion's tenth day, the dark goddess "Hekate carrying a light in her hands, met her"—her light reflecting the renewed moon. Hekate could not answer demeter's question, *Who had seized Persephone?* for she had heard cries without seeing. At Hekate's instigation Demeter asks Helios-Who-Sees-All: "No other immortal is to be blamed save cloud-gathering Zeus who gave her to Hades, his own brother, to become his buxom bride" ("To Demeter" ¶78–80). Imperceptible at night, the lord of darkness, appearing from below as masked Dionysus, is detected in the sun's presence, for, as Heraclitus reveals, Hades and Dionysus are one and the same.

Darvell's request that his ring be immersed in Eleusinian waters on a lunar ninth day in anticipation of his emissary's temple visit on the tenth, recalls Demeter's passion, for on the tenth day she arrived at Eleusis to eventually become reunited with Persephone. Polidori, indebted to Caroline Lamb for attributing "Ruthven" Dionysian characteristics and Byronian associations, understanding the implications of Darvell's ring, harnessed Taylor's *Pausanius* to their development.

With Aubrey about to leave Athens, his host appeared with "melancholy face" (272) to see him off; "Ianthe came to the side of his horse" (272), her mother was ostensibly absent. This dawn-lit tableau presages and mirrors the nocturnal incident in which the horse led Aubrey to a mystery destination from which it refused to advance. When we recall that Ianthe was within the nearby hovel, it seems as if the horse was determined to stand by Ianthe's side as Ianthe had stood by the horse as Aubrey set off. To review: Triggered by a Zeusian thunderbolt, Aubrey's mare, Demeter embodied, charged through an entangled forest, pulling up at the place of "orgies" that Ianthe's father, Okeanus-Zeus, had warned of— the *Telesterion*. "[T]he animal, at last, through fatigue, stopped" (273), leaving the spiritual to carry on. Blue light falling before Aubrey "to radiate at his very feet" (273) confirms Mystery Night's arrival. At a "hovel which hardly lifted itself up from the masses of dead leaves" (273), Aubrey hoped "to find some one to guide him" (273). When a woman's scream, Persephone's, compelled him to enter the structure, he "found himself in utter darkness: the sound, however, guided him" (273). Demeter has led Aubrey to her daughter. Aubrey struggled with a shadowy assailant who, unseen, disappears in a burst of light.

Clearly, during Aubrey's "unaccompanied" initiation into life's mysteries, Ianthe-Persephone, through her scream, "guided him" and remained his "conductress." The torchlight of those following the Sacred Way sent the Nocturnal One crashing into woods to disappear into darkness. Taylor teaches that Persephone was carried "through thick woods, and over a length of sea ... into a cavern, the residence of the dead: where by *woods* a material nature is plainly implied" (100). In examining the desolate dwelling they found only Aubrey, soot-laden thatch and earthen floor with a bloody spot.

Polidori's story unfolds within a sustained Neoplatonic projection. The hovels scattered across a landscape of material entanglements must be viewed as temporal abodes: Bodies that contained the spirit, once abandoned, are marked by soot, the residue of material man, a substance originating in Iakchos's Titan-fragmented, Zeus-incinerated body. An insistence on straw, an element associated with Dionysus in death, affirms this. Ianthe's spirit has quit a "hovel" to live a "Kashmere butterfly" upon a spiritual plane. With "a stillness about her face that seemed almost as attaching as the life that once dwelt there" (274), Ianthe, imbued with new beauty, personifies Persephone. Even in death, Aubrey sees her wandering "in quest of the modest violet" (275); "amidst the ruins he had formerly frequented, Ianthe's form stood by his side" (275).

Ruthven's death, too, was occasioned as the twin explorers processed along the Sacred Way:

> In consequence of thus neglecting the advice of the inhabitants they travelled on one occasion with only a few guards.... Upon entering, however, a narrow defile, at the bottom of which was the bed of a torrent, with large masses of rock brought down from the neighbouring precipices, they had reason to regret their negligence; for scarcely were the whole of the party engaged in the narrow pass, when they were startled by the echoed report of several guns, and by the whistling of bullets [275].

As Heinrich Schliemann points out, "at the foot of the conical hill of Poikilus, at the entrance to the defile, the Sacred Road appears to have to the right, whilst the modern way turns to the left. The defile is bordered on the right by Mount Icarus, on the left by Mount Corydallus" (122). The sanctuary of Aphrodite, situated between the temple of Daphnia Apollo at the Sacred Way's highest point and the Ploutonium at its lowest, stands just above the defile one must pass through to negotiate the Sacred Way. Repeatedly, the goddess of love, aided by the god of war, divides her two heroes, Day and Night. When Hobhouse and Byron passed though in January 1810, they searched for the place where Scirus was said to have fallen; the defile was later named after him.

In examining Ruthven's effects, Aubrey revisits Mystery Night's hovel,

The Sanctuary of Aphrodite along the Sacred Way. © Rarignac

transporting the reader into a detective story, a mystery. Although he seems to discover the murder weapon, it is written that Ianthe only bore teeth marks on her neck. While a vampire needs no knife, ceremonially spilling sacrificial blood upon the earth as a chthonian libation requires a consecrated blade "adapted to ensure the death of the victim" (277)—a Dionysian high priest's, a hierophant's—Ruthven's. The bloodied floor also marks the *locus classicus* where the earth gaped, the symbolic affirmation of Persephone's rape. As if Persephone, Ianthe, "Flower of Violet," was deflowered at Erineos. While Hekate's lunar Ruthven, Dionysian "Nocturnal One," accomplished the deed, it is Helios' solar Aubrey, Apollonian diurnal figure, who finds himself clutching the blade. This article's transmission manifests the protagonists' doppelganger bond.

At Eleusis, the ineffable goddess was summoned, a *Visio Beatifica,* from darkness; upon the Hierophant's command "a great light burst forth" (Kerényi 92), Persephone appearing. Polidori describes the occurrence: Aubrey "was again left in darkness; but what was his horror, when the light of the torches once more burst upon him, to perceive the airy form of his fair conductress brought in a lifeless corpse. He shut his eyes, hoping that it was but a vision arising from his disturbed imagination; but he again saw the same form" (273–74). Polidori writes that "lamentable cries, as they approached the city, forewarned the parents of some dreadful catastrophe" (274). As on Mystery Night of yore, calls of "*Iakchos!*" rang out. The clearest indication of the symbolic order employed is caught in the tangle of a gnarled sentence: "They were soon met by different parties who had been engaged in the search of her whom a mother had missed" (274). This mother, Demeter, searches this night for her *Kore.* Dispatched conjointly by Hekate and Helios, Demeter will soon arrive at Eleusis.

Dr. Polidori drew his image brilliantly, contrasting Aubrey's sketching with Ianthe's told tale: "In tracing the scenes of her native place; she would then describe to him the circling dance upon the open plain, would paint to him in all the glowing colours of youthful memory, the marriage pomp she remembered viewing in her infancy" (271). The marriage was Persephone's; the circling dance, that performed in great antiquity around the temple complex's *Kallichoron.* Although Ianthe had quit her temporal abode, Aubrey remained upon the material plane to mix with Ruthven in a vacillating relationship—like Apollo and Dionysus, bound at the *omphalos,* dividing supremacy over the Delphic temple. Mystery Night occurred 40 days before Dionysus's rebirth, perhaps explaining why Ruthven did not extract his oath, initiatory *apporheton,** and die with Ianthe, beginning his haematological new year then.

**Arrheton* refers to the ineffable secret; *apporheton* to that which is kept "secret under a law of silence." See Kerényi, *Eleusis*, p. 26.

The Kallichoron. © Rarignac

Aubrey's solar westward return, Ruthven in pursuit, balances Aubrey's eastward accompaniment of Ruthven. Solar-informed polarity has Death give rise to Life as East meets West. Although crepuscular Aubrey, red-faced, dies haemorrhaging from Ruthven-inspired lunacy, he will be as likely to reappear to share another eastward journey with Ruthven as the sun is to rise tomorrow. Ruthven and Aubrey, darkness and light, divide the year, returning us to Byron's Darvell, for Apollo's sister, Aubrey's in this *roman à clef*, is Artemis Hekate, virgin mother goddess venerated at Ephesus. Indeed, it is there, in the East, that Darvell awaits by an occult source for his wedding band to be returned from Dionysian depths on an Eleusinian tenth day, thereby effecting his return from beneath the sheltering soil, Aubrey having completed the mission Darvell set for his narrator.

Nodier's Vampires

Polidori's insightful novella, developing the theological aspect of the Un-Dead that Goethe first implanted in *The Bride of Corinth*, set the thematic direction for the Vampire Tale for the century to come while fixing as a ritual sequence of transformation numerous aspects of plot. This enduring influence however was not due to any great success of the tale in England or in English-speaking countries, but to its repeated and resounding triumphs in France.

On the heels of Ruthven's *New Monthly Magazine* apparition, Henri Faber translated *The Vampyre* into French, publishing it again, despite Polidori's protestations, as Byron's intellectual fruit, the Byronian attribution being accentuated to assure sales. Charles Nodier reviewed Faber's work in the 1 July 1819 *Journal des Débats*, heaping praise on *The Vampyre*'s author and scorn on its translator — an irony, considering a tendency to ascribe *The Vampyre*'s continental success to translator-engineered stylistic improvements. Nodier had to "admit the reader must make quite an effort to judge the merit of this work through the veil of lead with which the translator has covered it. The reader will not be able to enjoy its worth unless an author worthy of the pen of Lord Byron — and I am told that such an author is at present busy with this work of translation — repairs the unflattering homage that the French press has just paid him" (tr. qtd. Oliver 126), predicting that the anonymous translator "then will offer all these trappings of melodrama to one of the boulevard theatres; and what success will be in store for him!" (126). In complimenting Byron, Nodier praises himself, for he is himself the worthy translator that his reported rumour hails. Nodier's prognostication was proven just; as a Lord Byron whose attitude towards *The Vampyre* evolved over the years came to admit to Thomas Medwin, *The Vampyre* was only truly granted life once it "was got up as a melo-drame at Paris" (120): It was Nodier whose fatherly touch sparked that improbable life in the given-up-for-dead Vampire.

As early as 1813 Charles Nodier was writing on vampire lore he encountered while serving in Ljubljana as editor of *Télégraphe Officiel*, a Napoleonic propaganda organ. During this period Nodier fleshed out his major literary theme: transformative love, love forged from the chivalrous ardor of the medieval *romance*, tempered with a transcendental spiritual passion, ultimately Christian yet deeply mystic, seen as essential to man's resuscitation and renewal. A. Richard Oliver defines Nodier's conception of love as something which manifests itself through "eternal union, which could be achieved ... only beyond the grave" (124). While the Vampire expresses themes of renewal and resuscitation of a certain kind, the use of superstition to communicate Nodier's spiritually-charged love as a Christian force may appear problematic, but here is where a certain syncretism is brought to bear, or, rather, becomes a critical aspect of the Vampire Tale. Like Polidori, Nodier was a Catholic and a Mason and many of his novels feature initiatory plots, André Lebois going so far as to argue that Nodier's *La Fée aux Miettes* rivals Schikandere and Giesecke's *Die Zauberflöte* for discoursing on the rites of Freemasonry (27). Like fellow Romantic Johann Goethe, Nodier perceived Polidori's novella as an initiatic "fable," which undoubtedly furnishes one explanation for why he was drawn to the subject; but it is also true that Nodier, *intime* of the great melodramatist Pixérécourt, envisioned a new kind of Romantic drama even before *The Vampyre*'s publication. Polidori's subject offered a uniquely promising vehicle for founding a renewed melodrama that was not just moralistic, but supernatural, mystic, and cosmic, exactly what Nodier wanted. Polidori had also established a symbolic language that gracefully permitted the occulting of his tale's most profound essence, exactly what Nodier needed.

Complementing his several reviews and articles on the theme that appeared in the *Débats* and the *Drapeau Blanc*, two creative works published in 1820 link Nodier, ambiguously, to the Vampire: the *roman Lord Ruthwen* [sic], *ou les Vampires* and the melodrama *Le Vampire, ou Lord Rutwen* [sic]. If these titles read as anagrammatic, suggesting the melodrama is the *roman* inverted and vice versa, the *roman* bears little similarity to either Polidori's story or the melodrama, recalling only tales yet to be written. Perhaps to emphasize their divergent natures, Nodier modifies the spelling of the principals' names in the two works: "Aubrey" and "Ruthwen" in the fiction becoming "Aubray" and "Rutwen" in the play. As the theatrical work was the more enduringly influential, comments on the *roman* (to call it a novel would be misleading) and its innovations can be limited to a few remarks on notable aspects that may have been influential on Stoker's project.

In *Lord Ruthwen*, a shambling *Varney* before *Varney*, *Dracula* before *Dracula*, the Vampire's iconography is fixed for a century. More than a singular "dead grey eye," Ruthwen becomes a tall, thin, distinguished figure, draped in a long black cape; a smooth-talking, courtly gentleman when circumstances demand, seductive lady-killer when discretion permits. While Nodier signed the work's introductory "*observations préliminaires*," which, like the *New Monthly Magazine*'s "Vampyre" and the compendium *Fantasmagoriana*, includes distracting notes on the vampire phenomenon with references to Dom Augustin Calmet, Voltaire, etc., the novel's only authorial attribution took the form of the initials "C. B." along with the note "*publié par l'auteur de* Jean Sbogar *et de* Thérèse Aubert," referencing Nodier's better known contemporary works. For his entire life Nodier attempted to attribute the *roman* to his friend and non–author, theatre manager Cyprien Bérard, apparently fearful that his having written the piece might interfere with his eventually realized ambition of joining "the immortals" of the *Académie Française*, and securing guaranteed lifetime revenues. The speed at which the *roman* appeared following *The Vampyre*'s publication suggests that portions of the text existed when Polidori's story reached print.

The *roman* unfolds as a sequence of told tales, interweaving narratives from multiple sources fleshing out a meagre outline. The plot, easily summarized, is as familiar as *Dracula*: The Vampire attacks, is pursued for 400 pages by an expanding crew of raconteurs, and, when all their narratives have been related, is trapped in its grave. Lord Ruthwen himself tells two stories of the Vampire to listeners who are thoroughly sceptical as to the existence of vampires. Anticipating Stoker, Nodier has his hero, Aubrey, joined by confederates: the Venetian Léonti and Arab Nadour-Héli — three protagonists whose names index the solar: Aubrey, dawn; Nadour-Héli, midday; Léonti, mid–summer. Each of them having been deprived of a loved one by Ruthwen, they form a posse and pursue the Vampire across the woods and gardens of the Italian Renaissance, finally tracking it down and destroying it as the cadaver is rising from its tomb by burning its eyes out and staking its heart with a white-hot iron — a treatment akin to that Pitton de Tournefort actually witnessed performed on what he hoped was a corpse (though he suspected otherwise) on the Ionian isle of St George on the first day of the 18th century.

The 13 anecdotes and curious stories recounted by the *roman*'s various actors place it in the tradition of Boccaccio's *Decamerone* or the *Arabian Nights*, Nodier specifically attaching the Vampire to the *Tale's* Ghoul, Amina. Unfortunately, little represented action interrupts the told tales, resulting in an indirect quality that renders the work anaemic and antique. While it is tempting to make short shrift of its nearly 500 pages, several incidents and thematic departures merit mention. Sequentially, these are: the figuration of the demiurge returning on a boat at a hybrid of the Dionysian festival of *Anthesteria*, *Festa della Sensa*, and Carnival; a Tyrolean fortune-teller's construction of a mysteries nexus; Ruthwen's initial attack; the forming of the posse; a vampire–infected female called to return from death; the triumph of Christianity that allows her to aid her betrothed defeat the Vampire; Demeter's incest refigured through the love of Thelemy [the Will] and brother Oscar; Artemis–Diana personified, preserved yet desecrated. Most importantly, across the entire work Nodier depicts the hunter becoming the hunted, the enduring motif that motivates *Dracula*. Once Lord Ruthwen is disposed of, the dead are released to rest in peace and the novel ends.

The *roman*'s introduction of the Vampire again returns the story to Byron's *Fragment*, finally published in June 1819, and Darvell's instructing his comrade to throw a mystical ring into the waters of the Bay of Eleusis (290). The Doge's marriage to the Adriatic, accomplished by throwing a sacred ring into the waters of the lagoon, brings a figure floating ashore as if the ancient Dionysus approaching his awaiting faithful aboard his *carrus navalis* at Anthesteria. Should the lord of Venice take the sea as his bride, Ruthwen, underworldly Dionysian lord, will take his own Basilinna from among Venice's maidens, choosing the Lido's pale beauty Bettina, fiancée of Léonti. At the evening festivities, a Tyrolean seer sings and dances for the revellers, sounding a theme worthy of Thomas Taylor as she proclaims that the "'stars consulted in the fields of Chaldea, the mysteries honoured on the banks of Egypt's shores, and the famous oracle of Greece have revealed to us their formidable secrets'" (18–19). With that as an introduction and a rattling of her tambourine, the Tyrolean peers into Bettina's palm and is horrified to find reflected there Bettina's sacrifice to the Vampire. Ruthwen drives away the gypsy before she can say more. Later that evening, in the early pre–dawn hours, Ruthwen, having granted Léonti a commission in the Scottish army, will have him arrested for treason to Venice. Ruthwen then tricks Bettina into accompanying him to a secluded woods where he claims Léonti awaits her. There he will drain her life away.

When the body of Bettina revives after her mortal encounter with Ruthwen, an angel appears to her in an annunciation-like scene: Because of her exquisite purity and chastity, she will be spared from an eternity of vampirism. The angel commands her to go to the Adriatic where an oarsman awaits to take her to the East, her soul undergoing a return to the eternal on a barque from the sea of death. As Bettina's soul is saved, grieved fiancé Léonti wanders Venice, searching out the murderous Scottish nobleman Ruthwen to exact vengeance. He is at last gratified to find the unholy criminal by a canal. Léonti is preparing his attack when, sensing a melancholy air of sadness about the man, he realizes the person he is about to kill is not Ruthwen. It is thus that Léonti comes to meet Aubrey, who has arrived at Venice from Scotland in search of his sister's killer. Through a shared resemblance, Nodier renders the Ruthwen-Aubrey doppelganger status clear.

In his tales of the material enwrapping the spiritual, Nodier makes frequent use of the image of woods and forests that enclose magical sources and clearings, places where the normally unknowable is revealed by the supernatural. As in Polidori's story, and following Taylor, through the representation of *woods* 'material nature is clearly implied" (100). Bettina now becomes the supernatural emissary who appears to guide endangered mortals to defeat the Vampire and thus gain her own salvation. For instance, Ruthwen's fiancée, the princess of Modena, separated from her party during a prenuptial hunt, is approached by Bettina in the heart of the wood with a message of warning about her betrothed's unnatural nature. Bettina also appears in an urban nocturnal pleasure garden, when she is afraid that Léonti will be seduced by a corrupt Roman.

In tribute to James MacPherson — the writer from the village of Ruthven, Perthshire, who claimed to resurrect Ossian, ancient bard and Celtic Homer — Nodier places a figure named Oscar (Ossian's son) in his *roman*. Oscar, a princely only son, falls in love with a girl given the Rabelais-inspired name Thelemy, daughter of her mother's trusted servant and confidante. Borrowing from the Persephone myth, Thelemy is pictured in a delightful garden weaving a scarf for her lover, knotting his name into its fabric. Oscar is torn with jealousy until he realizes that his is the name of the one Thelemy loves. They delight in each other among the garden's fruit trees, and consummate their love, ignorant of their consanguinity—for Thelemy is Oscar's illegitimate half-sister. When they belatedly learn the terrible news from the mouth of their nearly mad mother, their torment is augmented by the punishment of the king, who, visiting the garden, overheard their story and learned of his wife's infidelity. The wood and garden, constant elements in the novel's many tales of love and wonderment, doubly frame Oscar and Thelemy's story, taking the ill-fated lovers from an enchanted garden where love blooms to a savage wilderness where guilt-wracked, despairing Thelemy is lost. Thelemy's story ends with the discovery of her veil, partially entangled in a wild willow's branches, floating on the waters of a torrent.

In his introduction to the collected works of Bryon, Nodier warned of the epistemological difficulties emergent from the "contemporary social revolution," saying,

> Thought has become a torture to man; as the old stand-bys fell away and he became more individualistic, a wave of doubt concerning his ability to know and understand swept over him, and in the succeeding chaos man experienced a kind of voluptuousness in plunging into nihilism. Romanticists, wanting to pierce to the reality of things, ripped away the veils of Isis in the horrible expectation of finding a corpse [qtd. Oliver 137–38].

The announcing of various incidents or their denouement through the "rustling of a garment" or the shedding of a veil is frequent and may be attached to Nodier's image of the goddess being unveiled.

Nodier, tellingly, finally inserts the story of a Diana-like figure, Cymadore, who, having been sheltered by a priest of the old beliefs, survived into the modern era, hiding in the ruins of a classical-era Greek temple by a blessed bay near Athens. She is pictured with her bow and arrows, one breast exposed, virginal, and a huntress. Nadour-Héli, as he traveled near Athens, glimpsed her and fell painfully in love. Armed with a lyre rather than a bow, he managed to win her confidence through his music, enchanting Cymadore with his voluptuous Lydian mode and the story of Timothy's lyre's seventh string. The octave-defining seven strings associate musician Timothy of Miletus with Saint Timothy, first bishop of Ephesus (said by Paul to play his congregation like a lyre), who was martyred for attempting to stop Diana-Artemis's licentious annual festival. Love-struck Nadour-Héli was so worshipful of the virginal beauty that the normally solitary misandrist Cymodore agreed to grant him a further audience to continue his effort at love-making. This was her downfall. When Nadour-Héli arrived at the appointed hour he was greeted only by Cymodore's distant cries for help. While she awaited the musical Arab youth, Ruthwen had seized her. Cymodore is represented in chains leaving on a galley with Ruthwen as her captor, Nadour-Héli watching helplessly from shore. Later, Cymodore is discovered defiled, Ruthwen having sold the pure virgin and huntress into a potentate's harem. While the old goddesses are defeated, the Christian Virgin and her agent Bettina will help assure Ruthwen's defeat.

Nodier's Melo-drame

Soon after his novel's publication, Nodier's melodrama *Le Vampire, ou Lord Rutwen* opened at the Porte Saint-Martin Theatre on the Boulevards, listing stage manager Carmouche and backer Jouffroy d'Abbans as co–authors. This time Nodier dared add his own name to the play. Nodier's reworking of the Polidori novella as melodrama was immediately influential, spawning a veritable craze. Though frequently mentioned, this genre–transforming play is little considered by researchers. Like *Fantasmagoriana*, that French anthology of German Gothic tales being read at Villa Diodati when Byron threw down his "ghost story" challenge, which (when considered) is always approached through Mrs. Utterson's related-though-materially-different *Tales of the Dead*, English-speaking commentators on Vampire literature content themselves with James Robinson Planché's adaptation of Nodier's play as if it were Nodier's own, with nothing made of the differences between them. Even then, discussion of Planché's *Bride of the Isles* is usually limited to repeating E. F. Bleiler's story that the play was set in Scotland because of a stock of kilts in wardrobe (xxxviii), a blatant distortion of Planché's statement:

> *The Vampire, or the Bride of the Isles*, was produced at the Lyceum, or English Opera House, as it was then called, on August 9, 1820. Mr. Samuel James Arnold, the proprietor and manager, had placed in my hands, for adaptation, a French melodrama, entitled *Le Vampire*, the scene of which was laid, with the usual recklessness of French dramatists, in Scotland, where the superstition never existed. I vainly endeavoured to induce Mr. Arnold to let me change it to some place in the east of Europe. He had set his heart on Scotch music and dresses — the latter, by the way, were in stock — laughed at my scruples, assured me that the public would neither know nor care [Planché 39–40].

The Scottish connection was hardly due to Gallic recklessness. Remaking the Ossianic connection Lady Caroline Lamb's novel *Glenarvon* established with her character Clarence de Ruthven, Lord Glenarvon, Nodier infuses Rutwen with a Celtic dimension anchoring the vampire in the turbulent cross-currents of the classic *and* the Romantic, ultimately attracting the Anglo-Irish. As Montague Summers aptly observes, *Le Vampire* costumed the

Athenian revenant "in the true transpontine tradition of Ossianic attire" (307). Nodier, having set his revolutionary melodrama on the arch–Romantic Isle of Staffa, left Planché no choice but to follow suit. Pierced by Fingal's Cave, the island of Staffa, which was "discovered" in 1772, attracted to its cathedral-like, sea-washed cavern such Romantic luminaries as Turner, Keats, Wordsworth, Scott, Tennyson, Mendelssohn, and Nodier.

Developing the Ossianic element, Nodier introduces the entire MacPherson-embroidered Ossian genealogy: Oscar, Malvina, Cromal and Fingal and their druidic transmigrating soul take up roles in the Vampire drama and eventually inform Stoker's plural Quinceys. Moreover, Nodier's insistence on Scottish rites seems hardly accidental, and may be due to something beyond Romantic love of highland mists. Nodier, son of Besançon's Masonic lodge's orator, was also a lodge member; recent years have seen repeated claims he was head of the Templar-like Magdalenian Gnostic cult Dan Brown features in *The DaVinci Code,* the Priory of Sion (431).

Polidori penned an initiatory drama that nonetheless reads as a grotesque comedy. In it the principal, the Rutwen-Aubray duality, traces a comic circuit that, after the course of a year, pirouettes towards the tragic on the 366th day's final reversal, when, in a race against midnight (one o'clock), Darkness extinguishes Light. English critics decried this departure as "odious"; a Parisian theatrical public would hardly have reacted more kindly. As melodrama insists on light's triumph as its perfect plagal cadence, plot changes were unavoidable. Even with changes, one French critic, particularly complaining of an offstage attack on a young woman whose pursuit spills across the proscenium, forcefully questioned the play's moral foundation, demanding to know how government could allow such a "hideous and immoral play" (Collin de Maury back notices "*de Quelques Nouveautés*" 271) to be performed. To liquidate Rutwen, Nodier prolongs Polidori's plot by minutes; too late for the Vampire to renew his lease on life through his annual marriage-feast, he, soulless, is condemned to the "void," primordial chaos.

Nodier's three-act composition begins nearly where Polidori's circuit reaches completion, with Aubray returned home from his voyage east. The scene, transported to the Western Sea's isle, is given an emphatic Gothic quality. An interlude of light in darkness constitutes a prologue that flows from Byron, *Manfred*'s Faust-inspired first scene. The curtain rises to darkness, nothingness, "the void." As gaslights flare, a basaltic cavern, *grottes de Staffa,* is progressively revealed, the *grottes* reflecting the subject's grotesque nature. Roughly carved geometrical tombs, pyramidal, cubic, columnar, fill its depths. A sleeping beauty sprawled across the ground in this place where "all breathes of trepidation and terror" (330) brings forth protective spirits: Ituriel, angel of the moon, issues from above the proscenium; Oscar, genie of marriage, from within the cavern's depths. Ituriel evokes the angel of *Paradise Lost* whose spear unmasks the diabolic, no matter its disguise; Oscar incarnates Ossian's son. Night's first moonbeams transform the Caledonian cavern into a Celtic Telesterion.

A Shakespearean tempest drove the ingénue, who is due to marry on the morrow, into the malignant basaltic womb. The innocent fiancée hardly suspects that instead of falling into Love's embrace, she risks falling into Death's clutches, the sage Oscar observes. Ituriel demands an explanation, could it be "true that horrible phantoms sometimes appear, and under the pretence of exerting seigniorial rights of the hymen, cut the throat of a timid virgin to drink her blood?" (331) "Such monsters are called Vampires" (331), specifies Oscar, remarking that one such, having desolated 20 countries, must add one more soul to his infamous roster within the coming hours. "He can take any form, make use of any language, ply any seduction" and though he appears alive, "his eyes expose his veritable status" (331). As a distant clock strikes one, the tombs yield their dead. A specter in his death shroud leaves his downstage grave; approaching Miss Aubray he cries out "Malvina!" In a line Stoker would adapt, he claims: "She belongs to me!" (334) "She belongs to God," retorts Oscar, "and you'll soon belong to the void" (334). The pure, antique spirits watch over the maiden and spout Christian dogma as the clock's somber tone fades and the darkening stage depletes vision.

The tolling clock announces a French classic "unity" of time; the Vampire's tragic day, like the Dionysian Anthesteria, runs from night to night, provoking a question as to whether a Dionysian imperative underlies Aristotle's maxim on confining a tragedy to a single circuit of the sun, or not much exceeding.

Act one opens in Castle Staffa with servants discussing Malvina Aubray's return, after their having searched her out all night. Hearing that she was lost near the grottoes, Scrop, a servant, remarks, "By St. George; that's the only bit of forest that we neglected to search," thereby connecting St. George to the literary vampire for the first time. The domestics huddle to listen to forbidden lore of the House of Staffa's last heiress, who, on the day of her nuptial to a Scottish lord, disappeared near the caves, to be found soon thereafter covered in blood, her throat slashed. Her betrothed was never seen again. With the lord of Staffa having disappeared, Castle Staffa passed into the family of Sir Aubray. Periodicity, stressed from the beginning, is endowed with added resonance, as the murderous marriage occurred precisely 100 years prior. In possible incestuous reference, Scrop claims his grandfather's great-uncle had heard from his grandmother's grandfather that the lovers were victims of vampires. When Malvina's domestic Brigitte thanks the gods that she had till then avoided the caves, Scrop derides her fears, saying that vampires only crave maidens' blood.

1820 etched handbill by "Berthe" advertising *Les Vampires* and representing the prologue of Charles Nodier's influential *mélo-drame*. Public domain, published with Collin de Plancy's *Histoire des Vampires et des spectres malfaisans*.

Malvina's fiancé, Count Marsden, though endowed with vast holdings on the mainland facing the western isle, is unknown to all. Scrop chides fellow servant Edgar that the new lord should arrive just in time to witness his wedding. Enter Malvina, claiming to feel fine despite her ordeal, though her soul is agitated — the fruit, she's certain, of ill-dreamt dreams. She recalls phantoms leaving their graves, most particularly, the face of a young man who emerged from the pyramidal tomb of Fingal. His handsome features, uncanny paleness, and suffering appearance seemed to plead for her aid. As her heart melted in sympathy, his face decomposed, eyes becoming as hollow as the cavern. She dreamt she was destined to serve as victim to a devouring monster, but an unseen force wrenched her away and she found herself, suddenly awake, wandering the forest. An old man set her on a path towards the avenue where she almost at once encountered her brother Aubray who was out searching for her.

At her mention of his name, enter Aubray to discuss wedding plans. Although he has never met Marsden, he declares Marsden's brother Rutwen the "most seductive" (350) friend a man ever had. Having met in Athens, each an enthusiast "of Nature's beauties and monuments to the Arts" (351), they became boon companions in travel and "in pleasure" (351). Sensing something superhuman in Rutwen, Aubray was intent on their knotting a closer relationship. Rutwen sufficiently admired Aubrey's miniature portrait of Malvina for him to suggest an alliance through marriage, an idea which Aubray eagerly adopted as his own.

With Polidori, a miniature of Marsden had revealed Marsden as Ruthven to Aubrey; Nodier, in substituting a feminine subject while maintaining the motif of the miniature, alters the image's function, it now serving to replace the drawing-room as a vehicle of introduction. Similar inversions are evidenced in the exposition that Aubrey provides in recounting to Malvina Rutwen's fatal day in Athens.

One day Rutwen headed into the Athenian countryside to attend the wedding of a maiden whose dowry he had the generous urge to underwrite. Later that afternoon, as arranged, Aubray set off to rendezvous with his friend some miles from Athens. Before he could reach their appointed meeting place however he unexpectedly crossed Rutwen's path, the latter charging by, racing the setting sun towards the city. Rutwen had just enough time to warn Aubray to flee before brigands fell upon them and forced Aubray to the ground. Rutwen had the gallantry and foresight to cover Aubray with his own body, but his heroic act cruelly rewarded him, for he absorbed a mortal blow, seemingly in Aubray's place. Despite their absolute advantage, the assailants then vanished into the dusk. Rutwen proclaimed himself honored to have preserved Aubray's life, regretting only to die without becoming his brother-in-law.

Urging Aubray to escape lest the murderers return, he asked only to be turned so he might look upon the moon, "*astre de la nuit*" (352) to comfort him. Aubray complied, before leaving in search of his cowardly servants, all of whom had abandoned him to the brigands. Within the hour he returned to the place where he had left Rutwen to discover him gone.

Nodier thus amalgamates Polidori's twin Grecian death scenes, Ianthe's and Rutwen's. Rutwen's banditti have no interest in robbery or in Aubray; they were either hunting dark Death, whom they managed to kill, or seeking vengeance and the expiation of a crime — imperatives now satisfied.

Aubray concludes by noting that when he forwarded Rutwen's effects to Venice where Rutwen's brother Marsden had established residence, he included Malvina's portrait among the affairs in tribute to a heroic friend and his ill-fated betrothal. He was both delighted and surprised when Marsden wrote back to offer to accomplish what Rutwen no longer could and to unite their families through Malvina's hand and his own. As Aubray completes his story, Marsden is announced. Malvina, too overwhelmed by her ordeal to welcome her fiancé, retires.

Marsden, whose resemblance to Rutwen dumbfounds Aubray, admits that he is in fact Rutwen, miraculously saved from death. In a further twist of fate, brother Marsden died in Venice, leaving Rutwen heir to the mainland estates. A second recognition scene soon follows, for upon being presented to her fiancé, Malvina faints; his is the spectral face that invaded her cavern dream. Barely recovered, she finds herself under a spell when Rutwen takes her hand. She breaks away, begging leave to consider anew his proposal. Rutwen urges Aubray to expedite the wedding; though he is not at liberty to explain his reason, he must reach London within 36 hours on a life or death matter.

Aubray takes his leave of Rutwen to speak to his sister about advancing the wedding. A servant, Edgar, takes advantage of the interlude to step forward and request Lord Rutwen's presence that afternoon at his own marriage to Miss Lovette, servant of Castle Marsden. Rutwen readily accepts, and orders his launch to be readied. Returning with the happy news that Malvina has consented to wed that evening, Aubray insists on accompanying Rutwen to the mainland to witness their servants' nuptials.

At Marsden, Lovette and her father Petterson, the estate manager, eagerly await both Edgar and their new master. Edgar appears first to inform Petterson that Lord Rutwen, the new master, was arriving. Petterson, believing Rutwen dead for several years, suspects a fortune-hunting impostor, but when Rutwen appears, despite a seven-year absence, he instantly recognizes his unchanged features. When Petterson presents daughter Lovette to the lord, Rutwen ogles her. When Petterson orders the lovers to dance for the nobles, thunder growls.

When Rutwen declares his desire "to crown the maiden's head" (371) by contributing to her dowry, it rolls to a crescendo. A bard, Oscar, emerges from out of the highland fog. To Lovette's offer of drink, the old man promises that in exchange he'll chant an epithalamium to her happiness and pray that the "Great Being" watch over her sleep.

"Young virgin of Staffa," his song begins, "burning with the first flame to set your heart a-trembling.... At the moment of uniting with the lover of your dreams, Be on guard of the kiss that brings Death." With each successive strophe, Rutwen's agitation increases. "When the desert sun no longer gilds the peaks, then the angels of hell come to caress their victim. If their sweet voices lull you to sleep, Pull back" (374). Oscar teaches that the Vampire is of night, winter, and approaches his victims through their dreams. Discerning Rutwen's perturbed state, Petterson interrupts Oscar and sends him away. To Lovette's request that he visit her the next time he crosses the valley, Oscar replies that the morrow may be too late.

Although Oscar's "Great Being" is specifically Platonic, his bardic role emphasizes the Celtic, Ossianic frame. Not only does Oscar, son of Ossian, wander the stage as a bard, but Rutwen emerges from the tomb of Fingal, Ossian's father, usurping heir to a godless reign. In giving Aubray's previously anonymous sister the name "Malvina" to wear, Nodier attributes to her the name of Ossian's granddaughter, blind Oscar's daughter, conductress, muse, and survivor: "Then come thou, O Malvina—with all thy music, come; lay Ossian in the plain of Lutha: let his tomb rise in the lovely field" (from MacPherson "Berrathon: A Poem" 193).

As Petterson toasts his "virtuous master," Aubray excuses himself to go to inform outlying lords of the Count's return so their presence might "*ajoute à l'éclat de ton hymen*" (376), ambiguously referencing either the "splendour of thy marriage" or "bursting of thine hymen." As the cast files off, Edgar offers Lovette his arm to join them. Before they can leave, however, Rutwen interrupts. "Lovely Lovette," he begins, "honour me by hearing me out" (376). Lovette answers that she is no longer her own mistress. "I hope that your betrothed..." (376), continues Rutwen, bowing towards Edgar. Edgar, in recognition of his subservience, implores Lovette to indulge his lordship's wishes, and exits.

Rutwen orders the girl to come to him, but she hesitates. He urges her to fear not: "If you only knew what seeing you does to me" (377), he sighs, claiming she rekindles love's once extinguished flames—again he burns! "But sire," starts Lovette, no doubt thinking of Malvina, "the one you love...." "Is dead!" he interrupts (376). He begs Lovette to indulge him and revive the presence of his departed "celestial" (376) lover. Word by silvered word, he gathers control over the lassie. Oscar's reappearance with a renewal of his refrain allows Lovette to break away. Released, she begins to cry. Rutwen, claiming her tears as his, insists she be his totally. She refuses a purse he places in her hand; an addition to her dowry, he says in encouragement. Just then, they are surrounded by people; compromising circumstances force Lovette to accept Rutwen's binding gift, equivalent to the golden chain of the Corinthian bride.

As her wedding feast begins, Lovette senses something has possessed her; her soul, like Malvina's, is strangely altered. Feeling ill, she leaves the gathering; Rutwen follows in pursuit, Edgar pursuing the pursuer. A scream stops the revel. Lovette, clothes torn, rushes on to the stage, crying to her father to save her. Rutwen appears, Edgar at his heels. Edgar curses Rutwen and fires a pistol. "Ah, I am dying!" (382) moans Rutwen as he collapses. The chorus encircles him; Lovette swoons. Action freezes.

Aubray, coming to console his friend, restores the clockwork's movement. He sends away the crowd. In the intimacy of life's final moments, Rutwen exacts from Aubray twin promises: to keep his death secret for 12 hours, and to carry him to a rock where he might pray while gazing upon the "*astre de la nuit.*" The act ends with Rutwen's corpse, reunited with his celestial lover at last, bathed in moonlight.

In a brightly lit Gothic hall, Brigitte reasons that if Oscar can tell the future, he can read her heart. Oscar replies that she wishes his reassurance about her mistress's fate, but to save Malvina she must get her away from the castle before the new day's first hour strikes. As Oscar withdraws, Malvina enters, sparkling with pre–nuptial joy. Rutwen has just told her they must be off to London as soon as the ceremony has ended so he can present her to the king, undoubtedly referencing himself.

Enter Aubray. Malvina asks her brother if he has seen Rutwen. Aubray sighs, burdened terribly by his sad news. "Milord ... alas!" (389) he struggles to begin. Malvina effervesces about wedding preparations, the voyage to London, how pleasant it would be should her dear brother accompany them. Heartbroken Aubray impatiently tells her to forget the wedding. When Malvina continues, claiming that Rutwen pledged love eternal but moments earlier, Aubray thinks her deluded. As he begins to reveal Rutwen's death, Rutwen appears to remind him of his pledge. Aubray, revolting against a "phantom," continues. As if Jesus with Thomas, Rutwen challenges Aubray to touch him. Malvina, with Rutwen's encouragement, concludes that it is her brother who is mad for believing Rutwen dead. Aubray commands her not to wed, exposing the circumstances that led to Ruthven's death. "Remember your pledge!" orders Rutwen "in a terrible voice" (393). Rutwen has Aubray seized as a madman. As he is carried off, Aubray tries to exact a promise from Malvina not to wed before the clock strikes one.

Strengthening the incest motif, Malvina confesses that her brother is a father to her, she can hardly act against his wishes. Rutwen tenderly laments his friend's insanity and woos Malvina with phrases rehearsed on Lovette: She has rekindled a love once dead. He exacts from her a pledge to marry as planned. On Brigitte's return, Rutwen exits.

Malvina voices bright hope for the future; Brigitte, through asides, scepticism. Addressing Malvina, Brigitte insists that with Sir Aubray possessed the day will end badly for all. Devastated, Malvina moans that it is her wedding day. On those words, the strains of a severe march initiate the ceremony. Enter Rutwen. A door to a chapel opens; within, several servants attend. Rutwen orders Malvina to come. To hurry her along, he grabs her by the wrist and begins to drag her towards the chapel. From the wings, Aubray calls "Sister, my sister!" (399) Struggling against his servants, he enters. She is being led to the tomb, he warns — the priest is a minister of Death; the torches are funeral flames. Aubray incites the household against Rutwen. Deaf to their cries, Rutwen insists, "This woman is mine" (400), still pulling Malvina along by the wrist. With his free hand Rutwen pulls out a dagger and is about to stab brother and sister both when a bell tolls once and thunder rolls. "*Le Néant! Le néant!*" (401) cries the assembly: The Void! Nothingness! The dagger falls from the hand that clutched it. Featureless shades climb out of the earth to drag Rutwen into the underworld. Above the stage, an exterminating angel appears on a cloud; lightning flashes; the curtain falls on a hail of fire as Light triumphs over darkness.

The names Rutwen and Aubray unambiguously reference Polidori's *Vampyre.* In adapting Polidori's novella, great efforts were made to maintain Nicolas Boileau's "classical unities" of action, time, and place. Only in terms of "place" is Corneillean convention violated, permitting the day-night polarity's materialization in Aubray's Isle of Staffa and Rutwen's Estate of Marsden. Western Aubrays and Eastern Rutwens, inhabiting contiguous estates and destined to be joined through marriage, have been each other's heirs for a century, though they must visit a spot near Athens to make one another's acquaintance. From Marsden, solar Aubray disappears to visit other districts. When Rutwen grabs Malvina by the wrist to drag her towards her marriage, the scene is literally mimetic, imitating the mythic act of Plouton who, appearing from the gaping earth, grabs Persephone by the wrist. It even might be imagined that Persephone is the dead true love Rutwen describes to Lovette and Malvina. This time, however, the gaping earth and enveloping shadows swallow Rutwen alone.

Nodier has introduced a new grotesque to the stage, personified an antique god, and placed it in a new form of melodrama influenced by Byron's "classical" *Manfred.* Rutwen has been contained by a melodramatic form, a comic form, and has thus been rendered non–threatening; no Byronic hero, he becomes in the public's mind a pure villain, leaving Aubray to share the hero's role with Oscar. In having his modern grotesque dispatched to nothingness, Nodier has also constructed a cautionary tale attached to his concerns for the epistemological difficulties of agnosticism, the direction of the "new" Romanticists, warning anew against "a kind of voluptuousness in plunging into nihilism" (qtd. Oliver 138). In representing "the idea upon which is founded those romantic fictions which belong to an order of seething passions unknown to the ancients, but too real and exalted not to be poetic" (qtd. Oliver 138), Nodier represents the Byronic. When Rutwen succumbs, he depicts the Byronic undone, falling to modernity's inescapable nihilism.

The Bride of the Isles

Samuel Arnold, proprietor of London's English Opera House, remarked *Le Vampire*'s wild Parisian success, and, to cash in on the vogue, commissioned James Robinson Planché to adapt and translate Nodier's melodrama. Planché's play, scored by Joseph Binns Hart, premiered in August 1820, barely two months after Rutwen's Parisian debut. The success that greeted Arnold's project was such that the play was exported to France, running before sold-out houses in Paris concurrent to those for Nodier's at the *Porte Saint-Martin*. Critics raged now at a fashion, not an aberration.

Planché's trimmed two-act "Romantic Melodrama" resembles Nodier's, but its discrepancies are noteworthy. The play opens in the familiar cavern on Staffa, Planché labeling his prologue "Introductory Vision," a terminology suggesting an affinity with "vision scenes" of later melodramas. Miltonian Ithuriel becomes a Shakespearean Ariel; Oscar is replaced by Unda; Malvina is rechristened Lady Margaret, likely in homage to Goethe. Outdoing Nodier, the set inverses the function of the proscenium, positioning the audience as if it were looking out from within the cavern at sea and sky. Unda rises from the depths and works an incantation; reinforced by a new presence, an unseen chorus, she summons Ariel: "By the sun that hath set, In the Waves I love; On the eve that renews: The fair moon's birth." The chorus chants, "Appear! appear!" (14)

Winged Ariel, draped in a star-spangled white muslin gown and covered by a skyblue robe, descends on a silvery cloud from above the proscenium, head crowned by a tiara, silver wand in hand. The spirits of Heaven and Earth set to work on the behalf of the sleeping virgin, a pearl enclosed in a grotesque shell. Unda, "Spirit of the Flood," explains that wicked souls exist who, through evil, "enter the dead forms of other men, Assume their speech, their habits and their knowledge, And thus roam o'er the Earth; but subject still, At stated periods, to a dreadful tribute" (15).

The reanimation of cadavers by "wicked souls" separates this vampire from Polidori's, in the words of the *Monthly Review* of 1819, "bustling inhabitant of the world" and Nodier's soulless body, to place it in a context of demonic possession. The spirits review a vampire's annual obligation of draining a maiden's blood to avoid being reduced to "nothingness, total annihilation" (15), inexplicably Heaven's worst punishment for a "wicked soul." Unda explains that the relics of "Cromal the Bloody," lie within and that it is he, in the form of the Earl of Marsden, who terrorizes the earth. Cromal intends to wed Margaret and thereby renew his terrestrial term.

Cromal brings the Vampire once again into direct contact with Ossian. Pagan Cromal, usurper of the theocratic order of the druids in order to assure his position as first hereditary chief, Vergobretus, has returned, replacing Nodier's Fingal in the tomb. It is he, blood-crazed temporal ruler, who must renew himself by activating Marsden's body. In "Fingal's rocky sepulchre," the spirits of air and sea conjure the chthonic Vampire before sleeping Margaret: "Let thy vampire–corpse appear To this sleeping maiden's eyes.... That the form she may know ... And shun thee, till the setting ray... Phantom, from thy tomb so drear, At our bidding rise!—Appear!" (16) To a peal of thunder, Cromal's tomb opens; the Vampire lunges at the maiden, claiming her as *mine.* "Down, down!" (16) Unda commands, driving the Vampire back to his grave.

In a variation on the *Arabian Nights*' "Tale of the Ghoul and the Prince" and certain incidents of Nodier's *roman*, Margaret was in pursuit of red-deer (15) when a storm separated her from her hunting party and forced her to shelter in the cavern. The image of virginal Margaret as huntress brings Diana and Darvell's Ephesian pilgrimage to the fore as embedded associations. Hunter shall become hunted, first with Margaret, then with Ruthven.

Planché, casually violating another of the Vampire Tale's conventions, substitutes Lady Margaret's father, Sir Ronald, for Aubray. Perhaps this was intended to mirror the Vampire's Fingal-Cromal generational shift. James MacPherson claimed Cromal, Fingal's father, died in battle at the precise moment of Fingal's birth, son renewing father, father being given new life, his son's, through blood, his own. A somewhat similar type of metempsychosis is already at work in Planché's *Vampire*. Ronald, traveling with his son Aubray, encountered the endearing Ruthven in Greece. A clash with bandits cost Aubray his life, but Ruthven, who saved Sir Ronald, filled the void in his father's heart, Ruthven effectively becoming Aubray. The father-brother inversion thus serves to intensify dangerous relations, a father vehemently wishing his daughter to marry a man he has come to view as his son, rather than one brother working to mate his sister with another. This innovation displaces a relationship fundamental to the Vampire Tale — sibling incest — without offering ritual justification. It also deprives Margaret of orphan status.

Changes of names and idiom little modify the play's first scenes, but when Marsden and Ruthven are discovered to be one and the same a second fundamental departure from canon occurs. When Margaret faints, her father escorts her offstage, leaving an agitated Ruthven alone. Planché has isolated his vampire to set up a soliloquy in which he expresses remorse, recalls a withered conscience, and portrays himself as an unwilling agent of murder:

> Demon as I am, that walk the earth to slaughter and devour! The little that remains of heart within this wizard frame, sustained alone by human blood, shrinks from the appalling act of planting misery in the bosom of this veteran chieftain. Still must the fearful sacrifice be made, and suddenly, for the approaching night will find my wretched frame exhausted — and darkness — worse than death — annihilation is my lot! Margaret! Unhappy maid! Thou art my destined prey: thy blood must feed a Vampire's life, and prove the food of his disgusting banquet [26–7].

Planché then labors to lend Nodier's double wedding what seems to him greater rationality. Hearing of servant Robert's marriage gives Ruthven the idea to satisfy his need for a ripe maiden's blood in time for his renewal while relieving him of the need to drain Margaret. This seemingly arbitrary coincidence explains his delight at learning of the impending marriage. Substituting himself for Robert, he can glut his thirst by exercising his *droits de seigneur* over the servile girl Planché lustily renames "Effie." When Ruthven declares his love, Effie is confused, flattered, repelled. Ruthven seizes her, carrying her off bodily, stage right. Robert enters stage left; looking afar, he cries out, "Villain!" (31) Drawing a pistol, he chases after them as the stage goes dark.

When the lights rise anew Andrew, the mainland bride's father, and Ronald, the island bride's father, enter, wondering what could have happened to Ruthven. The sounds of shots fired and Effie screaming "Save me!" send Andrew running off. Ruthven staggers on stage to say: "I die!" Stage directions indicate that the moon can now be seen rising. Ruthven begs Ronald to promise him the fulfilment of a last request. Ronald quickly promises, but Ruthven, unsatisfied, insists he make solemn oath. With the oath pledged Ruthven orders Ronald to "[c]onceal my death from every human being till yonder moon ... shall be set this night" (31). Resurrecting Byron, he explains that Ronald must take a ring "and, ere an hour shall elapse after I have expired, throw this ring into the waves that wash the tomb of Fingal" (31). As Ronald fervently repeats "I will, I will!" Ruthven dies, a reminder on his lips: "Remember your oath. The lamp of night is descending the blue heavens; when I am dead, let its sweet light shine on me. Farewell!" (31) In an apparent continuity error, Cromal's tomb has become Fingal's.

To music, Andrew, Robert and Effie approach Fingal's Cave in a boat to leave Robert with provisions for his survival until Ronald's anger has abated. After a farewell duet, Effie is rowed off by her father. Soon thereafter a boat carrying Ronald approaches the island. In the cave, Ronald proclaims that his soul has been altered and wonders what the ceremony he is performing could mean. Why would Ruthven wish his death kept secret till the moon set? He tosses the ring into the waters. Over rolling thunder Ruthven is heard intoning "Remember thy oath!" Ronald calls out, "his spirit speaks! Ruthven, my friend, my preserver!" (34) Robert steals forth from the shadows to claim his innocence and explain his role as defender of Effie's honor. Ronald grabs him, casting him into the sea. Boarding his launch Ronald declaims: "Ruthven, thou art revenged!" (34) As the boat pushes off, Robert is revealed clinging to a rock.

At the castle, the wedding is about to begin so that Ruthven can be off "ere daybreak" (34). When Ronald arrives, Margaret tells him to get ready, Ruthven will soon be there. Before he can explain that the wedding cannot go forward, Ruthven is among them. "Fiend!" hisses Sir Ronald. Kept in constant reminder of the oath, Ronald rages. Ruthven declares him mad, and has the servants restrain him. Ronald pleads with his daughter not to marry before the moon has set. Margaret can only manage to exclaim "Oh, my poor father!" before fainting into Ruthven's arms, a transference having been made.

As he is taken away, Ronald declaims: "A mist seems clearing from my sight; and I behold thee now — oh, horror! Horror!— a monster of the grave — a — a Vam —" (36). Although he collapses before he can utter the difficult word, Margaret suddenly snaps to her senses. Ronald has suffered a relapse of a condition developed when her brother's death inflicted a shock upon his reason, explains Ruthven. Margaret hadn't known of her father's fragility of mind, but finds his wish to delay the wedding until the moon sets reasonable. To Ruthven questioning if she loves him not, Margaret asks how could he doubt her? Ruthven then asks her to accept the ring so recently thrown into the sea as his sacred pledge. In a sublimated wedding ceremony, he kisses it and places it on her finger, proclaiming in an aside, "her fate is sealed — she cannot now retract" (37). Margaret, her conflicted heart ready to burst, is sent off to ready herself.

Outside the castle, Andrew and Effie aid sea-battered Robert. Having noticed Ronald's boat, they returned to the cave and rescued Robert. Robert insists on going to see Ronald: "I know his noble nature too well to fear a continuance of his anger" (38), he says of the man who minutes earlier attempted to murder him. Effie breaks into song. Another voice takes it up. Robert recognizes the singer as Ronald's "henchman." The servant staggers in, bemoaning his master's folly. Accosted by Robert, he explains Ronald's condition. Hearing that Marsden lives and the wedding is underway, they charge off to "foil the villain" (39).

In a chapel through whose "Gothic Window" "the moon is seen going down" (40), all await as music plays. Ruthven paraphrases Ariel and Unda: "Ere yon orb shall kiss the wave, the tributary victim shall be paid" (40). Thunder peals. Ruthven grabs Margaret's wrist to drag her to the altar. Margaret begs him to wait. "Nay ... Father commence the rites" (41), snarls Ruthven. Before he can, Robert, Ronald, Andrew, Effie, and attendants invade the chapel. Ronald forbids the marriage; Margaret now throws herself into her father's arms. A blast of wind blows open the casement. Ronald calls out that the moon is disappearing beneath the waves. Ruthven again grabs Margaret by the wrist and draws his dagger, taking aim for Ronald, but the servant Robert wrests the arm away. Margaret seeing the moon set, declares herself Ruthven's, to which he responds, "I am lost" (42). A great thunderclap announces Unda and Ariel; a thunderbolt strikes Ruthven, who disappears into the earth through the famous "vampire trap."

In his *Recollections*, Planché expresses satisfaction with his *Vampire*, noting that the play was continually in revival a half-century after its premiere.

Revelation

> "He had evidently forgotten all about the dark stranger, as in his illness he had forgotten all that this episode had reminded him of. I don't like this lapsing into forgetfulness; it may make or continue some injury to the brain. I must not ask him, for fear I shall do more harm than good; but I must somehow learn the facts of his journey abroad. The time is come, I fear, when I must open that parcel and know what is written" [156].

While the Vampire Tale retains to this day the Byron-implied Mysteries discourse Polidori so brilliantly embroidered, Polidori's *Vampyre*, characterized in the British press as "a filthy tale" "devoid of all merit" (*Edinburgh Monthly Review* 1819, 618–20), was doomed to oblivion until, as Byron phrased it, "it was got up as a melo-drame at Paris." The being that became canonical in Stoker's hands washed up on English shores not from Transylvania but from across *la Manche*. Planché's role in this transaction was both slight and pivotal, he hardly understood the thing he was hired to translate and badly wanted to re-costume, but in earning his daily bread he nonetheless brought the Vampire an enduring success with English-speaking theatrical audiences. It was Nodier who made the Vampire a stock character in a new and enduring *Commedia dell'Arte* where it has flourished ever since, a star of stage and screen, but he did so at a remove. In reforming Polidori's "trifle" Nodier bequeathed its occulted theme to later generations of French Romantics, most notably Théophile Gauthier, and Alexadre Dumas, *père*, and, through him, the Irish, and most particularly Abraham Stoker.

Nodier's *Vampire*, necessarily not Polidori's, was in fact scarcely his own. His *roman*, while defeating the pagan and positing a love beyond the grave, is most concerned with denigrating the amoral, agnostic turn of modernity, even staging a seduction scene in the Sistine Chapel, a Roman matron attempting to corrupt a Moslem Arab youth. His melodrama posits a pagan element, Celtic and Ossianic, existing without gods—the druids having been overthrown and banished by Cromal. In sending the Vampire back to its nihilistic origins Nodier simply defeats godlessness. Although Nodier claimed to be dedicated to making his work subservient to a Christian ideal, passing reference to St. George and the idea of annihilation as divine punishment for the soulless seem far too vague and grossly insufficient. The drama, manifesting little transcendent-yet-chivalrously romantic love, reads as a misshaped morality play, conceding the attractiveness of the *frénétique* while railing against its inherent nihilism.

Having interjected the Vampire into the theatrical world Stoker inhabited, Nodier abandoned it to pursue his further ambitions. It would wait to be reclaimed until Alexander Dumas, with silent partner Auguste Maquet, came along a generation later to apply a post–Restoration veneer to *Le Vampire* and to tint it with a dogma so faithfully Catholic that it would make Abraham van Helsing possible. To mitigate Ruthven's frenzied nature, Dumas injects him into a *féerique*, a traditional, trouvère–flavored secular theatrical form returned from the middle-ages and related to Adam de la Halle's *Jeu de la Feuillée* with Renaissance reverberations in Shakespeare's *A Midsummer's Night Dream*'s Green George and Celtic allusions. This contributory strand of French *mélo-drame*'s fashion ascended with Napoleon III at mid–century. Surprisingly, through the intervention of faeries and pixies, Dumas' homage, projecting a more clearly articulated statement of love and highly evolved appeal to Christian symbols, better serves Nodier's thematic priorities than Nodier managed himself. Dumas' particularly ludic play plays on the polysemous nature of Christian symbols, making his Vampire, as will be shown, narrowly and decisively relevant to Stoker's.

As much as any human agent, Nostalgia wrote this particular *Le Vampire*. Setting out at mid–century to draft *Mes Mémoires*, Dumas recalled arriving at the capital the proverbial callow provincial. Fortuitous circumstances on a glorious day of a sudden and unexpected Dionysian initiation conspired to have him see the opening performance of 1823's revival of *Le Vampire, ou Lord Rutwen*, in which Nodier adapts certain of Planché's innovations. It marked both the first truly Romantic confection Dumas had ever experienced and his illuminating discovery of melodrama. Through his recollection of that introduction to the Boulevard theatres and the vampire superstition, of his chance meeting with the baffling, erudite Nodier, his subsequent attendance of Nodier's weekly soirées at the Bibliothèque de l'Arsenal at which authors like Hugo and himself gained entry into the burgeoning Romantic literary scene, Dumas went back and consulted *Lord Rutwen*'s text. Seeing it all re–enacted in his mind, he was inspired, a long, successful quarter-century later, to rewrite the play. Nodier, dead for the better part of a decade at mid–century, had provided Dumas with exceptional insight into his thinking on the play, nearly in the way that Byron had privileged Polidori with his concept for the Vampire. This thus made the subject a perfect vehicle for Dumas to pay homage to a mentor. *Le Vampire, Drame Fantastique en cinq actes, en dix tableaux, en société avec M. Auguste Maquet* premiered at the Ambigu-Comique at 1851's winter solstice. The play, which formed the basis for Dion Boucicault's *The Phantom*, has only recently been translated into English. In that the translation, which remains obscure, fails to discern fully the symbolic system engaged, it will be useful to review the play as written.

Le Vampire, Drame Fantastique

Its curtain rises on a Spanish inn's courtyard. In an out-of-place nod to classicism, a dialogue between chorus and a gypsy sets the scene. Alternating, they sing about the ruins of Tormenar Castle. Who lives there? their song asks. A double answer returns: Terror by day, Death by night. Enter innkeeper Juan Rozo, his daughter Petra, her fiancé Botaro, and a servant ostentatiously named Lazarus. Rozo chases off the gypsies, saying he needs every inch of space. Lazarus muses he doesn't see how Senor Rozo will be able to lodge everyone. Botaro, too, finds it difficult to believe Rozo's inn will accommodate the entire wedding party. Boasting that his inn has already lodged "50 Christians," Rozo dismisses their concerns. Lazarus reminds his master the 50 Christians were swearing like 100 pagans by morning, and Botaro rejoins that the wedding party consists of 77, not 50.... But what does it matter, he adds, as long as the bride is well bedded! Lazarus accuses the groom of selfishness.

Botaro asks his soon-to-be father-in-law what he will do if travelers arrive. "I'll tell them there's no room!" comes the firm reply. Botaro wonders if his attitude is compatible with an innkeeper's vocation, to which Rozo declares that for his daughter's wedding, his house is simply his home, not an inn, though guests in residence will not be evicted.

As in Nodier's play, the audience is invited to a simple wedding. Rather than an estate keeper, an innkeeper is giving away his daughter. The sole and singular guest is a Moor who "only eats a few grains of rice ... with a pair of ivory chop-sticks" (402). Lazarus is convinced she gets up in the middle of the night "to eat olla podrida and garbachos" (402) since no human being could survive on her diet.

On Botaro's suggestion, it is decided that to make room at the inn Lazarus should find himself some other place for the night. As he is being escorted to the establishment's gates, visitors arrive. A husband, wife and children join the assembly. Lazarus greets them by advising that the boss says there's no room at the inn. Rozo calls over to Lazarus to find out what the travelers want, and Lazarus claims that they've journeyed since dawn and will accept any uncomfortable corner. The new arrivals said nothing of the kind — Lazarus is pleading in their stead. Botaro suggests they take the attic where Lazarus lodges, an idea that Rozo greedily pounces on, instructing Lazarus to conduct the family to his room. This sparks a series of protests by Lazarus, all dismissed. When Lazarus asks why he is being driven away from his resting place, Rozo reveals he is suspected of flirting with his daughter by her fiancé. Lazarus maintains he was only helping her with something in her eye. One might imagine that the something was desire. He is ordered off again. Protesting hunger, he is told to take a crust of bread and cheese. Here it is, the day of a wedding feast, and all I get is bread and cheese, he grumbles. A compromise is negotiated: He can eat at the inn, but must sleep elsewhere. Petra, who has observed the entire exchange, sighs, "Poor Lazarus!" (407)

Alone, Lazarus complains bitterly, "put out of doors, into the night, into a mountainous wilderness where evil spirits skulk along the pathways and at midnight the black château of Tormenar expels bats, vultures, owls, serpents ... all because I blew into a young lady's eye" (407). From a safe distance, he contemplates the Moor, troubled by what he calls her "evil eye." An odd pair of eyes, one desirous, the other envious, seems to be deliberately formed from the features of Petra and the Moor. While Lazarus ruminates, he is called for, but, since no longer attached to the household, rather than respond, he turns on his heel and wishes them to the devil. In the distance, he claims to spy mules, soon qualified as a single mule, with a lone voyageur, a woman.

Once arrived, the woman asks Lazarus to whom she might speak; he proposes himself. She asks if she hasn't arrived at a hotel. An inn, corrects Lazarus, that takes no guests. The woman is in need of a servant and will pay generously. Lazarus remarks she has come to the right place; he happens to be looking for work, proposing his service as mule driver, valet, cook. The lady, Juana, seeks a guide only. Lazarus, claiming to know every rock and crevice in the neighborhood, is hired on the spot and pressed to set out. "Now?" asks Lazarus; "Now!" answers his new employer. To Lazarus's next logical question, "Where are we going?" comes the only possible answer in this pared-down universe: "Tormenar." Comedy follows, Lazarus listing reasons to avoid Tormenar, but Juana is adamant, she must go there that night. She offers him ten times a guide's normal pay. He swears "not for one hundred, nay a thousand times the pay" (409) will he go. Juana says she'll find someone braver. "You'll see, senora!" Lazarus cries out, "*Hey*! Christians! *Hey*! pagans! *Hey*! everyone! The senora is ready to pay 10 piastres for a guide" (409). Volunteers come rushing. Lazarus continues, "to lead her to Tormenar!" The population of guides as quickly vanishes. In an aside, Juana says, "My God! But *he* will await me; he'll believe that I failed to keep my word" (410).

Innkeeper and betrothed enter into the fray, Lazarus identifying the boss to Juana. She sets out her mission, venturing that the innkeeper surely doesn't share in the pleasants' superstition. Hearing her destination, he exclaims: "Tormenar! Holy Virgin!" Botaro echoes his prayer, "Tormenar! Lord Jesus!" (410) Juana defiantly declares she'll go alone.

From the far side of the courtyard gate a voice calls. The innkeeper orders Lazarus to see who's there, but Lazarus, no longer employed, refuses. The voice, grown louder, demands the gates be opened, a group of eight horsemen and four ladies awaits. To the innkeeper's claim the house is full, the voice assures the ladies the gates will open. The innkeeper contradicts him. The voice, belonging to a Count Gilbert, says in such a case he should take down the sign advertising his inn, and offers to save him the trouble. Pistol shots explicate the sense of his proposition. Gilbert orders his companions to batter the gate. A storm threatens, he says, and the ladies have no desire to spend the night exposed to the elements. To Rozo's repeated refusal, the door is broken down.

With the company inside, Rozo continues pleading how full his house is, with aunts, uncles, cousins, brothers, and sisters. Gilbert, pointing out the Moor, snaps, there's a strange one, part of your family, too? Rozo explains her status as a lodger since the previous day. In asides, Gilbert declares the Moor "sombre featured"; she, looking him over, pronounces him "handsome" (414). Gilbert asks if there is no other place nearby, a house, an inn, a castle? Botaro volunteers there is a castle nearby, but... "But what?" (414) challenges Gilbert. The castle's malignant presence is recounted. Disparaging superstition, Gilbert urges his companions to follow him there. Before they leave, however, stories of what happens to the castle's visitors are related. Gilbert, suspecting bandits, is assured that corpses are found at the castle with their jewellery and gold intact. Gilbert reminds his party they wield eight swords, declaring himself unafraid. On Lazarus's suggestion, Juana asks to accompany Gilbert. She introduces herself as the Marquis of Torillas's only daughter, in flight from a convent where she was confined to prevent her marrying Louis de Figuerroa, to whom she is betrothed before God. She has come to this remote region because of a letter from Luis, Catalonia's most handsome nobleman, assigning a meeting that night at Tormenar.

Gilbert, too, reveals his origins. He hails from Brittany and has a tenderly-loved sister. Offering his arm, he promises to treat Juana as he would wish his sister treated should she find herself in a comparable situation. Lazarus, who has taken a liking to Gilbert, offers his services to this newly arrived hero, an arrangement that is never quite concluded. Gilbert asks the innkeeper for food if he has no room. The groom agrees to hand over part of the wedding feast to be rid of the intruders. Claps of thunder peal as the travelers take leave of the inn with cries of "*adieu*": "to God." The innkeeper's family sets off to dine, leaving only the Moor. "It will take you two hours to find your fiancé," she remarks. "I'll have caught up to him in three minutes!" (420)

Act two opens in a vast, column-lined salon. The opened frame of a large ruined window reveals a storm gathering over mountains. Old portraits in worm-eaten frames, Gothic furnishings, and an immense fireplace complete the décor. Immediately, the Moor skulks out of a doorway as a distant clock strikes 11. "He was young! handsome! ... and now here am I, young and beautiful once again!" (420) Approaching voices tell of Gilbert's arrival, he is heard helping a laughing woman. Promising, "till next year, Gilbert!" (420) the Moor, displaying a set of wings, flies off through the window.

Enter the travelers, admiring the room's magnificence. As some light candles and others gather scraps of wood, provisions from the wedding feast are laid out on a great table. Juana notes that though it is after 11 o'clock Luis hasn't arrived. Gilbert tries to comfort her, reminding her of the road's condition, the storm's force, and the trouble their party of 12 had climbing to the château. That is precisely what troubles her. Gilbert offers that don Luis is undoubtedly a brave cavalier, strong enough to face any adversary. Juana reminds Gilbert that some dangers cannot be combated by the sword. Gilbert refuses to believe her intimidated by "chimerical terrors." Juana is haunted by a sense of foreboding, distraught at not finding Luis at Tormenar. The Breton recalls how she had so recently been clutching his arm and laughing when the mule carrying their victuals, swept off its feet by the currents, was almost lost, joking that it had threatened to reverse the miracle at Cana by changing their wine into water. Her humor changed, she says, on entering Tormenar, whose cold chilled her soul; she daren't even look around. She describes a difficulty in breathing, and, as if recalling an incident of Nodier's novel, a sensation, in entering Tormenar, of being a bird who seeking a seed is trapped in a cage set to ensnare her.

Cursing Tormenar's blackened walls for afflicting her so, Gilbert, reinforcing the parallelism established between Juana's mood and Tormenar, proposes fire, food, wine, and conversation to banish gloom from her spirit and the castle walls. The candles on the table, says Gilbert, will serve as beacons to any lost traveler. Another of the company quips that should any ghosts be present they'll at least be able to see them. Gilbert says that, though a child of the Château de Tiffauges and practically godchild to the fairy Mélusine, he little believes in ghosts, but strongly in bandits of the Spanish Sierras. But, comes the question, why would anyone murder without stealing? In order to terrify and secure Tormenar as a base, reasons Gilbert, proposing to post sentries at strategic points throughout the night. He sounds a horn to summon the travelers to table. Gilbert insists they are 12 to have come to Tormenar, though at the inn, before Juana joined them, he claimed they were already eight cavaliers and four ladies — a continuity error serving to stress the importance the authors attached to constituting a party of 12.

Gilbert, offering Juana "two drops of wine" and some rabbit pâté, says, "We are in the country of Sancho, the kingdom of proverbs" (424). We are also with Nodier at the Porte Saint-Martin in 1823, for after a series of exchanges on Tormenar, superstitions, Bretons, Gilbert (alluding to an entr'acte conversation between Nodier and Dumas at Nodier's *Vampire*) asserts that he had never said he didn't believe in ghosts — only that he wasn't afraid of them and hadn't seen any recently. Intrigued companions ask when he had last seen a supernatural being. Gilbert answers, not since coming of age, admitting, however, a belief in the supernatural, asking why should man constitute the highest level of creation?

Another voyager remarks he has faith in the glass of wine in his hand because he can see it, drink it, but cannot believe in things imperceptible. Gilbert, further referencing Nodier, asserts the Marquis is mistaken; microscopic beings, though invisible, are every bit as real as themselves. He had seen them, with the aid of a microscope, only last year, which doesn't mean they hadn't existed for the last six thousand, adding, not a peasant in Brittany goes without an elf to help with his horses, or a sprite to assist with other chores.

He himself has a fairy residing in a tapestry, explaining that the lords of Tiffauges see the light of day in a chamber known as the tapestry room, indeed his own case. He spent his infancy there watching the fairy dance quadrilles to a silent melody, and can't say if it happened in any reality other than his imagination. Every night he would watch Mélusine sweep across the floor, while a hunter, also a tapestry resident, chased a stag around the room, and birds fluttered forth to fan him in his cradle. The fairy, pale and smiling, would sing him a song "whose melody and lyrics have since been lost in the noise and agitation of this world made up of materialism and the real" (427).

Another voyager, saying each country cultivates its native superstitions, tells of visiting Epire, where the population fears a terrible ghoul who appears immensely beautiful to attract handsome youths whose blood she then drinks with abandon.

Gilbert, hearing Juana express her horror, adds that if she had been French she would have known of such creatures through Antoine Galland (first European translator and, no doubt, partial author of *The Thousand and One Nights*), and how such a one, who would eat but a few grains of rice with ivory chopsticks at her familial repast, was discovered feasting on a bloody meal by her husband, who followed her during her nocturnal wanderings. Juana asks if any had seen such a creature. The Marquis had seen a woman reputed to be a ghoul. When he is asked what she was like, he says she was like every other woman but a little paler, thinner, with staring, owl-like eyes. To Gilbert asking if she were beautiful, the Marquis judiciously states, "more beautiful than not" (428).

Juana doubts such a monster could be beautiful. The Marquis terms such women "coquettish," as they carefully select their prey, choosing only men that are handsome or loved by another. "They hide in some desolate place, following in their victim's wake, to put him to sleep with the whisper of their great wings, and, once asleep, they suck his life's blood in a deadly embrace; then, invisible, they witness the pain of the fiancé whose tears they drink with the same voluptuousness as they had consumed the blood" (428).

Juana protests the subject's grotesque nature, Gilbert conceding the conversation's somber turn. She asks Gilbert if he won't go seek out Luis. Morning brings answers, he replies, outside "branches break, nocturnal birds, frightened, collide in the air; we, here, savour the innkeeper's wedding feast, drink to the health of those dear to us, and ourselves, holding hands, defy fairies, thieves, ghouls and vampires" (429). Unsatisfied, Juana renews her plea. Gilbert suggests they go to the balcony with torches and call out; if Luis replies, they can set out after him. With his proposition accepted, he escorts Juana out to the balcony with a torch, calling out for Luis as they go.

Meanwhile, the raconteurs continue, a second voyager telling that though he had never seen one, he once visited a family of Pern, Jews, who had a beautiful daughter whose portrait he had seen, and .... Juana's scream, her torch having been extinguished by the wind, interrupts the story's thread. Juana and Gilbert re-enter. The storyteller is urged on. The clock begins striking the midnight hour. The traveler says that a noise of the wind, much like that which they were then listening to, continued to howl at the moon as the clock began to strike the ultimate hour, now years ago, when suddenly, at the last chime of the midnight, the door slowly opened to reveal a vampire.

At that point in the traveler's tale, midnight's 12th tone was, as in the narration, striking. When, in a *mise-en-abîme*, the door to the chamber of Tormenar squeaks open, the startled members of the party all want to know "Who's there?" "Oh, excuse me, Mesdames, messieurs, I am so sorry to disturb you," replies a stranger. "I'm but a simple voyager" (431). His name is Ruthven, Lord Ruthven. Having seen the signals from below, he came seeking shelter for the night.

Gilbert demands pardon for their lack of cordiality, but his arrival was so unexpected. Looking at Juana, Ruthven apologizes for any shock he has occasioned. Juana says, in fact, it was merely that his arrival coincided so strangely with their conversation. Ruthven asks what they were discussing. A voyager discloses that they were speaking of vampires. The raconteur insists that in Hungary it's not rare to hear of such devils. Ruthven readily agrees, but remarks that what is truly rare is to see one of those monsters. He had been in Hungary and heard the stories, but never actually saw a vampire; he begs they change the subject to something gayer.

The assorted nobles present themselves. Gilbert receives an affirmative reply when he asks Ruthven if he is armed. And your provisions? They follow with a servant, a servant undoubtedly aware of Tormenar's legend which might considerably slow his progress. But, protests Gilbert, they may be lost. Ruthven does not think so. He has hired a local lad encountered in the vicinity of the nearby inn. Taking Luis' place, Ruthven joins the party, the 13th at table.

Enter Lazarus, declaring he hadn't believed that any man could have lived through the torments of fear he'd just experienced. Juana and Gilbert greet him warmly. Having already missed two chances to visit Tormenar, a third opportunity decided him on coming. When a traveler remarks that Ruthven neither drinks nor eats, he replies that the cold has stolen his appetite. Lazarus finds the cold's effects curious, declaring he hadn't his master's nature: He is famished. The travelers ask about the legend of Tormenar. Lazarus, too afraid to tell the castle's story in the castle itself, refuses to recount Tormenar's history. Offered a glass of wine, he drinks it, but still won't talk. More wine is forthcoming. When the comic interlude ends after three large glasses are downed, Lazarus is interrogated not on the castle but on the count of Tormenar, and initially denies that any such prior exists. He soon qualifies his absolute.

Fifty years earlier, or some say one thousand, while others insist that none of it ever happened, there were three counts of Tormenar, brothers. Today, if Tormenar has a master, it would be a great-great-cousin who didn't bear the Tormenar family name. Each count of Tormenar had a Catalonian castle. The youngest and most villainous invited his brothers to dine at the table where they now gathered; he brilliantly lit the castle as if he awaited his brothers. To Gilbert asking about the "as if," Lazarus explains they never arrived, being assassinated along with their children en route. The youngest brother inherited his elders' properties. But each time he came to dine, he found one of his brothers awaiting him, the same thing happened when he went to bed.

Enchanted by the story, Ruthven promises to double Lazarus's wages.

The remaining count had three sons; one studied at Salamanca, the second at Valladolid, the third at Coïmbre. The father decided to visit his castles in their company. At the first castle, the eldest died; at the second, the second died. Reluctant to venture farther, he left his third son to visit the last alone. When this son died, he dared not return to any of his estates, going instead to a convent to confess his crimes. He repented and led a holy life to die with the odor of a saintly man. Since then, the three castles had been deserted but for fresh corpses regularly found within.

Ruthven concludes that he is unlucky then, since misfortune always befalls the last to arrive, which was he. Lazarus, having taken Ruthven's place at table, corrects him *he* was the last to arrive. Everyone compliments Lazarus on his narration but Gilbert asks what happened to the heir, the great-great-cousin — why doesn't he visit? Lazarus reasons that he surely wishes to avoid a broken neck. He struggles to recall the heir's name, finally coming up with Figuerroa, Luis de Figuerroa. Juana begins gasping, begging God's help. Gilbert vainly struggles to console her. She repeats that every heir to cross Tormenar's threshold dies. Ruthven interrupts, suggesting it's time to locate a safe place for the ladies to pass the night.

Gilbert orders Lazarus to distribute blankets. The Marquis insists that no one need take care of him or the ladies, his wife and daughters; they have heated up a small salon for the night. Juana maintains that she will stay where she is. Gilbert objects that the room is exposed to the wind; opening a door to an antechamber, he tells her to rest there until dawn. Juana replies that the room is as dark as an abyss, or, more literally, a gaping pit or sinkhole: "*on dirait un gouffre!*" (440). Gilbert proposes to stay by her, but she won't hear of it. Ruthven salutes Juana, saying "Senora." She trembles. Gilbert alerts her to the fact that Ruthven is bidding her farewell. She timidly says "Milord," her eyes downcast. In an effort to cheer, Gilbert observes that an hour has already passed since the clock struck 12, the catastrophic fatal hour ending only by their welcoming a new companion, no ghouls or vampires. To Gilbert asking where he will lodge, Ruthven replies that he shall seek, and he shall find, bidding the *dames* "*Adieu*!" and the *gentilshommes* "*Bonne Nuit.*"

Gilbert cautions his comrades to sleep with two pillows but watch with both eyes, which Lazarus finds amusing. Gilbert asks if Lazarus weren't going to follow his master, but before Lazarus can respond Ruthven calls back to forbid it. Gilbert reassures his little sister once more, promising that her least sigh will bring him running. In wishing her goodnight, he asks her to pray for him as his sister Hélène is undoubtedly doing at Tiffauges, noting how privileged he is to dwell in the thoughts of two angels. Juana, approaching the open window, says he deserves prayerful consideration. To Gilbert asking where she is going, she observes that the moon is soon to rise, illuminating the way for lost travelers. Gilbert persuades her to sleep. She asks Gilbert, should he see Luis before her, to tell him how much she loved him. When Gilbert utters "Oh!" she corrects herself: "How I love him" (443).

Exit Juana. Gilbert expresses his pity for her, conceding that Luis' absence is worrisome and causing her to shed tears. Lazarus agrees she is crying a little, offering his opinion that it might help her ... like him, if he could only....

Gilbert interrupts to say "cry?" "No, laugh!" (443) replies Lazarus. Gilbert encourages him to indulge himself but Lazarus says it's as impossible for him to laugh as it will be for him to sleep. Gilbert invites Lazarus to stay with him, should he wish: an offer immediately accepted as Lazarus claims to always feel better in Gilbert's company. Although he's not sure why, his master frightens him. Gilbert proposes they retire to an adjoining room, warning Lazarus not to awaken him.

As Lazarus enters, he shrieks. Imbecile! scolds Gilbert. Lazarus apologizes, but someone is already in the room. A comic routine about a person's presence or absence ensues while Gilbert's torch penetrates the darkness. Stage directions have Gilbert enter the chamber, Lazarus holding his torch at the threshold. They report finding a cadaver bearing a letter from Juana and a wound on its throat, leaving no doubt as to the corpse's identity.

A scream and Juana crying out "I'm dying!" propel Gilbert towards her. He draws his sword as he advances, calling "my sister!" Rushing towards the room sword first, he is arrested by Ruthven stepping out. "Lord Ruthven, in Juana's room!" (446) observes Gilbert, stating the obvious. Ruthven, raising his hand, stops Gilbert's thoughts from advancing further. Ruthven heard Juana's call, and ran to her aid. Seeing her try to extricate herself from her room, Ruthven entered to rescue or to avenge her. "You have cut me, Count Gilbert.... I am dying" groans Ruthven.

As travelers gather around Juana, Gilbert asks, but the assassin? Escaped by that window, no doubt, Ruthven ventures. "Oh Juana! Oh Lord Ruthven...!" (447) sobs a bewildered Gilbert. Ruthven replies, "Gilbert!" Hapless Gilbert blurts out, "I've killed you!" (447).

Ruthven insists Gilbert send everyone away. Once alone, Ruthven says, "Count, in the religion I profess, it is customary for the dead to be exposed freely on the earth, and not enclosed in tombs.... Promise that after my death, you will carry me to the incline of a mountain, exposed to the rays of the rising moon; promise me this, Count, and I forgive you my death, and you will have given me justice" (447).

Gilbert promises and starts to rise to seek help, but Ruthven declares it useless, asking only that Gilbert renew his vow. Lazarus, complaining about losing another employ, brings the scene to its end.

The act's concluding tableau shows Gilbert carrying Ruthven's body on his shoulders. He places the body face up, stage directions specifying that he face west, at the mountain summit. Gilbert prays an instant over the body and climbs back down. Once he is gone, parting clouds reveal the moon. Moonbeams inch up the cadaver; reaching the head, Ruthven's eyes pop open, a smile twisting across his face, he half rises, then becomes totally erect, and, like the Moor, spreads his now apparent wings and flies off, thanking Gilbert.

Act three unfolds in the *cour d'honneur* of the Château de Tiffauges in la Vendée. The circular sequence of hours continues: It is morning, but six months have elapsed. A new cast of characters is introduced. Hélène, delighted Gilbert is returning, plans his welcome with Jarwick. Gilbert is arriving sooner than expected, and should be there by noon. They must let everyone know quickly. A servant, Lahennée, remarks that for six months she had received no word from her brother and now on the eve of her wedding he appears out of nowhere. Hélène muses her happiness will now be complete. Some commotion signals that Gilbert is on his way. Lahennée asks if Lady Hélène isn't going to inform le Baron de Marsden. Hélène claims Lahennée has read her mind, instructing him to send word of Gilbert's arrival. Enter a group of peasants.

Greeting them, Hélène sees they have heard the news, since their arms are filled with flowers. A peasant woman answers, yes, wild flowers — we know they're your favorites. Hélène notices the cornflowers and says she will make herself a crown. A peasant says he daren't offer her the daisies and buttercups he's gathered, since she has such beautiful flowers in her garden. "Give them to me, Yves," says Hélène; "a garden's flowers belong to man; wildflowers belong to God." They inundate her with wildflowers. She asks they keep some for Gilbert "our hearts' true lord" (451). They promise to strew flowers everywhere.

Hélène, calling for the village musicians, sends everyone to dress in their finest to celebrate Gilbert's return with a dance. When one demoiselle sighs Hélène interrupts to tell her a new dress awaits her at home. The girl replies, "May Our Lady of Clisson watch over you" (451). Hélène gives a golden cross to another, instructing that her fiancé should fasten it around her neck, and to a boy, she presents new ribbons for his pipes, a medallion for his cap. They all shout "*Vive la comtesse!*"

Once alone, Hélène describes her happiness. Every morning, in the sun's rays and the meadow's fragrance, she senses God smiling upon her. She is giving thanks for her brother's return when Lahennée interrupts. He has been to the baron of Marsden's château to find him absent. A messenger arrived the previous evening insisting the Baron be awakened, and no sooner had spoken with him than Marsden saddled his black steed and rode into the night, leaving instruction Hélène be told to expect him at noon. Hélène, hearing a commotion, asks Lahennée to run on high to see if it's her brother. Lahennée says there is no need as he has dispatched trumpeters to the château's towers to sound a fanfare as soon as Gilbert comes within view.

Enter Jarwick, urgently calling out "Mademoiselle!" A messenger has come from Spain with word from Count Gilbert" (453). This is surprising as everyone thought Gilbert had left Spain long ago. Jarwick is confused because at first the messenger had said Spain, but changed name of countries so often he can't remember them all.

Soon the messenger appears, followed by peasants. It is Lazarus: "Yes my friends, from Spain, from Egypt, Greece, Dalmatia, we have gone 'round the world" (454). He's seen the Red Sea and entered Jerusalem, he continues, then pauses to ask if everyone is Catholic. Hearing that they are, Lazarus starts to fetch a bottle of River Jordan water from his affairs when he sees Hélène. Stopping, he declares her so beautiful that she could only be Hélène. She confirms her identity and asks about Gilbert.

Her brother has encountered a small accident. My brother has had an accident! she repeats. No, his horse, answers Lazarus, describing how in Beirut they rode camels, but in Nantes, near Clisson, all four horseshoes fell off Gilbert's horse at once. So he was sent on to announce Gilbert's imminent arrival. Hélène notices that Lazarus is pale and trembling. Lazarus, glancing down, notices that indeed he is. When asked why, he says it is because he is Spanish and sensitive to disagreeable things. When pressed on which things exactly, he says that many disagreeable things happen when travelling; in Constantinople, there was a lion; at the Nile, he threw some stones at a trunk of a tree which turned out to be a crocodile; in Circassia there were bandits — all kinds of disagreeable emotions. When asked to be more specific, he says one league from the castle, he noticed he had to pass between two broom-covered hills. Afraid of becoming lost, he paused.

Further questioned, he begins by recalling his old master, Ruthven. When Hélène stops him to say he is mixing up two stories and will never get to the end that way, he replies that if there were but two he'd have no problem. He was carrying a lot of money (*de l'argent et je veux dire de l'or*) jangling in his saddlebags, and worried what would happen if robbers heard that telltale sound. Slowing down, he noticed the branches of a bush quivering on the hill to his right, "in the middle of the leaves, a face covered with a mask, a horrible mask" (457). Told to pass quickly or die, his horse shot off, carrying him to Tiffauges. Hélène thinks his story strange, as there are no bandits in the region. On second thought, she wonders if the masked figure might not be an enemy of Gilbert's. She instructs everyone to mount up to hunt down the masked man. Lazarus asks if he can't first store away the money he has, that of his deceased English master. Hélène scolds him for contemplating such a thing when Gilbert might be in danger. But here he comes now, exclaims Lazarus as a fanfare blasts.

Enter Gilbert, hailing his dear sister, who thanks God. Gilbert remarks she looks as though she'd been crying. She confesses she had, first for worry for his danger, now for joy. He wonders how she knew he had faced danger. Lazarus told me, she answers. But how could he know? She asks if he hadn't encountered a masked man. Indeed he had, exactly where Lazarus described. As Gilbert approached the twin hills, he noticed a beggar woman, a poor, curbed Breton. As he approached to give her a few coins, she grabbed his coat, pulling him towards her, and, God help him, she gave him a kiss! That is strange, observes Hélène. Yes, agrees Gilbert, but stranger still is that at the instant she so brusquely yanked me to her, a shot rang out, the bullet whistling by my ear. If not for her, I'd be dead. "My God!" exclaims Hélène as Lazarus, shuddering, asserts "That's could have been me!" Gilbert says his first thought was to make for the woods, but the woman whispered to him "flee" and whipped the horse with a briar branch. A second shot was fired, but, according to Gilbert, he was streaking like lightning. When Gilbert looked back, the woman had disappeared. Hélène suggests they find and reward her. Studying Gilbert, however, she declares him terribly pale. Gilbert explains that much happens during a year's journey.

To Hélène inquiring if Lazarus is in his service, Gilbert says yes and no. He is attached to him by honest affection, but his money comes from a deceased master. Neither Lazarus or Gilbert are forthcoming as to how this master died, however, Lazarus only noting that he expired in Gilbert's arms. Gilbert refuses to provide more detail, but Lazarus volunteers that Gilbert promised if no one reclaimed his master's goods in six months, they would be his by default, adding that the term ends that night. To be rid of him, Gilbert tells Lazarus to take possession of the goods now and be gone. Lazarus says he is right to love Gilbert. Lahennée reminds Gilbert that his sister had wished his arrival to be festive, but if he is sad.... Gilbert declares himself happy and commands the dancing begin!

The peasants lead Gilbert towards Hélène. In an aside she again mentions his paleness, expressing relief "Georges" is not there. She will break the news before introducing her fiancé. Gilbert, approaching his sister, calls her Tiffauge's guardian angel and, reinforcing the wildflower-bearing peasant's statements, claims that her prayers cause the meadows to flower and the fields to yield grain.

Hélène replies she loves him as would an only sister. This comment brings to Gilbert's mind Juana, who was, for an evening, his second sister. Remarking tears in Gilbert's eyes, Hélène asks the cause. Gilbert evasively asserts that tears can be joyous, swearing himself the happiest of men. Can't she see the reflection of her felicity shining in his heart?

Hélène seizes on the word felicity, to thank God again for his return so that her felicity can now be as infinite as God's goodness. Gilbert imagines she is not only speaking of him, but also of her feelings towards their childhood friend Philippe, but when he intimates as much, Hélène corrects him. Three months earlier she told Philippe she could not love him and he left Brittany.

Gilbert defends Philippe as the best of men; Hélène cannot know love's meaning. She corrects him again: She is in love, a love that dissolves everything in a "devouring passion" (464). After lonely months peering down the road in search of her returning brother, she has Georges. That's why she asked Gilbert to hurry home. She'd set tomorrow as a limit; had he not come, he would have returned to find her a woman married without the honor of having a brother's escort to the altar.

Stunned, Gilbert asks if she is loved. She believes so. Inquiring into the man, he is told the groom is rich, honored, and living nearby for the past five months: the Baron Georges de Marsden, believed to be of Scottish origin. His age is difficult to determine, perhaps 30 to 35 years. She begs Gilbert to be neither harsh in his judgments, nor stubbornly loyal to Philippe. Her love is a sweet belief in sympathetic resonance, in souls seeking out their mates. She warns that if Gilbert should find Georges' face a bit too pale, his brow a bit too sombre, pity him, for he suffers from excessive love for her.

In accepting his sister's choice, Gilbert asks reciprocation, her loving generously one she must soon call "sister." Traveling from Almira to Spalatro, he was attacked by bandits; suffering wounds, he was sheltered in a nearby villa where a blonde Dalmatian, Antonia, lived with her mother. Antonia's incredible beauty was hidden under a long black veil whose mystery he has penetrated. Indeed, Gilbert would be married were Antonia not still mourning her father. Looking at his sister Gilbert says, in Dalmatia, I inhabited "a paradise that lacked only you, Hélène" (467). He promised to return for Antonia in six months, when her mourning period would be over.

Hélène proposes they go to Spalatro together to trade Antonia's black veil for a white gown; Marsden, she adds, is a great traveler. Gilbert, asking when can he meet her charming baron, learns he is arriving at noon, but Hélène excitedly suggests she could fetch him now. Gilbert claims to know every step of the sun's journey and noon will soon arrive. He calls his sister's attention to the gaily dressed peasants arriving with great pomp as if a living, moving bouquet.

Enter Lazarus to ask Gilbert to lend him a scribe to inventory his heritage, so he can acquire property and marry. Gilbert says he can have Lahannée's help, for the favor of neither mentioning Spain nor his heritage again. Exit Lazarus as the baron is announced. Seeing Marsden, Gilbert exclaims "My God!" Ruthven coolly greets "Monsieur le Comte," recalling their last encounter. Gilbert asks Hélène to send everyone off while he treats with her fiancé.

Ruthven explains that his wound, finally, wasn't mortal. He had lost consciousness and was as good as dead. Coming to, he called for help, but everyone had gone. Once recuperated, he came to Brittany to thank Gilbert for saving his life in not burying him. He asks for Gilbert's hand in fraternity. Gilbert, suspicious, wonders about his change of name. Ruthven explains his elder brother died, bequeathing him the title. All very natural, concedes Gilbert, but why had he hid their acquaintance from Hélène? Ah, begins Ruthven, he hadn't wanted to reveal that her brother had — or had thought to have — killed him. Gilbert deems everything "strange." When Hélène reappears, Gilbert admits his fatigue. He's told his room has been prepared. A peasant woman approaches Gilbert and, whispering, instructs him to sleep in the tapestry room. He recognizes her as the life-saving beggar; the audience, as the Moor. Advising in an aside that he'll retire to the tapestry room, Gilbert exits. The Moor suddenly disappears.

Ruthven, staring at the spot where the Moor had stood, murmurs, "Vanished!" Enter Lazarus, talking to himself: "Thirty-six thousand pounds! What I wouldn't give to see the dead man's shade to say 'Thank you, Lord Ruthven!'" (472) Ruthven speaks up: "Ah, there you are, Lazarus! Tonight we'll sleep at Tiffauges, my friend. Bring my things and my treasure" (472). Lazarus curses his ill fortune, declaring himself "ruined" (472).

Tableau 6 shows a vast room with a tapestry representing the fairy Mélusine, a musette player, a hunter, bird of prey on his arm, sylphs, water sprites, etc., arrayed in a riotous landscape. On the wall at the stage's depth, a large frame contains the portrait of an ancient baron of Tiffauges, leaning on two knights.

Gilbert sleeps in a chair as Mélusine detaches herself from the tapestry to slowly approach him. She observes in verse that, like half the world, Gilbert sleeps; the world is divided into day and night — close your tired eyes, while, with mystery, the other half soundlessly revives. For on two powerful rulers the world depends: one named Light; the other, Darkness. Fecund Night is the mother of Dreams; sterile Day, tyrant of the real.

Turning, she addresses the tapestry's occupants. The day is dethroned, her verse continues, we for 12 hours reign. The night world is ours! Mortals sleep and we deliver them from their residences. Wake up brothers! Shepherd, the day, under the bower, hid from your silenced pipes their joyous sound; but, in darkness, your rustic quadrille rises to be danced in silent steps. Hunter, who, on your gloved hand, thrones the white gyrfalcon, proud suckling of the North, that in the woods the screech owl, bloodied, exhales her last cry under the lethal beak. Sylphs imprisoned in embalmed, perfumed rose; ondines, water sprites, enveloped in watery vapors; salamanders, rolling in smoky wafts; reed-sliding mysterious sprites: Hurry, descend, the fog moans, the rushes groan, but the poorest hearths retain, under their ash, some of yesterday's ill-extinguished flame.

She launches into a song of greeting, containing the line "You'll rekindle a fire in the desolated homestead, as God revived a soul in an inanimate corpse" (474). She summons fairies embodying Earth, Water, Fire, assuming herself the role of "Air" in elemental magic. She asks slumbering Gilbert to recall the song she would serenade him with in gone-by years. She summons the figures locked into the family portrait, who warn they are forbidden to inform men of the frightening world they abide, though able to talk amongst themselves. Mélusine calls them forward to share with the hope of their race their wisdom concerning Hélène, endangered by the misery the stranger brings. Their voices will penetrate like a dream that passes, the Night Angel, silently watching, allowing their thoughts to reach Gilbert's spirit. The old man and his lieutenants step down from their canvas. Mélusine asks who the dark stranger is: a cursed child of shadow, they deem, whose night is too dark even for their eyes, an immortal assassin whose trail is marked by his victims' graves. Gilbert turns uncomfortably in his sleep. No virgin can escape the determined bloodlust of this hideous oppressor who braves the elements and commands space, they proclaim. When Gilbert calls for his sister, Mélusine reminds him of Juana, Ruthven's victim. Gilbert calls out again, "Oh my sister!" Yesterday, declares Mélusine, this fiend tried to kill you to deprive Hélène of a defender. She leads a prayer for Gilbert against a vampire whose love is death. With the dawn imminent, she hurries everyone back to his representational frame.

Act four finds a deserted terrace. Enter Lazarus. Given a 3 A.M. rendezvous there, he complains about a master who doesn't sleep, eat, laugh, and when dead returns to life, depriving a poor man of his riches. He sent Lazarus searching for news of a nameless old woman. Lazarus misses his master Rozo, and Petra, blaming everything wrong with the world on Tormenar. His soliloquy ends with Ruthven calling his name. More comedy is indulged before Ruthven asks about "the woman." Lazarus reports the village holds 80 houses and 97 women, 39 of them elderly. He questioned all but five, three idiots and two paralytics: None had spoken to Gilbert.

Ruthven understands Lazarus had counted on inheriting his fortune, and, as he'd hate his return to life to penalize his servant, he has a proposition, indeed, part of an entertainment. If Lazarus affirms everything he might assert about the past, he'll give him a guinea; if it's about an important subject, he'll give him ten. Lazarus enthuses positively about the project, immediately gaining ten guineas. But, Ruthven cautions, if Lazarus doesn't support his contentions, he will be penalized by similar sums. The approach of Hélène interrupts the conference, Lazarus being hurried off. Momentarily alone, Ruthven concludes that if the woman who spoke to Gilbert were human, he would have uncovered her identity.

Ruthven greets Hélène as an unexpected pleasure. To her question of how long he has been there, he calculates about 15 minutes, which she finds uncanny: Love has planted something marvellous in her. Fifteen minutes earlier, in her sleep, she'd felt herself called to the terrace. What can I, who awake each day with the dawn, say? Ruthven wonders. He could not sleep himself. Why not? asks Hélène. He cannot tell — perhaps fever — at any rate he didn't want to return home, so he spent the night listening to the winds murmur her name.

He insists that she swear nothing will ever separate them. She dismisses the notion. He says the closer happiness approaches, the more one doubts, blaming a "fantastic and capricious demon. Console me, Hélène!" (483).

It's my brother, she surmises, isn't it? Ruthven mustn't hold anything against Gilbert, she pleads; he had always loved Philippe, and now needs time to adjust. Ruthven rejects her view despite Hélène's reminding him of Gilbert's tenderness and generosity. Ruthven recounts how Gilbert had welcomed him warmly enough, but the word of a single person was sufficient to empoison her brother against him. Hélène asks who had done such a thing? Ruthven can't believe she hadn't seen "that woman." Hélène hadn't, but listening to his description, recalls a beggar who had saved Gilbert's life. Ruthven asks, "Who would want to kill Gilbert?" (485) She swears that he has no enemy. Well then, do you seriously believe his story? Hélène protests that Gilbert had said it, beside, Lazarus saw the assassin. Lazarus?! replies Ruthven: A coward and a Spaniard, which is to say, superstitious! Hélène asks if he is suggesting her brother imagined it. Ruthven is sure he believes that he saw what he claims to have seen, but hadn't she noticed his altered behavior?

Gilbert is portrayed as mad due to a terrible accident; Gilbert believes he killed or nearly killed a friend in an accident, and he, Ruthven, is that friend. Now, when the sun sets, Gilbert's world is populated by phantoms, spectres, and supernatural beings, which explains Ruthven's cause for concern; he fears that Gilbert will oppose their union and she won't be able to resist his pressure. Hélène poses the fatal question: Is her word insufficient to assuage his fears? Ruthven obliges her to declare her willingness to marry at any time of his choosing. With her committment, he chooses that very moment and sets off immediately in search of the chaplain.

Hélène, left to bemoan her brother, is interrupted by Lahennée, chanting "Mademoiselle!" Going to wake Gilbert he had found him absent, his bed unused. Going downstairs, he saw him leaving the tapestry room, pale, haggard, and wild-looking. Hélène's concern is exacerbated.

Enter Gilbert, praising God he has found his sister. Asking Lahennée to leave, he falls into a chair to inquire as to Ruthven's whereabouts: He must speak to him. She says he's gone to the chapel. "Impossible," replies Gilbert, he wouldn't dare present himself before God. Hélène says he's gone to get the chaplain to arrange the wedding. Gilbert is more frantic than before to see Ruthven. Here I am, announces Ruthven as he enters. Gilbert asks Hélène to leave; Ruthven insists she stay. Gilbert, accusing him of Juana's murder, raves about his evil nature. Ruthven, however, has a ready, rational reply for everything that has happened. And the ambush in the woods? prods Gilbert. And how does a man, run through the heart, stone cold dead, come to live again? "You who killed Juana, why not kill me?" (493) Ruthven asks Gilbert what interest he could have in doing such a thing. "Yes, my brother: what interest?" (494) adds Hélène. What interest! That of separating a sister from a brother come to defend her. Don't you require, every year, two virgins to sustain your morbid life? In an aside, Ruthven curses, "He knows everything!" (494).

"You haven't responded, Milord" (494), continues Gilbert. Ruthven concludes that Gilbert is positively mad; Hélène sadly concurs. Gilbert promises to kill Ruthven before he'll let him soil his sister, and calls out for all to come. Hélène joins him in the call. Lazarus and assorted servants are soon at hand. Gilbert interrogates Lazarus, who begins re-earning his lost fortune. Lazarus states he doesn't know who killed Juana, whether Ruthven was dead or merely unconscious at Tormenar, and he ventures that he might have been mistaken about a masked man in the woods. Gilbert insists that all was revealed to him, repeating, "The man is a daemon, a vampire! His love is death!" (496). To Hélène's asking who told him this, Gilbert answers it was Mélusine and the spirits of their forebears. Ruthven orders Gilbert seized so he can't harm himself as Hélène begs God's pity. Gilbert is carted off, screaming "Murderer!" as he goes.

Pardoning Gilbert's wild accusations, Ruthven dispatches Hélène to console him. As she sets off, Ruthven hands Lazarus a purse. Lazarus protests that he only upheld his pronouncements three times, but in the purse there must be at least.... Ruthven sends him off, promosing they will settle at another time.

Alone, having deduced the identity of his traitor, Ruthven conjures the Ghoul. She magically appears, asking what Ruthven wants. Although they are forbidden to betray one another, he begins, she has done so. She claims to have done nothing that was not her right. But why? demands Ruthven. For love of Gilbert! declares the Ghoul. Ruthven asks if she doesn't know about Antonia? The Ghoul will worry about Antonia later; in the interim, Hélène's death would cause Gilbert's, which she can't allow. Ruthven warns her to beware or he'll expose her. In which case, you'll forfeit your life for having betrayed me, she counters. Ruthven reminds her that he has but few hours to live. Oh yes, Hélène's blood, interrupts the Ghoul. Yes, agrees Ruthven, I must have her! And I, Gilbert, retorts the Ghoul. When Ruthven insists she is asking for war, she corrects him, saying, no, only love. Warning she'll soon learn what he is like when he hates, she vows he'll discover her nature when she loves.

Tableau 7 shows an apartment lit for a party; at the far end, a large balcony overlooks an abyss. Peasants are cheering. "Vive Monsieur le Comte! Vive Madame la Comtesse!" As Hélène thanks them and Ruthven, Bringer of Wealth, tosses coins, they cry, "May Heaven bless you!" The clock strikes 11. Ruthven, remarking he hasn't a moment to lose, orders Hélène to send away the revelers. With the crowd retiring, Ruthven opens his arms. Hélène notes she has fulfilled all her engagements; Ruthven claims to be the happiest of men. If you are, says she, so much the better, but there is one less happy; let me go tell my brother of our marriage. Ruthven consents, but then suggests he would prefer to descend himself and tell Gilbert, if necessary, that he has abandoned his plan and is leaving, in order to restore his tranquillity. Ruthven heads down to the underworld of Gilbert's imprisonment.

Alone, Hélène wonders about a woman who, accepting a coin from her hand, whispered she should momentarily get away from Ruthven so a man can bring her a revelation. She prays, saying God knows she doesn't doubt her husband, but her brother's accusations have troubled her. If only her poor mother were living, she would confide in her. But, she reasons, as she was pious and faithful to the idea that the soul doesn't die when the body expires, is it not as if she were still alive? Addressing her mother, Hélène asks her intercession with God to grant a miracle by manifesting herself. Then, modifying her request in order to be more humble before the divine, she asks only some human sign indicating what she should fear and what she should trust. Just then, she spies Lazarus, at the threshold, gesticulating, signing for her to extinguish the candles. "Pfuh! phfuh!" he says, as if blowing. She asks if he wants her to extinguish the candles, and he speaks: "Yes!" When she ask why, he answers so that no one will see him.

Comic dialogue brings Lazarus's conscience to light despite the darkness. He swears Gilbert is sane; Ruthven perhaps did kill Juana; at any rate he was definitely dead and now he is resuscitated by mysterious means, though he overheard Ruthven claim to be a member of a sect that doesn't bury their dead. Hélène repeatedly exclaims, "My God!" Lazarus renounces the purse he received, saying that he values his body, but holds his soul to be more precious still. Hélène is proclaiming herself lost when Lazarus silences her, cautioning, "He is returning." Lazarus hides by the window overlooking the abyss. Looking down, he judges, "Five hundred feet, Ouch!" (507).

Ruthven calls Hélène, saying he hadn't the heart to awaken her brother. Looking at her, he declares her pale. Not as pale as he, replies she, calling his the pallor of the grave. He asks about the darkness and she claims the candles extinguished themselves. He finds that as strange as her trembling. She is afraid. When he takes her hand she finds him as cold as a corpse. "Yes, cold, Hélène, because your doubts freeze my blood.... Oh come, my spouse, come against my breast, against my heart" (508). She begs him to let her go, his heart doesn't beat.

To Ruthven's demand to know who came during his absence, she says no one. Approaching her, he steps on Lazarus's purse. "Ah! Lazarus has betrayed me" (508). Going to the door, he locks it, asking if she weren't his wife. She protests, "Milord, milord," and then cries out, "Gilbert, my brother!" On the balcony, Lazarus calls for help. With both shouting for Gilbert, Ruthven encourages them. Grabbing her, he curses her and her brother. As he carries her to another room, Hélène screams.

Lazarus is still yelling when Gilbert begins pounding on the locked door. Lazarus opens it, pointing out where Ruthven has taken Hélène. She screams. Before Gilbert gets to the door, it opens and Ruthven appears. Locking in combat, Gilbert drags Ruthven to the balcony where Lazarus knocks him over the head and Gilbert throws him over; the sound of his scream is slow to disappear. Calling to Hélène, Gilbert charges into the antechamber. Sobs of grief and Lazarus alone on the darkened stage end the scene.

Tableau 8 represents the bottom of the chasm. Gilbert scales down with a torch, exposing Ruthven's broken body. Declaring the monster truly dead, Gilbert rolls a heavy stone upon him. "Sister, though I couldn't save you, I have avenged you" (510).

Act 5 opens in a palatial room overlooking Dionysus's twin realms: the sea on one side, mountains the other. Lazarus is standing; Antonia, reclining on a divan, is fanned and entertained by dancing slaves. Once their performance ends Lazarus asks Antonia how she finds the palace. As the slaves file out leaving them alone with the Moor, now named Ziska, Antonia answers by saying that, thanks to Lazarus, she has been received like a queen. Lazarus corrects her, saying, thanks to Ziska! Antonia acknowledges her "beautiful Circassienne," as Ziska bows. Lazarus hopes Antonia doesn't miss her villa, but a palace, surrounded by the Caucasus Mountains and the Black Sea is impossible to improve upon. Antonia only regrets Gilbert hasn't arrived. Lazarus notes it is farther from Bretagne to Circassia than from Nantes to Clisson. Antonia asks if Gilbert knows this country. Lazarus believes so. She asks Ziska if this is indeed the palace Gilbert designated; Ziska signs affirmatively.

Ziska's exit has Lazarus comment on her stiffness; Antonia, too, finds her bizarre. Lazarus thinks it's her eyes, somehow feeling he's seen her somewhere before. Antonia asks why they've come so far from Europe. Beginning with Ruthven, Lazarus explains how he inherited a fortune, found a charming house nearby, and is thinking of asking Ziska if she wouldn't, that is, if no one objected.... Antonia interrupts to approve wholeheartedly. Lazarus asks leave to see some fishermen he befriended three months earlier and charged with finding him a brave domestic to replace Gilbert, now that he's marrying, since Lazarus feels more courageous having a courageous soul at hand.

Alone, Antonia muses that cowardice makes Lazarus a bit mad, though he at least brought her Gilbert's message fixing a meeting for that day—but where is Gilbert? He could either come over the mountains or by sea. If by sea, she would already see his sail on the horizon. Spying a white speck afar, she determines it's a sail, but storm clouds are gathering. Hurry, little barque, she prays. The storm intensifies, driving the ship before it. It is no barque, not even a fishing boat, but a passenger ship from Europe being ripped apart by the sudden storm. She prays aloud that Gilbert is coming by land and is not on the ship.

"You called me?" inquires Gilbert as he enters. Taking Antonia in his arms, Gilbert asks if she regrets joining him. With a thread from the virgin, she answers, his love could lead her to the ends of the earth. The thread is apparently to avoid getting lost in the labyrinth, and the virgin possibly references Ariadne, Persephone, or the Blessed Virgin Mary.

Asked if she is ready, she replies that is why she has come. Gilbert says that with her hand in his, his wounds will begin to bind. Antonia thinks it dangerous to let injuries of heartbreak close too quickly, or they will ill heal, saying: "Let the blood stop, but the tears flow" (516). Gilbert, requesting no more talk of Hélène to allow him to forget the last six months, resets the dramatic clock: One year has passed since Juana and Luis's murders and the Ghoul announced her rendezvous; six months since Hélène and Ruthven's deaths.

Hélène, says Gilbert, is with Juana in heaven, two angels, souls vast enough to be the heart's true country, praying for me. Antonia conjures another vision, saying God, in giving love, offers paradise on earth and cause to believe that Juana and Hélène are happy, as he must be too. Gilbert vows to be reborn, today marking his first sun, first smile, first love. Antonia, overjoyed, says she'll fear nothing now. These mountains have hidden us from the unknown danger that menaced our lives; here we can find happiness. Yes, chimes Gilbert, happiness, as long as we remain unknown.

Pointing out a small azure patch of sky, Gilbert declares it "felicity" and claims it as his own, maintaining that it will grow once Antonia is his. He has already been there six minutes, why aren't they married? Antonia requests 15 minutes more to shed her clothes of mourning. Gilbert complains that will separate them. She replies that if he wants her to go to before God wearing the garb of a widow and orphan, she will, but it would bring bad luck. Although she'll have enough joy in her heart to transform black into white when she utters "yes," in her country, sacred custom requires that the bride resemble The Maiden, the Virgin. She begins to ask Gilbert something, but, knowing her request, he interrupts: Get the priest! He proclaims an end to mourning, in their clothes, their hearts, and the heavens.

A thunderclap contradicts him. Recalling the distant sail, Antonia thanks God that Gilbert came by the mountains. Gilbert says he'd forgotten that anyone might be unhappy in the world. Antonia calls, and the slaves file in.

Noticing Ziska, Gilbert inquires about her. Antonia explains that Ziska assisted Lazarus in preparing everything. Gilbert finds her familiar, but when Antonia attributes it to his having previously visited the region, he shakes off his sense of uncanniness. Antonia orders a white dress and roses from the bower and exits.

Approaching Ziska, Gilbert remarks that she is trembling, which she admits. Reintroducing the envious evil eye, he believes that she threatened Antonia with hers, which she admits. He asks her also to admit that he knows her, even if he can't place the occasion. She calls him an ingrate. He recognizes her as the Breton in the thickets of Clisson. He asks what kind of creature she is to be so transformed. The Ghoul, confessing her love, responds if she could but change her heart. Gilbert claims she frightens him. She asks if that is his only response and he replies with a question: What else could you expect?

Take care, she warns, I've crossed the world for you, doing everything a lover could. Gilbert recalls she didn't save Hélène. Oh, I would have had I the power. Look at me, Gilbert, tell me you can't love me! He declares his heart is no longer his own. Ziska can't understand transitory human love. In which case, Gilbert replies, give yours to a god! Why should she do that if she can make him immortal? she asks. Gilbert is steadfast. Ziska says he only knows the shadow of love, while she offers him its reality. Gilbert politely declines. When Ziska calls his attention to the increasingly troubled skies, he says that even thunder can't drown out the joyous song in his heart and he is going to the chapel. Exit Gilbert and Ziska.

On the shore Lazarus calls frantically for help. A ship has broken up and all aboard are drowning. Watching the heroic actions of others, and rationalizing that he will be redeeming numerous sins, he throws a rope to a swimmer, pulling ashore Ruthven who quickly scampers off. Lazarus calls again for help. Gilbert comes, and Lazarus, comically afraid, declares them lost. Deciphering Lazarus's hysterical message, Gilbert learns of Ruthven's arrival. Six months after his death, the Vampire climbs out of the Black Sea near the spring equinox.

Gilbert is alone when Ziska returns asking where his intended is. Gilbert claims he has been considering all she said, and begs her forgiveness. Describing himself as a mere atomic particle, he gives himself to her under the condition that no new victim of Ruthven expire in his arms: Antonia must live!

She refuses the bargain. Then, pleads Gilbert, have us both die. Ziska asks Gilbert if he loves Antonia that much. When he answers affirmatively, Ziska provides him with a poisonous elixir, marveling at the couple's shared spiritual happiness. Noticing Gilbert's sword nearby, she takes it and exits.

Gilbert's short soliloquy is interrupted by white-garbed Antonia's arrival. Seeing him, she knows something is wrong. He is cursed, pursued by Death, he confesses. Everybody he loves must die, victim to a monster, a horrible secret she must learn. She names Ruthven. Yes, he has arrived, answers Gilbert. This man, begins Antonia, he is... Gilbert finishes her phrase for her — a vampire! Antonia pleads he not abandon her, but defend her. Then she suggests they flee, an idea he dismisses as futile. They pledge to die together. Gilbert declares that death will bring him supreme felicity. She reaches for poison, saying she will go first. He decrees they must die, hand in hand, looking deep into each others' hearts, his lips on hers, swallowing their last breaths.

Enter Ziska. Stop, she orders, tearing the flacon from Gilbert's hands. Gilbert snaps back, "Be gone daemon"; he insists she either help them live, or let them die. Ziska asks to speak to Gilbert alone. And what if Ruthven finds Antonia? Ziska swears there is no danger until midnight. Antonia withdraws.

To preserve Gilbert, Ziska wants Antonia to survive. Understanding the death of one means the other's death, she has given Gilbert's sword to Lazarus to be blessed by the priest coming to marry them; so armed Ruthven will retreat before him. Ruthven is a daemon, the Lord will be Gilbert's ally. Gilbert thanks her, and Antonia steps forward from a tapestry, staring.

Gilbert notices Ziska is staggering. She asks if he who refused her gift of immortality can't guess what is happening to her: She is making him a gift of her existence. To save Antonia and bring Gilbert happiness, she has violated laws binding her to Ruthven. He takes her hand, she kisses his, asking who loved him better, herself or Antonia. Saying farewell, she bursts into flames. Antonia comes to Gilbert's side as he screams and the clock begins to strike 12 o'clock. Gilbert springs to action, rushing to recover his sword. Alone, Antonia is confused. Her legs do not respond to her will as she feels Evil's approach. Looking towards the door, she gasps. Enter Ruthven.

Antonia screams. Enter Gilbert. Ruthven, seeing him, snarls, "you again!" This time, says Gilbert, there's a difference, invoking the Lord's name. Antonia enfolds her hero in her arms. Gilbert orders Ruthven to renounce Satan. He refuses. Gilbert insists Ruthven confess to God. He refuses. In that case, says Gilbert, die forever! He exposes his sword to Ruthven who retreats as Gilbert advances. Reaching the wall, they both go over. Enter Lazarus to support the faint Antonia.

Tableau 10 depicts tombs, crypts, and a "sinister and fantastic" (535) background. Snow covers the ground, a bloodred moon floats in the sky.

Gilbert is before Ruthven and an open tomb. "For the last time," he says, "adore God!" Ruthven refuses. "Then, despair and die!" (535) orders Gilbert, thrusting the sword into Ruthven. The vampire falls into the pit with a terrible cry. As a stone falls to cover the tomb, angels fill the sky. Hélène and Juana separate themselves from the heavenly host to greet Ziska, rising towards heaven. Enter Antonia, rushing into Gilbert's arms. Hélène says to Gilbert, "Brother, be happy"; Juana, addressing Antonia, chants: "Sister, be happy!" The curtain falls, leaving the sexual and spiritual union of "brother" and "sister" and their felicitous union with the divine to be imagined.

Dumas transports Nodier's prologue, Planché's introductory vision, to his finale. Cluttered with crypts and tombs, it features the descent of twin spirits from above the proscenium—Juana assuming the role of the spirit Unda, Hélène replacing celestial Ariel. Sister spirits, one dark, one light, from the celestial realm greet Ziska, who, with arms outstretched, is assumed into heaven. They join to form a joyous triune, welcoming sister Antonia into their spiritual family and blessing her union with Gilbert.

All that is known about Juana, beyond her convent upbringing and love-motivated revolt against paternal authority, is that she sees "a gaping pit" in the room where she goes to rest that fatal night, thus evoking the Homeric poet's language in describing the aperture from which Plouton, lord of the dead, emerged. She appears as the day exhausts itself and counts on moonlight to reveal her lover.

Fair Hélène's particulars are more ample: Gilbert's biological sister is said to make grain grow and to love the meadow's wildflowers, proposing to coronate herself with a wreath made from the deep blue cornflower blossoms the peasants had gathered in the fields where they work. Even the name Hélène, believed to derive from a vegetation goddess, designates her as an earthy avatar of Kore–Persophone, and of course the name of the beauty over whose love the Trojan war was fought.

Ziska, endowed with a more complex and contradictory character, will be considered more fully later, but she is introduced as the drama's only guide that leads, Lazarus being figured as the guide that follows. The Christian-pagan tensions that Goethe introduced with "The Bride of Corinth" are quickly dismissed in the first scene when both Christian and pagan guides are called by Lazarus but collectively refuse to lead towards the superstition-inhabited domain of Tormenar. Ziska arrives before the others to deprive Luis of his life and to set a rendezvous with Gilbert for the following year, date of the climactic scene.

In the brother-lover figure joining Juana, Hélène, Ziska, and Antonia, a solitary Apollonian entity is readily discernible. Wherever he goes, Gilbert brings light, often being figured as carrying a torch, urging a fire be built, even firing a pistol. The extinguishing of light on the other hand brings forth Ruthven. A doppelganger pairing of Gilbert and Ruthven replaces the traveling companions Byron introduced and Polidori and Nodier furthered. Gilbert and Ruthven, both great travelers, move independently, even as they are seen to advance in pursuit of one another. In Dumas' rendition, Gilbert is more man of the world than neophyte, his only ostensible binding connection to Ruthven comes from inadvertently running him through shortly after their initial meeting. Ruthven nonetheless poses mortal danger to all the women that bask in Gilbert's love. Ruthven, massively connected to the material through his mountaintop affinity, is regenerated through the feminine, moonlight and the lifeblood of Gilbert's sisters combining to effect his resurrection.

Ruthven's Tormenar death is finally a mere skirmish in a biannual battle for predominance, Gilbert and Ruthven each struggling to obliterate the other. Underscoring their interlocking destinies, they are alternately served by the Sancho Panza of Lazarus, who works for each, opportunistically shifting allegiance between the living and the dead, diurnal and nocturnal, good and evil. When one is in the East, the other remains in the West, their paths crossing only every sixth month. The final contest falls near the spring equinox, snows still covering the ground. At Tormenar they met at midnight, at Tiffauges the encounter occurred at noon, 182 and a half days later. Dumas has understood the mythological underpinnings of Romanticism's vampire and happily reworks the symbol system he claims as heir. It is a drama pitting the sun, Sol, assisted by Mélusine, against the black force of death and darkness for the love of a multi–faceted feminine Luna. It simultaneously sets an explicitly spiritual Christian force against a diabolic nemesis rooted in the material and the corporal.

Dumas, at first glance, seems to use the Vampire to articulate a radically new discourse, wedding *frénétique* horror to *féerique* fantasy. The comic lightening of the subject does not change its essential symbolic content. Embellishing Nodier's melodrama by importing the Ghoul — a female blood fiend on whom Romanticism's vampire was constructed — from Galland's *Tales of The Arabian Nights*, and the Mélusine *deus ex machina* from folklore, Dumas complicates plot. Perhaps he was recalling the Arsenal Library of the 1820s, for under Nodier's direction the new library acquired many works on supernatural folklore and the occult. Montague Summers, while failing to understand why Dumas would have introduced the Ghoul, celebrates Mélusine's heavy-handed apparition:

> Lazare is a capital character, but the intrusion from Oriental legend of the ghoul cannot be considered happy. On the other hand the appearance of Mélusine, whose legend was collected about the end of the fourteenth

> century by Jean d'Arras, is certainly effective and entirely in keeping with the history, since according to Paracelsus she was an occult power, and in folk lore she is often represented as protecting ancient houses [311].

It is said Mélusine migrated into French Medieval folklore from Celtic mythology, where she was perhaps a banshee queen. In the 13th century, William de Portenache composed a no longer extant *Chronique de Mélusine* which is understood to have provided the basis for Jean d'Arras's *La Noble histoire de Mélusine* that Summers references. Mélusine was sufficiently revered in pre–Renaissance France for several prominent feudal clans to actually claim descent from her, the Lusignan family of Poitou in particular, but the Parthenays, Rochefoucaulds, Sassennages, Saint-Gelais, the ruling family of the Duchy of Luxembourg and ancient royal lines of Cyprus, Bohemia, and Armenia all traced their lineage back to her as well, and, indeed, as with all such ambivalent, bipolar figures, it is possible Mélusine was occasionally understood as the protector of these noble households.

Mélusine is depicted as a beautiful maiden from the waist up, but, like the mermaid, from the naval down, she is a slithering scaled being of blue and white coloration, though she is finless. Instead of being half-fish, she is half-serpent, a veritable phallic woman, making her more likely a castrating hag than guardian. To add to her incongruent mix of features belonging to species apart, she is at times represented with articulated wings like those of a bat, marking her as closely related to the Welch leather-winged night-hag Gwrach-y-Rhybyn.

Henri Donteville connects Mélusine to *Luc* or *Lug* from which derives Luncine, Lucinius, Licinius and transmits the idea of light and the root *mer*, confounding in it the notions of water and maternity, eventually leading him to suggest Mère Lucine. More pointedly, why not Mère Éleusine: Demeter? In the fairy Donteville sees, all at once, the serpent and the bird, or at least the appearance of the bird, since he perceives her as chthonian. The serpent and the bird recall Darvell's death in Byron's *Fragment* as does Mélusine's association, as part of a feminine triune, with hidden fountains and sacred oaths.

Pierre Martin-Civat associates Mélusine with water sources and megaliths. According to d'Arras, she was first perceived at the *Fond de Çé* or Fountain of Thirst; numerous legends make much of her bathing. Her role as a builder of towers and architectural wonders supports the second contention. She is specifically attributed with having given rise to three castles in a single night: Talmont, Partenay, and Tiffauges, explaining Dumas' insistence on Tiffauges in the play. A further connection to Tiffauges also seems consequential; it was to Tiffauge's that the young Maréchal Gilles de Rais retired after his role in the Hundred Years War.

At Tiffauges, as he matured, Baron de Rais pursued vulgar alchemy, spending fortunes to produce gold, maintained a ruinously lavish court, and gave unrestrained vent to a pronounced bloodthirstiness. His sadistic orgies drained the Vendée region of male children, consumed as so many containers of blood for a monstrous appetite, his servants hunting victims far and wide to sate their master's pleasure. Gilles liked to coddle the youths, stroking their hair, caressing their cheeks, talking sweetly, earning their confidence before slitting their jugulars and watching their lives drain away, as the look of intelligence and humanity vacated their disbelieving eyes. He would often sexually violate his victims' lifeless remains. Rais' confessional statement concludes by his begging to be forgiven for his sins and spared from excommunication.

No stranger to the romantic tale, Gilles, it is said, inspired Charles Pérrault's *Barbe-Bleue.* This tale recounts how, despite a troubling blue beard, ladies find Barbe-Bleue irresistible. Marrying a young beauty, he gives her the run of his castle but for a single forbidden chamber. Handing her the keys to his domain, he explains the function of each, repeating his injunction before setting off to tend to business in outlying districts. During her master's absence, the bride's curiosity overcomes her will to keep her matrimonial oath. Opening the forbidden door, she discovers her predecessors' bloody remains. Retreating in horror she locks the door anew, but the key has somehow become indelibly marked with the crimson color of blood. The ogre returns home and sees what has happened. He pursues his young wife from room to room, but before he can add her corpse to his pile of decomposing wives, the woman's brothers appear and succeed in killing him instead.

Dumas, it seems, quite clearly suggests that Gilbert is Gilles' descendant and heir. When Dion Boucicault liberally adapted the play into English as *The Phantom*, transporting it all to Raby Castle in Wales, his only reference to the Tiffauges scene survives through a mention of Bluebeard and the insertion of an alchemist. When Mélusine encourages the residents of the play's family portrait to come counsel young Gilbert, Dumas undoubtedly represents Gilles and his execrable lieutenants. The common phoneme of the given names of Gilles and Gilbert signifies "oath," "pledge," or "promise"—Gilbert denoting "Bright pledge."

While Tiffauges offers a bloodied key to uncovering the darker aspect of Gilbert's identity, Mélusine's utility remains more obscure, though her mythological and genealogical background too turns on the oath betrayed. Obviously there is the Celtic connection, maintained since Nodier; the relationship between the Eastern vampire, Oriental ghoul, and figures like the banshee; the bond between Greek, Celt, and perhaps even Indian mythologies; but whatever his reason, Dumas manifests Mélusine's importance by placing her at his drama's center as its omphalus with her magical companions of the tapestry arrayed around her. She is the point from which the recognizably human changes into the monstrous and fabulous. Introduced by Gilbert through expository dialogue in act two, she only manifests herself in the third of five acts to prepare the denouement.

Mélusine, who spends her time launching a quadrille, explains Dumas' compositional structure. The term "quadrille" refers to a rustic dance of the 18th century (long after the epoch of Gilles de Rais or the weaving of narrative tapestries) and its accompanying music. American square-dancing retains much of the quadrille's élan — both in its choreographic and musical dimensions; calls such as "dosey-doe" are recognizable as the corruption of the French quadrille's "*dos-à-dos.*" Dumas' quadrille, like all others, is composed of five movements; its dance requires four couples who, criss-crossing, trace geometric patterns upon the floor that permute from the basis of the square, a quadrille, and whose complexities come from the changing of partners, one figure substituting for another. The basic quaternary form insists upon the inviolate cross intersected by dancers moving diagonally from quadrant to quadrant in a saltire "X" pattern, relating these movements to Scotland's St. Andrew's cross. This and the elemental agents seem intended to exploit the alchemical motif associated with the historical Gilles de Rais.

The alchemists' quaternity device seeks to join opposing base elements and energies into one synthetic, transformative molecule of divine matter. The population of the tapestry, largely related to Mélusine's complicated heritage in myth and to Vendéan folklore, is insufficient to perform any quadrille. But the salamanders, ondines, sprites and other mythical beings black, white, red, and yellow, align air, earth, fire, and water in cruciform order along axes north, east, south, west, as they attempt to rekindle the fires that have gone out — even as a solar figure appears from the east to struggle with a deathly dark hero who has inhabited the neighbourhood since their last meeting — by having others respond to their symbolic order. In her incantation, Mélusine makes it clear that they are effecting in the material world that which Jesus accomplished within the human body, making explicit the analogy between the house and the body previously introduced at Tormenar.

The added element of the hunter and the stag seems intended to embody the Celtic hunter, the "White son of Night" the Welsh call *Gwyn au Nacht*, and his game, the mythic wild stag best recalled as Cernunnos. Their hunt is the Wild Hunt of ancient myth, the hunt of the God of the Underworld. There is an analogous hunt pitting solar Gilbert against the palely luminous Ruthven or vice versa. As the hunt races to its inconclusive conclusion, hunter becoming the hunted, the inhabitants of the tapestry attempt to set the fictive world to dancing. In so doing, they play both upon the notion of the alchemists' *Chymical Wedding* and the ultimate Christian symbol, the cross.

The five movements Dumas provides take the form of his five acts; the four couples he proposes are Penta and Rebozo, Juana and Louis, Hélène and Ruthven, Gilbert and Antonia. Left unformed are the dreamed-of couples of Lazarus and Ziska and Ziska and Gilbert, though the latter's spiritual love was at the final moment realized through exchange and reciprocation. Moreover, it ignited an all-consuming fire which released Ziska from her mortal form and endowed her with a soul. In each act but the third, a couple is either formed or sundered, and it must be argued that a couple is also forged in the third, consisting of Gilbert and Ruthven, who cease to operate independently but become firmly linked, each vying to dominate their shared identity. In the given theatrical context, one seeing the other as a masked figure references vegetation-god Dionysus as the embodiment of all doppelgangers, the fact that one arrived in Circassia from the mountains and the other from the depths of the sea, reinforces the Dionysian nature of the doppelganger. Lazarus firmly states he saw a masked figure in the leaves: "Suddenly, I notice the branches of a shrub that waved on the hill on the right hand side, and, in the middle of the leaves, I see ... a face covered by a mask...!" (457) thereby marking Ruthven as related to Green Georges, *Feuillu*: Saint George.

The motif of ruins, preoccupation of Byron and Polidori abandoned by Nodier, is restored by Dumas. In châteaux and simple rooms, we find the figuration of a material realm, a body, contrasted to the astral, the spirit. One structure, the inn, is figured as too full of life; a deserted mountain castle is established as its polar opposite. Juana senses Tormenar as a place of the dead on entering its "blackened" walls, the walls functioning like those of Polidori's soot-encrusted "hovel." For Luis, Tormenar is his inheritance and destiny; in entering its confines, through the curse of an original sin, he attains the realm of his mortality. The structure is but the husk he has invited his fiancée to wed. Their marriage will be purely spiritual, for they are joined that night as spirits liberated, he at the hands of the Ghoul, she at Ruthven's.

The pattern of the quadrille is displayed in a particularly artful maneuvre: The wedding feast of Penta and Botaro is transported between settings from the first act to the second (Rozo's Inn to Tormenar), to be served in a celebration transposed. We were taken from the marriage of Petra and Botaro to the holy union of Juana and Luis; from the physical plane of the wedding bed to the spiritual plane of the grave, a wedding feast marked by the bride and groom through abstention, present absence, and absent presence. In Tormenar's geography, a small chamber, offered to Juana for her repose, is her place of death; Luis' lifeless body occupies a similar space. The blackened chambers yield pale white bodies. Tributary to Tormenar's large hall, these figure as chapels in a cathedral of darkness and lend greater sense to the title of Baron of Marsden — Mars' den. Peering into her room from its threshold, Juana describes it as "gaping." The blackened walls project constructs — bodies — abandoned by the spirit, as Mélusine's rhyme declares. Ruthven, like Bluebeard, confines his deadly missions to closed rooms that are afterwards left dark and deserted. Luis, Juana, and Hélène emptied, are each confined to a deserted room of a noble mansion.

In act two, when the Ghoul pledges to see Gilbert in a year, she suggests he will then provide her nourishment, for the Ghoul, who must annually feed to maintain existence, only preys upon men who are loved by a woman or who foolishly fall in love with the Ghoul. This contrasts to the Vampire who, it is later revealed, requires a biannual transfusion of life, at the ends of winter and summer.

The insistence on the wedding and sacrifice of the maiden, featured in various plots of the Vampire Tale since Polidori, is retained by Dumas. It remains a story of a priest, Ruthven, leading a maiden by the wrists to the altar where she will be sacrificed and dragged into the underworld. Yet it is not merely the draining away of a victim's blood that effects the Vampire's renewal, as in each instance represented it occasions the Vampire's death immediately after the Maiden's sacrifice. It seems the Vampire first joins his bride in death before resurrecting to life. Polidori inserted an interval between Ianthe's death and Ruthven's. Not so Dumas.

The play ends with a failed attempt at exorcism, as Ruthven, unrepentant yet cowering before God's name, falls to a consecrated sword, strengthening Christian overtones first heard in Nodier's pseudonymous novel. Unlike in previous works, Ruthven, rather than being killed twice, experiences a triple death, each killing strengthening Gilbert's role. Previously, Aubray was a passive victim who aided his friend when another hand delivered the mortal blow, but Gilbert repeatedly, and with increasing deliberateness, kills Ruthven. Gilbert's ultimate victory over evil is also novel. The solar figure actively defeats his nemesis in the name of Jesus.

Act one introduced three characters who are present throughout the play: Lazarus, Ziska, and Gilbert. That Ziska would provide the sacred key to defeating Ruthven becomes improbable if she were indeed Moorish. The Spanish set was apparently designed to cast this character as Moorish, an Arab-speaking invader of the European heartland. She is presumably staying at the Rozo's inn because she is stalking the well-loved Luis de Figuerra. Her quality of "Moorish" would indicate her to be Arab and Moslem, yet legend's ghoul is not Moorish, but a pre–Islamic Mesopotamian fiend. What Dumas wishes to signify by assigning her the task of informing Gilbert of Ruthven's Achilles' heel at the cost of her own existence, beyond illustrating Nodier's Christian love, is not immediately clear. No doubt Ziska's beauty, somber features, and Christian character, yet closeness to the Mesopotamian, were to be resolved in ultimately assigning her Circassian origins. Circassian women were celebrated in mid–19th-century France as harem beauties of the Ottoman sultan.

Ziska's appearance in Brittany is particularly curious and perhaps clarifying. She intervenes and, in cooperation with Mélusine, saves Gilbert and initiates him into spiritual knowledge. The ambush between two hills of Polidori's novella is refigured with greater clarity and directness: The masked Dionysian component of the doppelganger attempts to assassinate the Apollonian, the attempt thwarted due to Ziska's intervention. On several occasions, feminine characters — Hélène, and a peasant girl — thank "Our Lady of Clisson," likely referring to the miraculous *Notre Dame du Roncier*, meaning "Our Lady of the Brambles," venerated by Olivier de Clisson, (it is also the name of a 15th-century basilica he built and a still-extant structure in which he chose to be buried). Notre Dame du Roncier is introduced when Gilbert is miraculously saved by Ziska, who spurs his horse on with a crop made of bramble branches. The confusion of Notre Dame and Ziska is furthered by the prayer scene with Hélène, who asks the intercession of her holy mother which neatly conforms to the advice of Ziska to await a revelation. Indeed, Lazarus appears with a revelation and to renounce the purse he finally received from his master.

The parallel between Ziska and Mélusine is further developed through their entourages. Ziska's slaves in Circassia are introduced dancing around the couch of Antonia and fanning her. This is precisely the treatment Gilbert describes receiving in his infancy from Mélusine and her companions. There seems to be an intersecting and indeed thorny supernatural feminine presence that joins several avatars, malefic and beneficent, into a single identity — Ziska is last shown being assumed into heaven and welcomed by Hélène and Juana, whose Luis she murdered. This regranting of eternal life to a sanctified Ziska apparently justifies the demand that Ruthven repent. Repentance will open the gates of the heavenly inn, even to those intrinsically without souls of their own. Ambiguously, Mélusine seems to celebrate the Romantic quality of darkness in contrast to the rigid world of light, though she wants nonetheless to rekindle the extinguished flame. The old baron qualifies that some beings and acts are too dark even for him, and Ziska declares the real that men love is but a shadow of the love of the immortal. Dumas compensates for this lack of coherence with enthusiasm.

By beginning the play on the theme of "no room at the inn," Dumas raises a question as to what type of nativity to expect thereafter. By positing two localities, the dramatic universe is polarized. Yet the shifting settings between acts are both transformational and curiously static. There are courtyards: that of the inn and Tiffauges; large, formal chambers: Tormenar's dining room, Tiffauge's Tapestry Room, its large salon where the marriage feast is celebrated, and the Circassian palace's hall. Visible from their windows and balconies are pits, abysses, and cliffs, no longer caves as with Nodier, but Tartarus, or more properly, the issueless pit of Christian damnation and neighboring region to Circassia. Dumas has taken the Vampire from celebrating pagan mysteries to subsuming them in a restored Christian order, Christian iconography and credo being immediately stressed through Lazarus.

The New Testament makes two references to one of that name. First, there is the Lazarus of Luke 16.19:

> There was a certain rich man who used to clothe himself in purple and fine linen, and who feasted every day in splendid fashion. And there was a certain poor man, named Lazarus, who lay at his gate, covered with sores, and longing to be filled with the crumbs that fell from the rich man's table; even the dogs would come and lick his sores.

This is very much the man, being turned away, sent off into the wilderness, encountered in the opening scene. Luke tells that when both the rich man and poor die, their fortunes are reversed. Lazarus is regaled "in the bosom of Abraham" (16:22) while the rich man suffers in hell. When the rich man asks Abraham to have pity and send Lazarus to soothe his suffering by carrying him some water, Abraham refuses. The rich man then asks Abraham to restore Lazarus to life and send him to his family "that he may testify to them, lest they too come into this place of torments" (16:28). Abraham coldly maintains that were Moses's commandments and the Prophets' words insufficient to keep his kin mindful of God, then Lazarus's return from the dead would be of no avail. Dumas represents Ruthwen as the Rich Man, always offering but never yielding Lazarus his fortune.

In John 11, Jesus does what Abraham would not, working a miracle to keep mankind mindful of God, "for the glory of God, that through it the Son of God may be glorified" (11:4). Jesus returns Lazarus to life after four days in the tomb. Considering the role Dumas attributes to light and fire, much of what Jesus says during the incident is noteworthy. "Are there not twelve hours in the day?" He asks. "If a man walks in the day, he does not stumble, because he sees the light of this world. But if he walks in the night, he stumbles, because the light is not in him" (11:10).

> These things he spoke, and after this he said to them, "Lazarus, our friend, sleeps. But I go that I may wake him from sleep." His disciples therefore said, "Lord, if he sleeps, he will be safe." Now Jesus had spoken of his death, but they thought he was speaking of the repose of sleep. So then Jesus said to them plainly, "Lazarus is dead; and I rejoice on your account that I was not there, that you may believe. But let us go to him." Thomas, who is called the Twin, said therefore to his fellow disciples, "Let us also go, that we may die with him" [11:11–16].

With the spreading word of Lazarus's revival, great crowds begin to follow Jesus. He habitually addresses them in parables evocative of the discourse of a Mystery religion: "Unless the grain of wheat falls into the ground and dies, it remains alone. But if it dies, it brings forth much fruit. He who loves his life, loses it; and he who hates his life in this world, keeps it unto life ever lasting" (12:24–25). Returning to his comments on the 12 hours of day and night, Jesus teaches, "Yet a little while the Light is among you. Walk while you have the Light, that darkness may not overtake you. He who walks in the darkness does not know where he goes. While you have the Light, believe in the Light, that you may become sons of Light" (12:35–36). This gloss on darkness and light articulates the operating principle of *Le Vampire*'s theme, as Mélusine makes clear in her appearance. What will be born in *Le Vampire* is Light in darkness. It also marks Ziska, only recognizable through her staring and envious eye. Luke 11:33: "The light of the body is the eye: therefore when thine eye is single, thy whole body also is full of light; but when thine eye is evil, thy body also is full of darkness." When Ziska out of love puts aside envy and protects Gilbert and Antonia, she becomes part of light.

A reference to the wedding feast of Cana in which Jesus reportedly turned water into wine, is transformed again: The wedding scene becomes a kind of memorial feast. Dumas has reconstituted, on his post–revolutionary, Restoration stage, a Renaissance tableau quite like DaVinci's *Last Supper*, Ruthven portraying Judas Iscariot and Juana the Paschal lamb in a cruel ceremony of salvation in which wine becomes blood. Juana is first offered a few drops of wine, but then, through substitution for the traitor, it is Lazarus who tosses down glass after glass. Three glasses of wine bring forward the story of three brothers and three sons.

After the biblical Lazarus was restored, a banquet, rehearsal for the Passover Last Supper, was given at which "Lazarus was one of those reclining at table" (John 12:2). In the case of Juana's last supper at Tormenar, Lazarus is eventually pictured receiving a pouch of coin for betraying Gilbert, but in abandoning the purse he betrays Ruthven. Dumas retains another interesting twist on the New Testament that Nodier inserted; it is the resurrected Ruthven who challenges Gilbert and Lazarus to touch him, to verify his true existence, as Jesus had challenged Thomas.

The representation of the supper of twelve plus one required a determined construction. The Last Supper reference demands seating 12 plus the individual to be sacrificed and transformed. Dialogue repeatedly insists on the party's 12 members, even when the arithmetic doesn't make sense. Ruthven takes the place reserved for Luis, but he does not eat. Lazarus in turn takes his place, but consumes the wine and bread of the sacrificial lamb Juana. The dinner-table conversation makes clear Dumas' intent to mark *Le Vampire* as a tribute to Nodier, for it largely follows the lengthy conversations *Mes Mémoires* recalls as occurring during the entr'actes of 1823's *Vampire* when he, by chance, found himself seated next to Nodier, the play's author.

Gilbert is always heralded before he appears, heard before he is seen. He is awaited by trumpeters, or announced by Lazarus, or called by his lover. Ruthven's appearances, on the contrary, are unexpected, surprising. While Ruthven was in the West in la Vendée, Gilbert was in the East, Lazarus making much of the Red Sea, the River Jordan, Jerusalem, and his having seen the misperceived wonders of the ancient world. The Jordan is of course associated with the rebirth of baptism; the Red Sea is also a sacred symbol of rebirth and death, a point where God grants his faithful new life and crushes his enemies, turning the water into blood with the lives of the damned. Jerusalem marks the particular point of spiritual renaissance for humanity that came on 3 April 33 with the Crucifixion, an event followed by earthquakes and the conjunction of solar and lunar eclipses. Gilbert's fiancée, bears the name of the fortress Rome built to protect Temple Mount—"Antonia." Most importantly, it is only when solar Gilbert becomes sanctified in Christ that he finally is able to defeat darkness, even beneath moonlight.

When we meet Ruthven in 1851, he has consumed the lives of Ianthe, Miss Aubray, Malvina, Margaret, Juana and Hélène. With each passing year, Ruthven drains two more lives. Dumas has fixed both spatial and temporal poles. Amplifying the relationship between the inn and Tormenar, he marks a town by the Western Sea as the western extremity of action, and the Black Sea coast as the eastern. Dumas is careful to limit each of his episodes to one portion of the Earth's rotation, accumulating a period of 24 hours or slightly exceeding from fragments of days, but he has bound his dramatic action by the actual revolution of the earth around the sun, covering the events of exactly one year, each act being separated by precisely six months. Three months before Gilbert arrives at Tiffauges, Philippe left for parts unknown; three months after the arrival at Tiffauges, Lazarus visited Circassia, befriending fishermen who promised to find him a servant. We are even told in act 5:3 that the scenes visited are at moments approaching equinox (the ides of March), suggesting a deliberate strategy involved in opening the play at winter solstice. During the season of darkness, from autumnal to vernal equinoxes, Ruthven was present and courting Hélène at Tiffauges. From that point on until the return of the season of dark, when Ruthven is pulled from the Black Sea, he was believed by Gilbert to be dead. He was present at Tiffauges in the season of light, invisible in the season of shadow. Conversely, solar Gilbert knows every moment of the sun's journey, proclaiming "Je suis le soleil," ambiguously stating either "I am the Sun" or "I follow the sun." That the forces of day and night, light and darkness, summer and winter are doomed to eternal battle and ephemeral victory should come as no surprise. The antique god has died, the New God triumphed.

Claims that Stoker's Count is as indebted to Gilles de Rais as he is to Vlad Tepes can only be speculative—the extent to which *Dracula* was influenced by either is completely unknown. It can be confidently stated however that the six-month interval Dumas imposed on his *Vampire* informs Stoker's novel. More definitely, in commenting on the 13 visitors who recount stories until the entrance of the Count at the stroke of midnight, Stoker indexes Dumas' *Le Vampire*, act 2:2. Dumas' act 2:3's "last supper" pays homage to the 13 told tales of Nodier's novel as well as the Sunday evening soirées at Nodier's *Bibliothèque de l'Arsenal* at which Dumas was a regular attendee. At these soirées the thirteenth arrival, excluded from conversation, was relegated to a separate table (Zimmerman 164).

Daniel Farson's oblique suggestion that Stoker's knowledge of French was limited to *vin*, *pain*, and *bain* (464) is dispelled when Stoker lists a work by "Maury" in his references (Rosenbach #43a *Notes* 173). This would be Collin de Plancy's (a.k.a. Collin de Maury's) never translated *Histoire des Vampires et des Spectres Malfaisans* of 1820. Should French influence on Stoker's opus remain obscure to Anglo-American researchers, *Dracula* makes them wholly apparent.

Revolution

> "It was as though my memories of all Jonathan's horrid experience were befooling me; for the snowflakes and the mist began to wheel and circle round." [317].

As if to mask his vampire, Bram Stoker covered his best-known work with a preface:

> How these papers have been placed in sequence will be made manifest in the reading of them. All needless matters have been eliminated, so that a history almost at variance with the possibilities of later day belief may stand forth as simple fact. There is throughout no statement of past things wherein memory may err for all the records chosen are exactly contemporary, given from the stand-points and within the range of knowledge of those who made them [5].

Masquerading as bundled narrative fragments, the conceit of *Dracula* has every character save the eponymous anti–hero contribute some textual artefact to a chronologically determined documentary jigsaw puzzle. The project is opposed by Count Dracula who, masquerading as his green solicitor guest, attempts to corrupt chronology by sending extorted post–dated dispatches from "Bistritz, the post town" (10) and by burning all the documentary evidence he encounters.

The tale begins with a sole coach-bound chronicler, Jonathan Harker, hurtling down a road "not yet ... put in order after the winter snows" (14), past "a bewildering mass of fruit blossom" (14) into spring's last "fine, powdery snow" (19) and towards a schismatic fault-line where Roman and Eastern churches fracture as they impale themselves on Islam's crescent, and institutional religion dissolves into the ethers of unforgotten paganism. The forested terrain Harker crosses, Transylvania, is alive with sub-continental and gypsy superstitions that reach beyond forest and mountain to an earlier time-space in which the Celts appeared in Nysian lands that stretch from the Black Sea's shores to far off Erin, and Dionysus descended from his mountain fasts to liberate the pre–Hellenic lands of Greece. Stoker's empiricist hero, unable to isolate himself from the theological, the mythic, the superstitious, confides to his journal a dialogue that consigns the spiritual, the realm of Good and Evil, to a divided temporal frame, as he recalls an old woman pleading with him not to undertake his professional maiden voyage due to a question of time:

> "Do you know what day it is?" I answered that it was the fourth of May. She shook her head....
> "Oh yes! I know that, I know that! but do you know what day it is?" On my saying that I did not understand, she went on:
> "It is the eve of St. George's Day. Do you not know that to-night, when the clock strikes midnight, all the evil things in the world will have full sway?" [12].

Here, Christopher Frayling steps in to complain that Stoker has purloined his text, writing: "references to the swallow as the fowl of the Lord, the crow as unlucky and the dates of St. George's Day are all taken verbatim from Emily Gerard's *Transylvanian Superstitions*" (345).

Gerard reports that Transylvania welcomes St. George with "occult meetings" held "at night in lonely caverns or within ruined walls, and where all the ceremonies usual to the celebration of a witches' Sabbath are put into practice" (333). "In the night of St. George's Day ... treasures begin to burn, or, to speak in mystic language, to 'bloom' in the bosom of the earth, and the light they give forth, described as a bluish flame resembling the colour of lighted spirits of wine, serves to guide favoured mortals to their place of concealment" (333). Gerard's "mystic language" concerning a "bloom" in the "bosom of the earth," "bluish flames" comparable to "spirits of wine," and occulted "treasures" revealed to "favoured mortals" expose at the core of the St. George beliefs a mysteries discourse with Dionysian overtones. The occult gatherings, necessarily concerning the upcoming growing season, identify St. George as a vegetation god of resurrection, a solar Other of a Dionysian dying-god. On St. George's, Transylvanian peasants deploy the same amulets, buckthorn, and pitch that Athenians of yore used to ward off revenants during the Lesser Mysteries at Anthesteria, the Dionysian festival of the Dead.

Given this, it is unsurprising that the Ionian isle of Saint George is denoted as the place of predilection for the cremation of vampires in Tournefort's 18th-century *Voyage du Levant*, or that James George Frazer ritually links Saint George, or "Green George ... in Carinthian, Transylvanian, and Romanian customs" (93), to Slavic sacrificial rites of spring in his *Golden Bough*. William Anderson maintains that British St. George legends derive from "the Celtic sun god Belinus," further remarking that, 1,000 years ago, Arab scholars "compared St. George with the Mesopotamian vegetation god Tammuz" (28–9). As Tammuz conforms to the ideal of a dying-god of fertility, St. George embodies his Christianization. Sabine Baring-Gould, whom Stoker cites as a principal source for information on the vampire superstition, takes the relationship between St. George, Tammuz, and other solar gods as his major theme in his lengthy essay on Saint George in *Curious Myths of the Middle Ages*, correlating St. George's Day and Beltine.

While it is not impossible that Stoker lists the festival's date and information concerning totemic beasts and protective amulets merely to pad his text, it seems far more likely that the occult import of the superstitions is in keeping with his authorial intent. If Stoker has plagiarized, it in no way diminishes St. George's significance as the point of departure for a spiritual epic; quite the opposite. Isaac Newton calculated that the likely date of the Crucifixion fell on St. George's of A.D. 34 In Roman Catholic traditions, St. George, a martyr who suffered seven deaths but experienced six restorations, was honored by the recitation of the Little Office of the Virgin. While these elements may be significant, Stoker's veritable investment in St. George, who is known as "The Quick to Hear," only becomes manifest when *Dracula*'s plot concludes at Castle Dracula, precisely six diegetic months after Jonathan's arrival there and at the instant of his return.

The exchange Jonathan so diligently transcribes, beyond exposing St. George's narrow import, underscores the signifying, sense-bearing role of the novel's chronological dimension. Mina Harker affirms "'In this matter dates are everything, ... if we get all our material ready, and have every item put in chronological order, we shall have done much'" (198). A notion that Stoker has Dr Seward second: "'What a good thing Mrs Harker put my cylinders into type!'" he dictates. "'We never could have found the dates otherwise'" (199). Indeed, *Dracula*'s every constituent voice recording, journal entry, newspaper column, memorandum, telegram, and shipping bill is datelined or postmarked; the narrative not only knits "together in chronological order every scrap of evidence" (199) regarding the Vampire, it comments on discrepancies between Julian and Gregorian calendars. Stoker's intrigue charges the Harkers, Jonathan and Mina, with "an exact ordering" (254) of the papers that the novel purports to be; but everybody inhabiting its pages concurs: narrative is about time. As Seward excitedly reports: "Harker has gone back, and is again collating his material. He says that by dinner-time they will be able to show a whole connected narrative" (199).

So it is; as St. George's Eve bleeds into St. George's Day and Castle Dracula's gates swallow Jonathan whole, a mad adventure begins. His mysterious coachman, master of wolves: vanished; the fortress ruins: apparently deserted; Harker stands before a massive door wondering what to think when he perceives "through the chinks the gleam of a coming light" (21). As the door opens, Count Dracula hierophantically appears, "clad in black from head to foot" (21), "an antique silver lamp, in which the flame burned without chimney or globe" (21) in his hand. He demands the ritual engagement of his visitor's volition, insisting he cross the threshold *proprio motu*. And so Harker does, to find himself confined, isolated from all but the mysterious, priestly count. For nine days, Jonathan will remain sequestered, before being initiated into vampirism by a lamia triune.

Harker's prison consists of a bedroom, a library, and an octagonal room, antechamber to each. This latter room's form is manifestly important, for Stoker insists upon it in both the novel and its stage adaptation. Still, no functional reason for introducing this space, or theatrical means for its representation is discernible. A passageway, "seemingly without a window of any sort" (22), containing but a single lamp, linking a space given to dreams to another dedicated to the written word and representation, reads as a symbolic and formal device of the author. The single lamp ambiguously suggests both sun and moon; the eight-sided shape more definitively projects the octave, eight-step cycle of return, as intrinsic to a way of passage. At cock's crow, Harker is left alone at the chamber's threshold, "all in a sea of wonders" (24). He who had so recently detected Dracula's approach as a "coming light" observes that he could not "help experiencing that chill which comes over one at the coming of the dawn, which is like, in its way, the turn of the tide." He muses "that people who are near death die generally at the change to the dawn or at the turn of the tide." (30). His sense of uncanniness serves to situate the novel's foregrounded principle-though-dual motif, liminality set against the temporal tides that pull Light from darkness.

The journal entries that form *Dracula*'s body are often dated around noon or midnight; several, begun at dawn, are continued at midday, as if to emphazise the importance of these liminal temporal markers. An infected Mina experiences "sunrise and sunset" as "times of peculiar freedom; when her old self can be manifest without any controlling force" (286), since Dracula's "'power ceases, as does that of all evil things, at the coming of the day'"(211). Dracula, confined by moon and sun, is a transformational being only able to "'pass running water at the slack or the flood of the tide'" (212), only empowered to "'change himself at noon or at exact sunrise or sunset'"(211). Yet, as Helsing remarks, he "'can see in the dark, no small power this, in a world which is one half shut from the light'" (211). Not only in the quotidian cycle of day and night is the world half shut from the light, but, as already seen, in the annual solar revolution as well.

Within Castle Dracula's library, Jonathan happens upon a worn map of England, and notices "certain places little rings marked" (29), each indicated site — Whitby, Exeter, London — foreshadowing some future scene of Dracula's invasion of England — what Jonathan rightly terms Dracula's diabolical scheme. Within the geography plotted out in his novel, Stoker, circling dates on a calendar, executes his own diabolical scheme, placing in conflict two notions of time: It *can* be the fourth of May and something more ephemeral, something beyond an empiricist's purview. Certain of *Dracula*'s plot events occur programmatically at lunar/monthly intervals. For example, Jonathan meets the Vampire on May 5; Renfield's "zoophagy" is diagnosed on June 5; Dracula sails for England 31 days later, arrives at Whitby 31 days after that; Arthur transfuses Lucy the following month; Mina insists on serving as telepathic spy on the Vampire the next; and the vampire chronicle breaks off 30 days later.

The calendric monthly interval, functioning mechanically like the watch that Jonathan had become "rigorously accustomed to wind ... the last thing before going to bed" (44) each evening, lends Stoker a periodic metric for blocking out plot. Beyond modernity's linear time, however, a cyclical, antique, pre–Copernican time pervades the novel to delineate a *Ciruclus mythologicus* and shape the story's dramatic envelope. The solar year — halved by solstices, quartered by equinoxes, inter–cardinal intervals bisected again — is contained by eight nodes, a vision of the annual cycle typical of post–Neolithic agrarian societies. An ogdaodic division of the planetary ellipse is defined. The Celt's sacred solar calendar, for instance, while observing the solstitial and equinoctial, celebrates their intermediates as true thresholds of change: Beltine (Walpurgisnacht, or, in the East, St. George's Eve) signals the season of light's arrival, Samhain (Hallowe'en and All Souls), the dark's. Mid-summer was observed in August, at Lughnasadh; mid–winter, in February, at Imbolic.

The month of 30 or 31 days is, nevertheless, pure paradox, being a solar, sun–defined metric rather than a true lunar, moon-dictated *month*. Yet it is repeatedly stressed that the Vampire is sensitive to both solar and tidal, hence lunar, fluctuations. Through a tactic to which he makes repeated recourse, Stoker, using the voice of Seward in this instance, poses a rhetorical question: "Can it be that there is a malign influence of the sun at periods which affects certain natures — as at times the moon does others?" (110). The answer eventually provided suggests that times of close coincidence between lunar and solar calendars, the former retained in liturgical affairs, provide conjunctive opportunities that Stoker is particularly keen to exploit. According to the lunar-driven calendar promulgated by the Book of Common Prayer, in the Christian era Beltine, or "Summer's Day," also accommodates Whitsun or Pentecost, the feast that commemorates the descent of the Holy Spirit upon the Apostles seven Sundays after Jesus' Passover self–sacrifice on the cross and

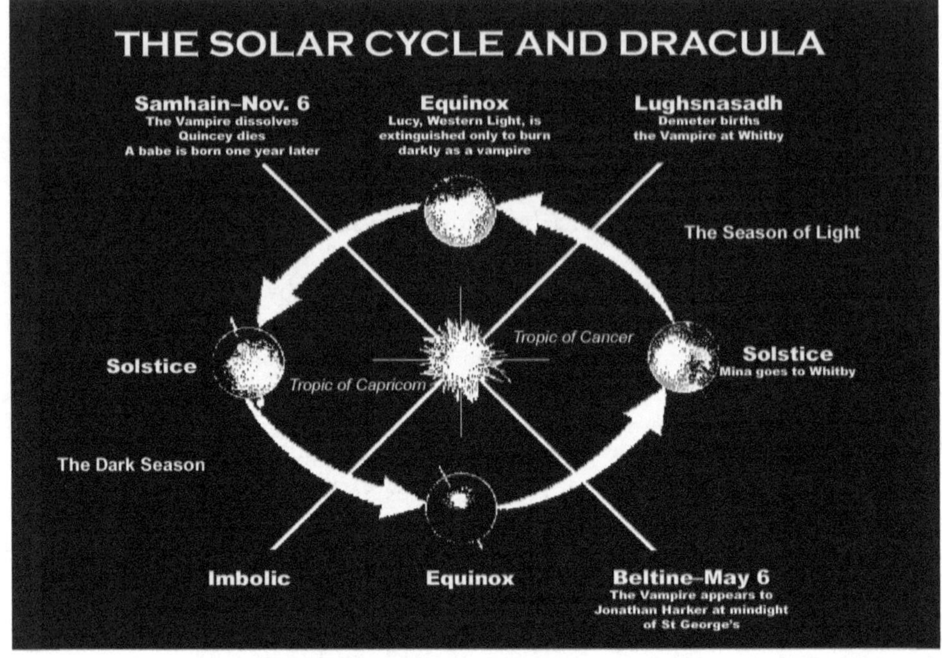

The solar cycle and *Dracula*. © Rarignac

His ensuing Resurrection. More often than not, dependant on the alignment of solar and lunar calendars, Whitsun, the traditional occasion for baptizing professing Christians during historical periods in which infants were considered volitionally inept for sacramental life, follows upon St. George's Day. Since Englishman Jonathan arrives at Castle Dracula upon St. George's, the timing of his shaving accident or his encounter with lamiae may very well have coincided with Whitsun as the moment of Jonathan's "baptism of blood" (297).

What can be stated definitively is that *Dracula*'s central event is precisely pegged to the novel's temporal midpoint, Lughsnasadh. On 7 August at Whitby, "shortly before ten o'clock the stillness of the air grew quite oppressive, and the silence was so marked that the bleating of a sheep inland or the barking of a dog in the town was distinctly heard, and the band on the pier, with its lively French air, was like a discord in the great harmony of nature's silence. A little after midnight came a strange sound from over the sea, and high overhead the air began to carry a strange, faint, hollow booming" (76). A crewless ship, carrying in her hold 50 cases of earth — listed on the shipping bill as an agricultural experiment — soon appeared out of the storm to run aground miraculously at East Pier.

Stoker names his ghost ship *The Demeter* after the dark goddess worshipped at Chthonia; the 50 cases she transports contain consecrated soil from Castle Dracula and the remains of its lord. Demeter—*mater* and matter, The Mother and the material—births the Vampire. Iconographically associated with wheat fronds and snakes, theologically with fertility, mythically constructed as the fruit of incest, she accepts blood sacrifice to graciously assure agricultural abundance and fertility. The Mother's daughter, Persephone, embodies her spiritual dimension. Virgin bride of Plouton, Persephone rules over the realm of the dead, but resumes earthly life each spring, returning from Hades with the blossoming vegetation when the flowers appear. Ironically, it was as Persephone gathered spring flowers that the lord of the underworld, hidden within the earth, appeared to ravage her and make her his queen. Demeter and Persephone jointly bestow the secret to eternal life to those who undergo the Eleusinian Rites. One secret that must figure prominently amongst those they reveal is that Plouton, whose unrepresentable visage is reserved for Hades, lurks behind Dionysus's masks.

Near the summer solstice, a half-season prior to *The Demeter*'s grounding, Mina had traveled to Whitby to visit her friend Lucy. Together, the two witnessed the scene of shipwreck. Three months later—that is, a half-season after the mysterious grounding, as the autumnal equinox neared—a wave of death swept across Britain that claimed bride-to-be Lucy. Preceding Lucy below by mere hours were her mother, her fiancé's father, orphans Mina and Jonathan's benefactor and Jonathan's partner and virtual adoptive father—all simultaneously dispatched to the underworld. The peeling away of a ripened, elder generation, and the offering of a sacrificial lamb, served to render neophytes initiates. Death and the rites it requires brought together the story's various strands in the persons of the novel's diarists and chroniclers. Death granted them awareness, gnosis. Through Lucy's funeral, Helsing discovers Mina, accesses her knowledge of Lucy's vampire contacts, obtains Jonathan's Transylvanian journal, and initiates the ordering of the papers. Communally, Lucy's orphaned friends could penetrate the mystery of her demise and resurrection, defining her relationship to a many-named lord who, questing for his queen, suddenly appeared from out of the earth in Lucy's garden. Time would be needed for the vampire hunters to form a posse, but on 25 September, the date of the Eleusinian Mysteries, they dedicate themselves to hunting down and destroying the Vampire.

Although the tale begun on St. George's ends six months later, the 183-day luminous half-year running from 5 May to 5 November projects a shadow-obscured Other, its dark double occupying the void between 5 November and 5 May. Metaphorically, the agrarian universe *is* contained by "a small octagonal room lit by a single lamp" (22), life-without-end turning

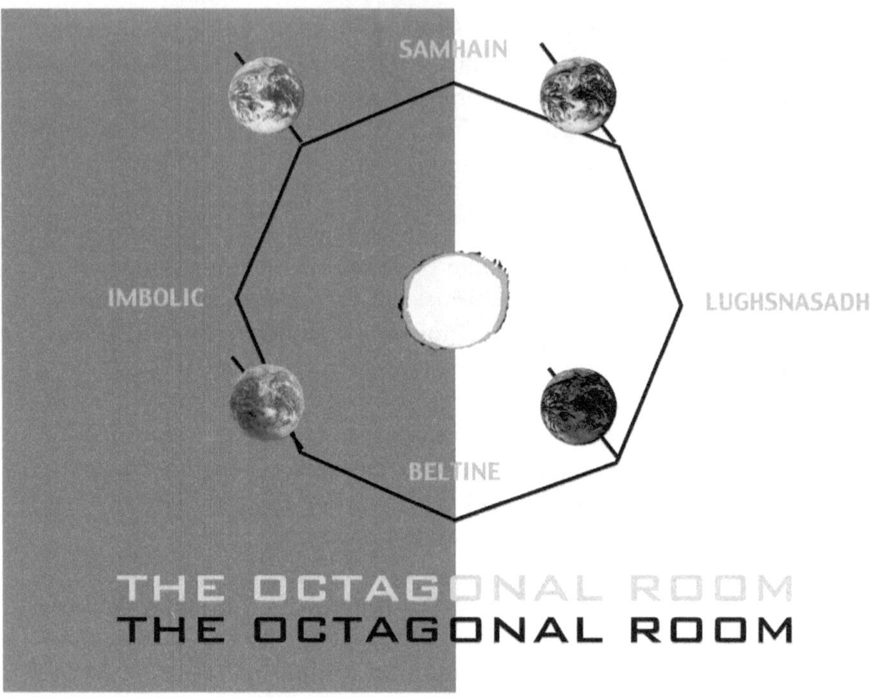

The Octagonal Room. © Rarignac

with the seasons. As Jonathan observes, we are always "simply going over and over the same ground again" (18).

The oracular Pythian Temple at Delphi was time-shared, Apollo seizing priority during the annual period of Dionysian absence, when, the 53rd Orphic Hymn tells us, he withdrew to Persephone's Hadean abode. Walter Otto notes that "we can even talk of a specific date, the eighth of November, as the day of his awakening" (194). Stoker suggests that that date is a bit off; the Dionysian renaissance should occur on 5 November, 40 days after the Mysteries' conclusion. Stoker's is a story of the Dionysian setting off to conquer the Apollonian, Dracula audaciously risking visibility for the possibility of triumphing over Light. During the season of light, Count Dracula, Plutonian avatar of a Dionysian god, remained visible to his pursuers, hunters of the hunter, who were themselves confined by the sun's light. Dracula disappeared from the Apollonian as Dionysus ascended the Delphic throne to reign over darkness, until, come spring, he must return to Hades to rule during Persephone's hiatus.

While it is often remarked in the critical literature that Lucy Westenra's name evokes "sunset," the sustained interplay between light and darkness Stoker invested in his novel remains little discussed, beyond being reduced to simple polarities yoked to ideological readings. Like much vampire fiction, *Dracula*—hardly Gothic—is less about the deathless body than the encapsulated soul. The well-chosen name Stoker bestowed on the vessel communicating Dracula to England furnishes means of understanding one of Helsing's otherwise incomprehensible speeches:

> When the corn is grown, even before it has ripened—while the milk of its mother-earth is in him, and the sunshine has not yet begun to paint him with his gold, the husbandman he pull the ear and rub him between his rough hands, and blow away the green chaff, and say to you: "Look! he's good corn; he will make good crop when the time comes" [111].

When Seward complains of the obscurity of these remarks, Helsing offers continuation in way of clarification:

> The good husbandman tell you so then because he knows, but not till then. But you do not find the good husbandman dig up his planted corn to see if he grow; that is for the children who play at husbandry, and not for those who take it as of the work of their life [111–12].

This, what seemed to Seward a perplexing discourse, is founded on several classical references. The discourse on the husbandman versus the child seeking amusement recalls Plato's *Phaedrus*. That the farmer becomes "the good husbandsman" (111) aligns the Socratic speech with Jesus' proverbial shepherd. The ear of corn clearly indexes the Mysteries of Eleusis, their initiative rites and the gestures that accompanied the mystogogues's prayer: "Let it rain, and bear fruit!"

From the sewing of seed to the threshing of grain, *Dracula* reports on events across the season of light. Yet by 4 November, it is "so cold that the grey heavy sky is full of snow, which when it falls will settle for all winter as the ground is hardening to receive it" (313). As the first flakes announced the end of Transylvania's period of fertility and the sun's last rays birthed Samhain, Dracula's end came: "It was like a miracle; but before our very eyes, and almost in the drawing of a breath, the whole body crumbled into dust and passed from our sight" (325). Crossing the threshold from light into shade, the forces of darkness attain invisibility and, like Dionysus, perhaps only seemingly disappear. Shadow, so strong that it projects through solid objects, so uncanny it can lie undetected in the dark, reveals itself only to Light. According to Plutarch, the Phrygians believed that their god slept in winter, and woke in summer; it would seem that Dracula is that god's antithesis. Stoker has Jonathan Harker rhetorically wonder of his own nemesis, "Can it be that he sleeps when others waken that he may be awake whilst they sleep?" (49).

Demonstrating deep concern for the cyclic, Stoker sacrifices one crusading vampire hunter on that 5 November that the Vampire was cut down—

Quincey Morris succumbs to wounds suffered in action. Seven years later, the Harkers report in postscript that on 5 November of the year following Morris's death, Mina gave birth to a boy who was called "Quincey," the transmigration of a regal soul being implicit in their "Note." Death had given rise to life. It may be prudent, however, to recall that Dracula crumbled into dust nearly at the instant of Morris's death and that the infant was certainly conceived at the antipodes of the anniversary of *Demeter*'s arrival at Whitby.

Jonathan concludes by acknowledging that "among the masses of material of which the record is composed, there is hardly one authentic document" (326), thereby undermining his own prefatory comments. Jonathan then appends his notarial signature to a prophecy that the son born to Mina would "some day know what a brave and gallant woman his mother is" and "how some men so loved her, that they did dare much for her sake" (327). The cases of soil that Demeter, The Mother, carried westward contained, rather than simple dirt, the Earth itself; the treasure blooming in the bosom of the Earth and revealed to favored mortal Jonathan on St. George's Eve was a vampire who sought to replace Green George with his darkling self. God of death, chthonic Dracula—his luggage composed of boxes of earth—will rule the underworld alone during Persephone's foray into the Apollonian solar world come St. George's Day next.

Syzygy

> "Then came another rush of sea-fog, greater than any hitherto — a mass of dank mist, which seemed to close on all things, like a grey pall, and left available to men only the organ of hearing" [77].

Ernest Jones, James B. Twitchell, and a host of others would cast the Vampire Tale as a "crime and punishment" fantasy that both expresses incest yearnings and — accommodating associated guilt — serves to effect their repression. This template is so solidly established that the ageless monster that preys on adolescents freshly initiated into sexuality has become a perennial Hollywood revenant, from Count Dracula to Jason Voorhees to Freddy Krueger to Leatherface. David J. Skal and Elias Savada claim that it was precisely the dichotomous interplay of desire and repression that attracted Tod Browning to undertake the filming of Balderston and Deane's Broadway *Dracula* when Universal's Junior Laemmle acquired the rights — Browning enjoyed playing "not only to the public's appetite for extravagant sex fantasy but to its puritanical resistance as well" (93). Lorne MacDonald encapsulates the psychoanalytical take on the vampire *qua* universal figure of consciousness's underworld:

> In Stoker's novel, what opposes the evil power of sex is the pure power of love...: Mina, as an object of love, is opposed to the demons of the Pit, objects of desire [the lamiæ].... The novel articulates the split between affectionate and sensual feelings, between sacred and profane love, which Freud saw as endemic in civilized men. Freud attributed this split to the prohibition of incest, which forces desire away from the primary object of affection. (He considered that the psychopathology of civilized women was slightly different in this respect — that they were attracted to the forbidden, rather than to the degraded. This, as well as the identifications of male authors, may explain why female vampires, the objects of masculine desire, are notably more degraded than male ones, the merely forbidden objects of feminine desire.) And the idea of contagion symbolically restores the

> element of incest onto vampiric eroticism: since Dracula's victims are reborn as vampires, he is their father (and even, as the scene of Mina's baptism suggests, their mother) as well as their lover. The ever-widening conspiracy of vampires is a league of incest [202].

The charge of a conspiratorial "league of incest" echoes the accusation Byron believed Robert Southey* leveled against Shelley, Polidori, Mary Godwin, Clair Clairmont, and himself in an infamous commentary on the stormy May night that indirectly gave rise to *The Vampyre, A Tale...*, *Frankenstein*, etc.: "Extracts of a Letter from Geneva." Its author, vaguely correct (though, as Byron insisted to John Murray, stepsisters Mary and Clair were not genetically related), nevertheless allows righteous ire to blind him to artistic merit in the works that the league generated. Incest may well be the constant on which horror generically functions, but forcing the Vampire, and *Dracula* in particular, into this horrified interpretative frame limits our capacity to discern other layers of meaning germane to the Vampire, other efforts at signification that, even when considering *blood*, engage something more than simple consanguinity. *Dracula* is written, in Helsing's phrase, in "the language that was of bloom and blood" (277), Persephone and Dionysus, resurrection and crucifixion; as with Polidori's début-de-siècle *Vampyre*, Stoker's fin-de-siècle novel's ultimate concern is fertility, the cyclical, the soul, the sacred and *gnosis*, rather than taboo violated. It offers *laconic* as a keyword, though its evangelists be many. "They say much of blood and bloom and of others which I comprehend not, though I guess what they mean; but nevertheless they tell us all the things we want to know" (276).

The Vampire Tale's truest sense escapes the attention of those who insist on interpreting the story as mythic and end up with Freud. Mircea Eliade terms the underlying mythos "renewal." Incest, a given of renewal in Demeter myths and Isiacal rites, is too narrow a frame to produce a larger understanding of these works, even as their plots expose unfolding rites of initiation and spiritual metamorphoses. Therefore, we must approach the text of *Dracula* as Helsing might, that is, "have an open mind, and not let a little bit of truth check the rush of a big truth" (172), consider "big and little...; perhaps at the end the little things may teach us most" (253). In applying that method, Helsing could triumphantly report, "I did not look for any specific thing. I only hoped to find, and find I have" (148).

Having considered *Dracula*'s temporal similarities to *The Vampires* of Dumas, Nodier, and Polidori, further penetration into the mysteries "confined within the limitations of [*Dracula*'s] earthly envelope" (255) becomes possible.

*Byron suspected Robert Southey, who crossed paths with the Diodati group at the Hôtel de l'Angleterre, of having penned both the scandal-mongering "Account of Lord Byron's Residence at Mitylene," and the "Extracts of a Letter from Geneva...," the latter of which was used to preface Polidori's *The Vampyre.*

Excepting Planché's discrepant contribution, since *The Vampyre* of Polidori—whose Aubrey siblings are orphans, and whose Ianthe becomes orphaned due to her encounter with Ruthven—the Vampire Tale begins with the parentless child. Stoker, too, creates a heroic couple whose members are obliged to fend for themselves in the world. Jonathan Harker has no parents, though his employer and mentor, Peter Hawkins, treats him in a caring, even paternal way; Mina Murray, who becomes Madam Harker when she weds Jonathan about one-third of the way into the text, "never knew father or mother" (143).

The critical act of being united as husband and wife is far from the only rite to which these young people will be subjected, though it may be the most important. With plot fixing rites of transformation that the main character—the couple or syzygy—must undertake, the complex initiation imposed will repeatedly try Jonathan and Mina's commitment to each other. The mysteries of sensual love seem scarcely to be their problem as they are examined and tested. While their ordeals are parallel, the timing of their individual trials and the sequencing of rites undergone are often sympathetically inverted or reversed to accommodate their respective genders.

Stoker opens his novel with Jonathan, traveling with the *de rigueur* image of Mina, off on a career-establishing mission. He is to rendezvous at midnight with a Transylvanian nobleman. Expository dialogue set down as a journal entry has an old woman engage the youth as he prepares to set out on what seems to be the last stage of his journey. When she asks Jonathan if he knows the day, and he replies, "The fourth of May," she nearly scolds him:

> "Oh yes! I know that, I know that! but do you know what day it is?" On my saying that I did not understand, she went on:
>
> "It is the eve of St. George's Day. Do you not know that to-night, when the clock strikes midnight, all the evil things in the world will have full sway? Do you know where you are going, and what you are going to?" She was in such evident distress that I tried to comfort her, but without effect. Finally she went down on her knees and implored me not to go; at least to wait a day or two before starting. It was all very ridiculous, but I did not feel comfortable. However, there was business to be done, and I could allow nothing to interfere with it. I therefore tried to raise her up, and said, as gravely as I could that I thanked her, but my duty was imperative, and that I must go. She then rose and dried her eyes, and taking a crucifix from her neck offered it to me. I did not know what to do, for, as an English Churchman, I have been taught to regard such things as in some measure idolatrous, and yet it seemed so ungracious to refuse an old lady meaning so well and in such a state of mind. She saw, I suppose, the doubt in my face, for she put the rosary round my neck, and said, "For your mother's sake," and went out of the room [5].

This, the first represented act of Jonathan's initiation (though we know that he was previously dispatched to undertake the mission), places an "old woman" "on her knees" before him, in order to challenge his will. In accepting her gift, he in part accepts her theology. The cross, offered as antithetical to "all evil things in the world," is to be worn for "your mother's sake." Considering that Jonathan is an orphan, the mother referenced is necessarily his and our spiritual mother, *Magna Mater*, *Notre Dame*.

Jonathan's eastward procession leads him to an encounter with a hierophantic figure who will lead him through a portal, or cleft, "separating two atmospheres" (16) in the mountainous steeps of "God's seat" (14) at that indeterminate moment of hesitation between days old and new: midnight. As the disquiet of St. George's Eve expires, Jonathan is rushed through the gates of Castle Dracula and confronted by an ancient warrior who invites him to enter his abode. Harker has little choice but to obey the command to "enter freely," for, as the Count stridently reminds him, he has been indentured by his surrogate father: "When your master, employer, what you will, engaged that someone should come on his behalf, it was understood that my needs only were to be consulted" (37). The exchange between new master and neophyte is initially stimulating, Dracula being "like a king speaking" (33). "I wish I could put down all he said exactly as he said it, for to me it was most fascinating" (33). The empirically-led, sober, fashionable young man of law and property who entered the castle sure of his world, is soon shifting, considering that "unless my senses deceive me, the old centuries had, and have, powers of their own which mere 'modernity' cannot kill" (41). Jonathan is soon contrasting "bare, meagre facts, verified by books and figures" with "experiences which will have to rest on my own observation or my memory of them" (35–36). So many of the givens of Jonathan's conceptual frame have been challenged that as the long evening abruptly ends at dawn he confesses to discovering, or losing himself "all in a sea of wonders" (24).

Jonathan awakes and arises to find himself alone. When he is at last joined by the lord of the domain, the Count expresses his desire to master Jonathan's "tongue" and contends that he is "but a little way on the road I would travel" (26). He indeed dictates to Jonathan what he is to say to those who may be concerned about him to rationalize a prolonged absence. The solicitor, functioning as scribe, writes and postdates his letters according to the Count's calculations. Dracula informs Jonathan, "You may go anywhere you wish in the castle, except where the doors are locked, where of course you will not wish to go. There is reason that all things are as they are, and did you see with my eyes and know with my knowledge, you would perhaps better understand" (26). The youth is particularly cautioned to "not by any chance go to sleep in any other part of the castle. It is old, and has many memories, and there are bad dreams for those who sleep unwisely" (38). As Jonathan soon realizes, he has become its prisoner.

On 8 May, Jonathan is startled when shaving by the sudden awareness of a hand on his shoulder and a voice speaking in his ear, much like Aubray's uncanny experience at the drawing room on his return to London. Jonathan's start, due to the fact that he had heard nothing and had seen nothing in the mirror that reflected the whole room, results in his cutting himself. The blood sets Dracula's eyes ablaze "with demoniac fury" (31), a fury so consuming that "he suddenly made a grab" at Harker's throat, that is, until his hand made contact with the rosary that Jonathan was wearing, that sign of the Sacred Mother — habitually recalled as "Ste Mary" in Stoker's text.

> Bless that good, good woman who hung the crucifix around my neck! For it is a comfort and a strength to me whenever I touch it. It is odd that a thing which I have been taught to regard with disfavour and as idolatrous should in a time of loneliness and trouble be of help. Is it that there is something in the essence of the thing itself, or that it is a medium, a tangible help, in conveying memories of sympathy and comfort? [33].

It is, tangibly and inherently, no simple crucifix hung on a necklace of beads; it is a rosary, a prayerful cycle designed to mediate and to connect a petitioning soul — through the Virgin Mother — to the Son of Man and God the Father, and a meditation on a series of mysteries: Joyous, Luminous, Sorrowful, Glorious. Heaven knows, Jonathan requires comforting, for he is deeply afraid. "I am, I know, either being deceived, like a baby, by my own fears, or else I am in desperate straits" (32). "I start at my own shadow, and am full of all sorts of horrible imaginings" (38). Convinced that he is in the presence of Evil, Harker concludes that unless he acts, his days are few and limited to the dates already numbered and dictated by the Count.

One evening, Jonathan accidentally learns more of the Count's ways as he looks out a window. To evacuate his sealed castle, grandiose coffin, and access the exterior world, the Count slithers headlong down the walls of his battlements like a lizard. Assured that his tormentor has departed, the neophyte solicitor slips out of his rooms to discover a more appropriate means to escape his fortress-prison. He descends a long flight of stairs into the Vampire's netherworld: "doors, doors, doors everywhere, and all locked and bolted" (31–2). He finds a stairway rising into a distant wing of the structure. "At last ... I found one door at the top of a stairway which, though it seemed to be locked, gave a little under pressure. I tried it harder, and found that it was not really locked, but that the resistance came from the fact that the hinges had fallen somewhat and the heavy door rested on the floor" (40). He enters what he assumes was a room frequented by long-departed, courtly ladies. Installing himself at a writing table, he records his day.

> When I had written in my diary.... I felt sleepy. The Count's warning came into my mind, but I took a pleasure in disobeying it. The sense of sleep was upon me, and with it the obstinacy which sleep brings as outrider. The

> soft moonlight soothed, and the wide expanse without gave a sense of freedom which refreshed me. I determined not to return tonight to the gloom-haunted rooms, but to sleep here, where of old ladies had sat and sung and lived sweet lives whilst their gentle breasts were sad for their menfolk away in the midst of remorseless wars. I drew a great couch out of its place near the corner, so that, as I lay, I could look at the lovely view to east and south, and unthinking of and uncaring for the dust, composed myself for sleep.
>
> I suppose I must have fallen asleep; I hope so, but I fear, for all that followed was startlingly real — sitting here in the broad, full sunlight of the morning, I cannot in the least believe that it was all sleep.
>
> I was not alone. The room was the same, unchanged in any way since I came into it; I could see along the floor, in the brilliant moonlight, my own footsteps marked where I had disturbed the long accumulation of dust. In the moonlight opposite me were three young women, ladies by their dress and manner. I thought at the time that I must be dreaming when I saw them, for, though the moonlight was behind them, they threw no shadow on the floor. They came close to me and looked at me for some time, and then whispered together. Two were dark.... The other was fair, as fair as can be, with great wavy masses of golden hair and eyes like pale sapphires. I seemed to know her face, and to know it in connection with some dreamy fear, but I could not recollect at the moment how or where. All three had brilliant white teeth, that shone like pearls against the ruby of their voluptuous lips [41–2].

Jonathan is a victim of succubae.

> The fair girl shook her head coquettishly, and the other two urged her on. One said:
>
> —"Go on! You are first, and we shall follow; yours is the right to begin." The other added:
>
> —"He is young and strong; there are kisses for us all."
>
> I lay quiet, looking out under my eyelashes in an agony of delightful anticipation [42].

Back from posting Jonathan's letters at Bistritz, Dracula sweeps into the room like a summer storm, disengaging lamiæ and sending them off in a fury amidst a hail of accusatory words on the subject of love. When the lamiae beg for sustenance, the Count motions to a sack containing, it is suggested, a suckling babe torn from its mother's breast. He promises to surrender Jonathan to their appetites shortly, once he has finished with him. Morning dawns on Jonathan in his habitual bed, doubting his recollection of the previous evening, searching anew for documentary evidence.

Later, Jonathan again witnesses "something coming out of the Count's window" (47), wearing "the suit of clothes which I had worn whilst travelling here, and slung over his shoulder the terrible bag I had seen the women take away" (47). Within a matter of hours, an "agonized cry of a woman" (48) draws him again to his window. In the courtyard below, a *Madonna dolorosa* spies him; falling to her knees, she franticly implores him to return her child, accusing him of having stolen an infant, no doubt a child the Count and the voluptuous lamiae had feasted on. At a signal from the Count, wolves slink into the courtyard to end the mother's mortal ordeal.

Count Dracula eagerly prepares to depart and take possession of his new estates in England, where Mina, visiting with her bosom friend Lucy, anxiously awaits word from her fiancé. Before the Count is carted off, however, Jonathan steals into the chapel crypt to open his coffin and search his person for a key.

> It seemed as if the whole awful creature were simply gorged with blood; he lay like a filthy leech, exhausted with his repletion. I shuddered as I bent over to touch him, and every sense in me revolted at the contact; but I had to search, or I was lost. The coming night might see my own body a banquet in a similar way to those horrid three. I felt all over the body, but no sign could I find of the key. Then I stopped and looked at the Count. There was a mocking smile on the bloated face which seemed to drive me mad. This was the being I was helping to transfer to London, where, perhaps, for centuries to come he might, amongst its teeming millions, satiate his lust for blood, and create a new and ever-widening circle of semi-demons to batten on the helpless. ... A terrible desire came upon me to rid the world of such a monster. There was no lethal weapon at hand, but I seized a shovel which the workmen had been using to fill the cases, and lifting it high struck, with the edge downward, at the hateful face. But as I did so the head turned, and the eyes fell full upon me, with all their blaze of basilisk horror. The sight seemed to paralyse me, and the shovel turned in my hand and glanced from the face, merely making a deep gash above the forehead. The shovel fell from my hand across the box, and as I pulled it away the flange of the blade caught the edge of the lid, which fell over again, and hid the horrid thing from my sight [53–4].

This assault leaves an angry red wound, mark of Cain, upon the Count's forehead, and Jonathan, more desperate than ever to escape, imitating the Count's headlong descent of the castle walls as he sets off towards an unknowable future.

Directly or indirectly, the plot has: dispatched the initiate under order of his superior; required his wilful threshold surrender of volition; enforced the initiate's sequestration; established an unjustified taboo; provoked an incident generating motivational bloodshed; introduced a spiritual guide; produced a providentially revealed crucifix; encouraged the initiate to lose consciousness; admitted a misting fog and allowed for the materialization of Evil; engaged a terrifying act of initiation; imposed the appearance of an authority-asserting dominant male; portrayed, through the distribution of communion, his assumption of a priestly role; promulgated a confusion of identities that should lead to the initiate's inevitable death and rebirth in a transformed state.

> To see a world in a grain of sand
> And a heaven in a wild flower,
> Hold infinity in the palm of your hand
> And eternity in an hour
> [William Blake, "Auguries of Innocence"].

Dracula is a story of becoming that traces the symmetrical ritual paths taken by Jonathan and Mina as they are conjointly transformed into New Man and New Woman. The manifold symmetrical aspects of the novel—from the opposing hierophantic roles of Dracula and Helsing, and dual feminine figures of Lucy and Mina, to the balanced East-West-East itinerary of plot, its temporal design and solar equilibrium—extend into the plot's ritual aspects. Whereas Jonathan encountered an old woman who foretold danger and provided protection from evil in the name of the Mother, life-giving force, Mina comes upon a man with "a face all gnarled and twisted like the bark of a tree" (64), Sir Oracle (65), on her first day at Lucy's residence at Whitby. No doubt inspired by Coleridge's "Rime," this Ancient Mariner takes Mina as the wedding-guest in seating her on the stone of St. Mary's churchyard.

Concerned with life's ends, Sir Oracle, or Swales, holds court in a graveyard situated high upon East Cliff, overlooking the grounds of an ancient abbey and the bay. His first meditation, "a sort of sermon" (65), is on dualism and the falseness of death, which leads him to cast aspersions on the veracity of the surrounding gravestones, "simply tumblin' down with the weight o' the lies wrote on them, 'Here lies the body' or 'Sacred to the memory' wrote on all of them, an' yet in nigh half of them there bean't no bodies at all" (65). He later speaks on the conduct of Judgment Day, envisioning the truth of men's lives as cut in stone on their graves, each soul struggling to bear the weight of the heavy truth of his mortal existence. His Geordie manner of pronouncing the word *tombstone* forces it to approach the sound of "tomb stain." On a third occasion he concentrates on death's arrival and the trumpet call for the soul's surrender, saying, "For life be, after all, only a waitin' for somethin' else than what we're doin'; and death be all that we can rightly depend on" (74). Claiming to be ready to heed the call, he closes the interview by blessing Mina.

A week after meeting Mina, on the night of *The Demeter*'s delivery of Count Dracula upon England's shores, Sir Oracle dies. His distorted features lead Mina to speculate that "he had seen Death with his dying eyes!" (85). Yet, as with the comfort that the old woman's rosary brought Jonathan long after she was distant, the Oracle had not yet issued his last, unspoken word. It awaits his funeral. The stone bench, mercy seat, on which Mina and Lucy would sit listening to him hold forth while enjoying the view was, according to Swales, part of a suicide's grave, that of a man named Canon, only son of a widow, who killed himself to spite his very own pious, holy mother. From this spot of seeing and hearing, Mina watched the funeral cortège of *The Demeter*'s captain approach, climbing the hundreds of steps, even as a maritime procession honored the sailor on the waterway below. Swales, too, was to be interred by the East Cliff bench, and it seems that the identities of Swales and *The Demeter*'s captain are somehow strangely combined. In fact, it was precisely there, on that seat, that Swales had died. One of the Oracle's mates, a mild and silent man with a devoted dog, joined Lucy and Mina at the bench during the funeral service, though the dog kept its distance, howling in fright and alarm. When the man, seeking to control his dog, took it by the scruff of its neck and placed it upon the bench beside him, it cowered and trembled in fright and would not be calmed — apparently terror-stricken by its proximity to Lucy.

In Ste Mary's East Cliff churchyard, Lucy, locked in a somnambulistic tryst with the Count, had also and already sprinkled her blood upon that bench and literal *tomb stain*. She described the encounter to Mina in fluid images:

> A fish leaped as I went by, and I leaned over to look at it, and I heard a lot of dogs howling — the whole town seemed as if it must be full of dogs all howling at once — as I went up the steps. Then I have a vague memory of something long and dark with red eyes, just as we saw in the sunset, and something very sweet and very bitter all around me at once; and then I seemed sinking into deep green water, and there was a singing in my ears, as passing away from me; my soul seemed to go out from my body and float about the air. I seemed to remember that once the West Lighthouse was right under me, and then there was a sort of agonizing feeling, as if I were in an earthquake, and I came back and found you shaking my body. I saw you do it before I felt you [94].

Despite the blood spilt, with word of Jonathan arriving from the East, Mina bids Lucy farewell and hurries off to join her fiancé. The two orphans, Jonathan and Mina, become one in the double city Buda-Pesht's Convent of Saint Joseph and Saint Mary, to which Mina was summoned in the name of "God and St Joseph and Ste Mary" (95). Mina tells Jonathan, "You are nearest and dearest and all the world to me; our souls are knit into one, for all life and all time" (287). Just prior to the marriage ceremony, Jonathan presents her with his Transylvanian diary as if it were his very soul. In accepting it, she takes possession of his nightmares, and, using her wedding band as signet ring, seals the document with a sky-blue ribbon and wax (100), the transaction with a kiss. "And ... when he kissed me, and drew me to him with his poor weak hands, it was like a very solemn pledge between us" (101).

This holy unity of man and woman gains in status and wealth, prospering due to Jonathan's Transylvanian initiation. On 17 September, Mina writes to an already dying Lucy to tell her that Mr. Hawkins had named the newlyweds his heirs, and to announce a recently-formed partnership, "the important firm of Hawkins & Harker" (141). The firm's name, deliberately communicating the sense of "eyes and ears," "sights and sounds," calls attention to a constant representational gambit: Throughout the text the sensory and extrasensory are given contrasting play — particularly communicative acts that confound the senses: hearing what was to be seen, or seeing that which should have been *entendu*, and, of course, being visited by visions. Reality, however, often exceeds fantasy in embracing ironic happenings. No sooner had Mina finished posting her letter than Death initiated youth into maturity, for on the day following the writing of Mina's letter Mr. Hawkins unexpectedly dies at the height of a deadly harvest season in which "the Aud Man" (74) claims Lucy, Mrs. Westenra, and, at Ring, Lord Godalming, Arthur's father.

Now a man of property, Jonathan is more confused than on the day he arrived in Transylvania. He "begins to doubt himself" (141) and confesses that he no longer knows "what to trust, even the evidence of my own senses" (168). 'It was the doubt as to the reality of the whole thing that knocked' (168) certitude from him. Jonathan mostly doubts his own sanity, judgment, and abilities. In London, while returning from Mr. Hawkins' funeral, he becomes distraught as he observes a man who strongly resembles the Count, yet the Count as he might look renewed and rejuvenated. Troubled by the effect the tall, thin, cruel-faced man spied in a London street has had on her husband's psyche, Mina decides to "take the foreign journal, and lock myself up in my room and read it" (161) once they return home.

Mina, describing the silent abode that welcomed them in Exeter as a "house empty of the dear soul" (156), exploits symbolic language Polidori once employed to suggest mortal coils sloughed off. In this void, at this barren pass in the mountains, she receives a request from a stranger, one Dr. Abraham Van Helsing, for a meeting to discuss Lucy's death. While he is specifically interested in Mina's Whitby diary, she cannot avoid questioning an authority on "therapeutics ... of the continuous evolution of brain-matter" (215) on the record of her husband's Transylvanian experiences. Within a short period of time, joining West and East, Helsing determines that Lucy's death and Jonathan's diary are intimately related, writing to Mina, "You may sleep without doubt" (167), and vouching for Jonathan's sanity and capacity to recover from the shocks he has suffered. Jonathan confides to his journal that when Mina "showed me in the doctor's letter that all I wrote down was true ... [it] made a new man of me" (168). If previously he had "felt impotent and in the dark," he was now confidently predicting that "Van Helsing is the man to unmask" (168) the Count. The couple joins Helsing at his protégé Seward's asylum.

In joining together Lucy's diary and correspondence with the Harkers' personal papers, Helsing also gathers the journals' authors and the personalities that enliven their pages. As Jonathan was surrounded by the Count and his three ladies in Transylvania, Mina will be by Helsing and his three gentlemen in Britain. These latter, Lucy's former suitors all, will embrace Mina nearly as they had Lucy. Mina, who knows of them through Lucy, solicitously extends to them her heart—affirming to Jack Seward, "You will let me help you, will you not?" (197); explaining to Art Holmwood that she and Lucy "were like sisters; and now she is gone, will you not let me be like a sister to you in your trouble?" (203); and softly challenging Quincey Morris, "Will you let me be your friend, and will you come to me for comfort if you need it?" (204). At their first meeting, "The Professor stood up and, after laying his golden crucifix on the table, held out his hand on either side. I took his right hand, and Lord Godalming his left; Jonathan held my right with his left and stretched across to Mr. Morris. So as we all took hands our solemn compact was made," another "transaction of life" (210), joining the couple to Helsing's band.

Despite oaths of solidarity and joining of hands, Mina is soon isolated, not by the walls of a material fortress but by gender—the surrounding band of men think her participation inappropriate and dangerous. For Mina, "to accept their chivalrous care" (214) was "a bitter pill" (214). Although she is physically present at Seward's asylum, she is for Jonathan as much an image as she had been when he was in Transylvania. For noble-sounding, deceit-justifying paternalistic reasons he strives to exclude her from sharing in the group's collective knowledge. His reports reflect the depth of his gender chauvinism:

> I could not tell the others of the day's discovery till we were alone; so after dinner—followed by a little music to save appearances even amongst ourselves—I took Mina to her room and left her to go to bed. The dear girl was more affectionate with me than ever, and clung to me as though she would detain me; but there was much to be talked of and I came away. Thank God, the ceasing of telling things had made no difference between us [234].

Drawing a curtain that partitions their covenant, an initial foray into the count's demesne was launched without Mina's knowledge. Mina stoically accepts the situation. "Manlike, they have told me to go to bed and sleep; as if a woman can sleep when those she loves are in danger! I shall lie down and pretend to sleep, lest Jonathan have added anxiety about me when he returns" (214). While menfolk conspired and advanced against the Count's territory, the Count made their asylum his sanctuary, seeking out, "as though he owned the whole place" (245), its chamber of courtly ladies.

The returning men were jubilant: "More than all do I rejoice that this, our first—and perhaps our most difficult and dangerous—step has been accomplished without the bringing thereinto our most sweet Madam Mina or troubling her waking or sleeping thoughts with sights and sounds and smells of horror which she might never forget" (223), was Helsing's optimistic assessment of the foray he had led. Bidding his comrades good-night, Jonathan "came tiptoe" to find "Mina asleep, breathing so softly that I had to put my ear down to hear it. She looks paler than usual. I hope the meeting tonight has not upset her. I am truly thankful that she is to be left out of our future work, and even of our deliberations. It is too great a strain for a woman to bear. ... Henceforth our work is to be a sealed book to her, till at least such time as we can tell her that all is finished" (223). Mina's unsealing of Jonathan's book brought together Helsing's forces; the band's sealing off and cloistering of Mina has prepared her for initiation.

Despite Jonathan's innocent willingness to cross Castle Dracula's threshold, it was Mr. Hawkins who engaged the fledgling solicitor's volition by dispatching him to Transylvania in his stead; similarly, it is Mr. Renfield, "mouth ... nauseous with ... flies and insects" (225), who places Mina within the Vampire's grasp via his willingness to welcome the Count to his cell. In designating these particular wilful agents, Stoker, who had earlier proclaimed that "the God created from human vanity sees no difference between an eagle and a sparrow" (96), contrasts the mighty hawk (albeit, a hawk with "neither chick nor child" (140)) and the humble wren, picturing the former emerging "from under the shadow of your beautiful cathedral at Exeter" (36) while situating the latter merely "somewhere under this" (226)—that is, in a place beneath us. "[W]ith his fly business" (169), Renfield, variously depicted as disgorging "a whole lot of feathers" (71) and "singing gaily as he used to do" (239), is cajoled by Dr. Seward with images of flight and freedom from the bars of his confining cage: "A nice time you'll have some time when you're flying out there" (237), his status suddenly elevated. Seward duly reports: "He did not care for any of the things of mere earth; he was in the clouds and looked down on all the weaknesses and wants of us poor mortals" (235); yet: "Our bird when he found the cage open would not fly" (102). In choosing his birds, Stoker has perhaps borrowed imagery from Shakespeare's Richard III, Act I-3 or King Lear, Act IV-6, while equally attaching his work to couplets of the great mystic artist William Blake's "Auguries of Innocence."

Renfield, a legally-constituted madman, bribed by an implicit promise of the provision of millions of lives for his consumption—a bribe expressed, he makes clear, through gesture only—admits the Vampire into the asylum:

> He slid into the room through the sash, though it was only open an inch wide—just as the Moon herself has often come in through the tiniest crack, and has stood before me in all her size and splendour [245].

Lunatic, devotee of the Moon, Renfield claims he has previously been visited by Artemis–Hekate; he also "thought that somehow Mrs Harker had come into the room" (245). On the occasion of her first visit, "[s]he came into the room with an easy gracefulness which would at once command the respect of any lunatic.... She walked over to him, smiling pleasantly, and held out her hand." Before he could speak she said to him, "'Good evening, Mr Renfield'" (205).

One persistently posed question in *Dracula* is whether Mina, the only woman represented as appearing in Renfield's cell, will be figured as queen of night or of day. Madam Mina — that is, "My Lady Love" — is often portrayed as a celestial guide, pointing the way through darkness, "with such spiritual intensity that her eyes were like pole stars" (283); her given name, Wilhelmina, suggests "wilful (or desirous) protectress (or shield) of love." Unlike "radiantly beautiful" (179) Lucy Westenra, ruddy Light of the West, whose hair spreads in "sunny ripples" (146), Mina is constant and enduring. Addressing Mina, Helsing proclaims, "there are darknesses in life, and there are lights; you are one of the lights" (165), but she seems a light in contrast to darkness, as if a star in the night sky, or, indeed, the moon, seat of feminine fertility. Although it appears at times that Mina is diurnal as she confesses, "I do not understand Lucy's fading away as she is doing" (92), she seems unfamiliar with Lucy's brilliant habits; moreover, she guardedly controls access to the nocturnal world, repeatedly noting, "I keep the key of our door always fastened to my wrist at night" (92).

One often suspects that Mina is an Anglicized expression of Luna. Equally at home by day and night, "sweet" and "appealing" are adjectives repeatedly summoned to render "our sweet Madam Mina" (223): "She looked so appealing and so pretty" (205), "a sweet-faced, dainty-looking girl" (194). "So true, so sweet, so noble, so little an egotist" (169) that Renfield bids her farewell saying: "I pray God I may never see your sweet face again" (207). The thoughts of "her man's brain" become "her sweeter counsels" (269). She can also be brilliant and her happiness is shown in her "bright smile" (208). "Her lips are curved and the face beams with happiness" (282), and she "will not be content, I know, to remain in the dark" (197). Of herself, she reports: "I always used to make up the timetables, so as to be helpful to my husband" (293) (he is described as being full of energy "like a living flame." [263]), though she "shall not wonder if at first he mixes up not only the month, but the year" (100); it is Mina, with her husband's help, who organizes the dates and puts "all the papers into order" (202). Unsurprisingly, another word used in conjunction with Mina is "phase": "The new phases of things leave my mind in a state of wonder" (282). "If this new phase was spontaneous, or in any way due to her unconscious influence, she must have some rare gift or power" (206). "She seemed brighter and better than she has been for days" (292). Yet, on another occasion she self–consciously writes: "When coming home — it was then bright moonlight, so bright that, though the front of our part of the Crescent was in shadow, everything could be well seen" (91). Lunar Mina mediates that which is there to be seen and that which is not visible, the bright and the dark faces of the cosmos.

> The bat that flits at close of eve
> Has left the brain that won't believe.
> The owl that calls upon the night
> Speaks the unbeliever's fright.
> He who shall hurt the little wren
> Shall never be beloved by men.
> He who the ox to wrath has moved
> Shall never be by woman loved.
> The wanton boy that kills the fly
> Shall feel the spider's enmity
> [Blake, "Auguries of Innocence"].

On the evening of 2 October, the Count, not Hekate, appears to Renfield. Despite Renfield's most strenuous efforts, and at the cost of his life, the Count penetrates the Harkers' bedroom to conduct Mina's initiation. Through a dying Renfield, Helsing, Seward, Quincey, and Art learn of Count Dracula's presence in the asylum, and rush to the Harkers' room. When they finally penetrate the sealed chamber a rite of initiation is nearly complete and the moon has arrived.

> The moonlight was so bright that through the thick yellow blind the room was light enough to see. On the bed beside the windows lay Jonathan Harker, his face flushed and breathing heavily as though in a stupor. Kneeling on the near edge of the bed facing outwards was the white-clad figure of his wife. By her side stood a tall, thin man, clad in black. His face was turned from us, but the instant we saw we all recognized the Count — in every way, even to the scar on his forehead. With his left hand he held both Mrs Harker's hands, keeping them away with her arms at full tension; his right hand gripped her by the back of the neck, forcing her face down on his bosom. Her white nightdress was smeared with blood, and a thin stream trickled down the man's bare breast which was shown by his torn-open-dress [246–47].

Despite the room's "thick yellow blind," the moonlight is brilliantly illuminating, as if the light were generated by Lady Love herself. The kneeling initiate is, like the White Goddess, "white-clad"; the standing priest, "clad in black," is lost in night. His dress, however, is torn open like his flesh and the initiate is partaking of his body and blood. Although Helsing misleadingly terms this "the Vampire's baptism of blood" (280), unlike Lucy's baptism—which she described as "sinking into deep green water, and there was a singing in my ears, as I have heard there is to drowning men"—it is given the form and the discourse of a Communion.

Forced to taste the Count's blood, Madam Harker has become one with him, and he claims her as "flesh of my flesh; blood of my blood, kin of my kin" (252). This profaning act of Communion, de facto Marriage in which lunar Mina is wed to a being we believe to be one with the Night even as her flush-faced Apollonian husband silently, impotently witnesses by her side, is still far from the ultimate ordeal Mina shall undergo. Helsing, noting that Mina is safe until sunset, lovingly seeks to protect her further by blessing her with the Eucharistic Host. He solemnly intones, "On your forehead I touch this piece of Sacred Wafer in the name of the Father, the Son, and—" (258), at which point Mina completes her interrupted Persephone-like "scream, so wild, so ear-piercing, so despairing that it seems ... it will ring" forever (247), for "[a]s he had placed the Wafer on Mina's forehead, it had seared it—had burned into the flesh as though it had been a piece of white-hot metal" (258–9).

As Jonathan was returned to health by the sisterhood of the Convent of St. Joseph and St. Mary, Mina will be defended by a brotherhood, "ministers of God's own wish" (278) that Helsing construes "as the old knights of the Cross" (278). The Brotherhood's pledge, "to peril even our own souls for the safety of one we love—for the good of mankind, and for the honour and glory of God" (279), is solemnly renewed and a new covenant founded. Helsing, presiding over the Brotherhood in a priestly manner, counsels Mina: "You must struggle and strive to live, though death would seem a boon unspeakable. You must fight Death himself, though he come to you in pain or in joy; by the day, or the night; in safety or in peril! On your living soul I charge you that you do not die—nay nor think of death—till this great evil be past" (254). The brothers struggle and strive to re-sanctify the profaned consecrated earth of the Count's many transient resting places, gathered in a disused chapel that "smelled ole Jerusalem in it" (201). Helsing, rephrasing the Ophite's Gnostic phrase "The beginning of perfection is the knowledge of man, but absolute perfection is the knowledge of God" (King, 19), elucidates the theology of their mission: "It was sanctified to such use of man, now we sanctify it to God" (*Dracula* 260), for "[i]t seemed as though corruption had become itself corrupt" (221)—blackness had become blacker than black.

As consecrated ground corrupted requires renewed sanctification, Mina, aggrieved by her innocently-acquired pollution, becomes the object of a particularly solemn sacramental ceremony dominated by her volition. Mina tells her husband, "I want you to read the Burial Service" (288). "Oh, my wife, must I read it?" he asks. "It would comfort me, my husband!" (288), says she.

The formality of their exchange resounds with scriptural overtones. The old woman that was Mina must die to permit Mina's rebirth as a New Woman, and her husband must pray for her soul as Helsing had once done for Lucy's. This was soon undertaken; the prayerful source? The Book of Common Prayer or, considering Helsing's spiritual role, The Sarum Missal.

> The caterpillar on the leaf
> Repeats to thee thy mother's grief.
> Kill not the moth nor butterfly,
> For the Last Judgment draweth nigh
> [Blake, "Auguries of Innocence"].

The Brotherhood, *fraternitatis*, its core composed of hunters of beasts rather than fishers of men, is formal, and given the shape of a hand, Helsing and his "rude four-in-hand" (313); five men, repeatedly described as brave and strong, earnest and good, constitute its explicitly secret organization: "We are pledged to set the world free. Our toil must be in silence, and our efforts all in secret; for in this enlightened age, when men believe not even what they see, the doubting of wise men would be his greatest strength" (279). Comprised of "gentlemen, who by nationality, by heredity, or by the possession of natural gifts, are fitted to hold ... respective places in the moving world" (215), it constitutes an elect. Mina is central to the Brotherhood, not as a member but as its object of devotion, Helsing elevating her to nearly divine status: "We are men, and are able to bear; but you," he says, addressing Mina, "must be our star and our hope" (214). Her stigmata, characterized by Helsing as a cross to bear, cause the knights to gather around her and swear themselves to her sacred cause. "We men pledged ourselves to raise the veil of sorrow from the head of her whom, each in his own way, we loved; and we prayed for help and guidance in the terrible task which lay before us" (259). For "it may be that we are chosen instruments of His good pleasure, and that we ascend to His bidding as that other through stripes and shame; through tears and blood; through doubts and fears, and all that makes the difference between God and man" (259). She, tired of being "kept in the dark" (225), insists: "There must be no more concealment" (253).

Jonathan recovered rapidly from his "brain fever" (100) after Helsing made of him a New Man, but once Mina's flesh was corrupted by the Count, he becomes destabilized in a different way: rushed, rash, vengeful, the man who pledged himself "heart and soul" (169) to the defeat of the Count proclaims himself ready to "sell [his] soul" (265) to destroy him. He is called back from this new malady by Abraham, who would protect his soul, and Mina, who would save the souls of all the afflicted, including her husband's. They each implore him, "Oh hush!" (265, 269) in the name of God. Mina argues for compassion for the accursed Count and his kind, and for forgiveness. In her generous celestial spirit, Mina approaches the Holy Mother, modestly asserting that "women have something of the mother in us that makes us rise above smaller matters when the mother-spirit is invoked" (203). Indeed, Mina is celebrated for her goodness — Helsing proclaims her exemplar of the good woman and defines "good women" as those "whose lives and whose truths may make good lesson for the children that are to be" (166).

The final hunt is engaged neither to avenge Lucy, nor to rid the world of a monster, but to purge Mina of a pollutant within her that came of the impure "baptism of blood," Mina confessing to sensing "some of the taste of the original apple that remains still in our mouths" (164). Mina herself casts this hunt as a question of uncovering true selves, of locating a singular truth within a duality and a light within darkness, encouraging her heroes: "you must destroy even as you destroyed the false Lucy so that the true Lucy might live hereafter; but it is not a work of hate" (269). In defining their mission, Mina's mention of the true Lucy necessarily refers to divine light.

High mysticism resides in Stoker's text beyond its constant references to light and dark. Helsing, who becomes "The Professor" in a very evangelical way, assumes a priestly function in his distribution of sacred Hosts, theological and metaphysical discourse, and role as father figure to the entire order. Hailing from Holland, Low Countries or the Netherlands, Abraham — in contact with the underworld, but "come ... to do what [he] can of good" (184) — is prophetic, declaring, for example: "He have gone back to his Castle in Transylvania. I know it so well, as if a great hand of fire wrote it on the wall" (274). The Professor's very work is to arrive at profound understandings of things that at first glimpse seem transparently simple, to read with a "man brain" instead of a "child brain." As he says, "He have been blind somewhat; blind after the manner of men, since when we can look back we see what we might have seen looking forward if we had been able to see what we might have seen!" (273). He comes to see more clearly when "our dear Madam Mina is once more our teacher. Her eyes have seen where we were blinded" (306). His speech seems moreover prophetic to his companions:

> Then Van Helsing turned and said gravely; so gravely that I could not help feeling that he was in some way inspired, and was stating things outside himself: —
>
> "It may be that you may have to bear that mark till God himself see fit, as He most surely shall on the Judgment Day to redress all wrongs of the earth and of His children that He has placed thereon. And oh, Madam Mina, my dear, my dear, may we who love you be there to see, when that red scar, the sign of God's knowledge of what has been, shall pass away and leave your forehead as pure as the heart we know" [259].

He who mocks the infant's faith
Shall be mocked in age and death.
He who shall teach the child to doubt
The rotting grave shall ne'er get out.
He who respects the infant's faith
Triumphs over hell and death
[Blake, "Auguries of Innocence"].

They are all present, a glowing "hand of fire" (274), when in the East the sun sets on Judgment Day. *Dracula*'s East-West opposition has been remarked upon by several commentators and understood in colonial, racial, anti–Semitic, anti–Slav, or other xenophobic terms; it more rightly should be seen as scriptural discourse. What began with the arrival at Castle Dracula on Saint George's Eve reaches a Western nadir with the death — on the Western Isle and land of Saint George — of Lucy Westenra, but the solar circuit must be completed, concluding in the East again. When Jonathan reports, "We left Charing Cross on the morning of the 12th, got to Paris the same night, and took the places secured for us in the Orient Express" (289), we are invited to picture their departing from Charing Cross, heading east, expressly, inevitably, on a spiritual journey towards the Orient where they are to assume their divinely assigned places.

Charing Cross is not merely the name of a London train station but of London's historic omphalos and the *axis mundi* from which emanate all geographical measurements in the British vernacular. The word "Charing" is said to be a corruption of the French *chère reine*, marking the location as the place bearing the "cross of the dearest queen," as this site was fixed by a cenotaphic monument erected in honor of the beloved Eleanor of Castile, queen to Edward I. It was the last of 12 "Eleanor crosses" erected at the places of rest attained over a nearly two week period by Eleanor's funeral procession as the bier wended its way from the northern city of Lincoln, where she had died, to the capital. No simple cross, this multi-tiered, four-faced and octagonal monument can be further seen through its geographic function as the embodiment of Stoker's precious *Quatre Faces*. Since from Carfax the Count entered London through King's Cross station, it is only fitting that Mina would leave London through Cross of the Dearest Queen.

Time and space become confounded in Stoker's transcendental, transcontinental journey, the Professor expressing the final stage of their restless eastward voyage in cosmic terms: "For we are going up, and up; and all is oh! so wild and rocky, as though it were the end of the world" (316). The end of the world will coincide with the end of time. As the Professor foretold of Mina and as she herself had promised: "I must bear this mark of shame upon my forehead until the Judgment Day" (259). In her mark of shame, the circular scar seared into the flesh of her brow even as she had sealed Jonathan's journal with her wedding band, the Charing Cross is manifested.

Mina processes towards Castle Dracula as Jonathan once had, but with the Professor rather than the Count serving as coachman. Arriving to await Judgment Day in the shadow of the Count's Transylvanian retreat, Helsing shelters Mina as night descends, enclosing her within a lunar disc whose perimeter he marks with fragments of Sacred Host, situating her now as if within the Host itself, "the Holy Circle" (318) being the Professor's term, her person incarnating the Holy Spirit. Although he asks her to move beyond the ring, Mina is unable: "I rejoiced, for I knew that what she could not, none of those that we dreaded could. Though there might be danger to her body, yet her soul was safe!" (316). Seasons have been reversed since Jonathan faced a ring of wolves in the same spot, and in the gloom, "the snow flakes and the mist began to wheel and circle round, till I could get as though a shadowy glimpse of those women that would have kissed" (317) Jonathan. Now they call to Mina, as Juana and Hélène once called to Antonia: "Come, sister. Come to us. Come!" (317) mistaking her for their sister, but "God be thanked she was not, yet, of them" and they "could not approach ... Madam Mina whilst she remained within the ring which she could not leave" (317).

The symbol of the ring has been a constant across plot, surrounding Jonathan with a lupine "living ring of terror" (20), marking out the Count's English domains, sealing Jonathan's diary, ennobling Lord Godalming, sustaining the agonized sound of Mina's passion, marshaling the Syzygy that will cost Quincey Morris his life, joining the Brotherhood as a band, and securing its jewel: Mina. "And so the circle goes on ever widening" (190). Her spiritual transformation is complete when she is purged of evil through Dracula's death, that is, upon the perfection, confirmation of the sacrament that the Professor initiated but which was suspended when it resulted in Mina's branding. Yet to be cleansed of evil unavoidably requires the death of purity, embodied by Quincey, who, hurried in his "lonely walk between this and Kingdom Come" (60), sacrifices himself for the sake of Lady Love:

> With a sigh he took, with a feeble effort, my hand in that of his own which was unstained. He must have seen the anguish of my heart in my face, for he smiled at me and said:—"I am only too happy to have been of any service! Oh, God!" He cried suddenly, struggling up to a sitting posture and pointing to me, "It was worth this to die!—Look! Look!" [326].

The genesis of Mina's stigmata, rooted in a verbally-rendered Sign of the Cross, meets its ends in a cathartic rose light: "The sun was now right down upon the mountaintop, and the red gleams fell upon my face, so that it was bathed in rosy light" (326). After having skirted the Black Sea to attain a point east of our "Dearest Queen's Cross," Mina is reunited with Lucy

Westenra, rosy Light of the West, Stoker attributing, perhaps, a new sense to Charing Cross derived from "charring in the fire" (190): "the *charred, burnt* or *branding* cross," or even, "Cross of the Char Ring." Helsing was right: the Host had protected Mina until sunset, now finally come. As day gives way to endless night, queenly Mina is liberated. Mina's forehead, like Jonathan's hair, finds a white purity through her contact with the Vampire; having been stained by sin and re-sanctified, she, New Woman, can, in full knowledge of good and evil, claim true purity.

Every night and every morn
Some to misery are born.
Every morn and every night
Some are born to sweet delight.
Some are born to sweet delight,
Some are born to endless night.
We are led to believe a lie
When we see not through the eye
Which was born in a night to perish in a night,
When the soul slept in beams of light.
God appears, and God is light
To those poor souls who dwell in night,
But does a human form display
To those who dwell in realms of day
[Blake, "Auguries of Innocence"].

Through long sections of the novel, Mina—the novel's "fixed point" through which "the centripetal force is balanced with the centrifugal" (62)—is necessarily an ambiguous and divided figure, a woman united at once to a man in holy matrimony and a corpse in unholy servitude. Ambiguity also describes Messrs Hawkins and Renfield, to whom Stoker was required to attribute mixed functions in order to perfectly balance his symmetrical composition. Renfield's dual role is particularly complex, not merely a John the Baptist to diabolical Dracula, but a man for whom the struggle between light and dark is lived daily as his insanity, yet who, knowingly and courageously, defies the Count to protect Madam Mina. He selflessly serves the Brotherhood, which nevertheless fails to count him "amongst the best and truest of ... friends" (216). Sharing a priestly function with the Count, the lunatic-wedded-to-wisdom Renfield counterbalances the sage-wedded-to-folly (see 158) Helsing. When Helsing muses "Perhaps I may gain more knowledge out of the folly of this madman than I shall from the teaching of the most wise" (225), he is rightly greeted by Renfield as "the old fool Van Helsing" (225). Speaking as a Baptist-like figure, Renfield transforms John 3:29's metaphor of a marriage scene by substituting senses—sight for sound, watching for harking — and focus — feminine for masculine, deception for joy: "The Bride maidens rejoice the eyes that wait the coming of the bride. But when the bride draweth nigh, then the maidens shine not to the eyes that are filled" (96–7). The Professor, too, calls attention to this confounding of eye and ear, exclaiming as Thomas: "I could not have believe until such time as that fact thunder on my ear. See! see!" (209) — though the Professor also connects hand to foot, looking forward and moving back, admonishing "once our feet are on the ploughshare, we must not draw back" (193).

Stoker confronts several other scriptural sources, calling repeatedly on the Old Testament's first books, Genesis, Exodus, Numbers, and the apocrypha. His conceit turns on Genesis 9's command to Noah: "Every creature that moves and lives shall be food for you; as I gave you the green plants, I give you everything. But the flesh with its life — that is, its blood — you shall not eat" (Genesis 9:3–4). Renfield confesses, "I used to fancy that life was a positive and perpetual entity, and that by consuming a multitude of live things, no matter how low in the scale of creation, one might indefinitely prolong life.... 'For the blood is the Life'" (206). Yet Enoch becomes his model "because he walked with God" (Genesis 5). To Renfield's evocation of Enoch, Seward, too, confounds eye and ear, claiming "I could not see the analogy ... so I harked back to what he had denied" (236). According to Genesis 9, it is Noah, great-grandson of Enoch, who was said to "Walk with God." Stoker has Renfield refer to the Book of Enoch (published in translation from Ethiopic by Robert Henry Charles in 1893), a text in which apocalyptic depictions of the end time are rendered and scriptural and psychoanalytic imaginations coincide.

Enoch "the scribe" begins by saluting the elect and the righteous. He explains that, charged with petitioning the Divine on behalf of "the Watchers," he has seen and heard remote generations to come. The Watchers are archangels who, having formed a compact to defy the Great Glory, abandoned their heavenly home to descend to Earth and fornicate with the comely daughters of man, begetting a race of sinful monsters. Seeking redemption, they have engaged Enoch to record their petition. Enoch receives visions in his sleep that constitute the divine response to the Watchers' prayers. His dreams take the form of astral voyages through the elements in their wildest expressions, the bitter and the sweet, that take him west, to the place of heavenly lights; to the sacred omphalos, Jerusalem; and to the east where, beyond its deserts, a fertile land rises in far off mountains. He visits the Great Glory who charges the eternal Watchers with defiling themselves with the blood of women and with mortal flesh. Enoch is shown the fiery abyss in which the evil ones will pass aeons.

In their transgressions, the Watchers have introduced mankind to knowledge and sin. The petition that Enoch has scribed will not be granted, but the Watchers shall be known as evil spirits, and confined to the earth until they are destroyed with the ungodly while the elect "shall inherit the earth." Enoch is to inform the Watchers that they know not the true mysteries, only worthless ones, and to alert his grandson Noah to prepare for a purgative deluge. Several parables follow that sketch out an elect dominated by the Elect One, or Son of Man, final judge of all flesh, and particularly the judge of the mighty of the world. In a last section, great attention is paid to the movement of the sun, stars and heavenly lights in time, and the according divisions of time, Enoch arguing for solar rather than lunar division of the year.

Stoker, confounding eye and ear, replaces angelic Watchers with human (scribe and solicitor) Harkers. He also has Renfield comment on the Elect of the Purfleet Brotherhood as he is introduced to them, and he seemingly suggests that they represent four iterations of New Man: Jesus, Adam, Abraham, and Moses — the first being son of the Lord Godalming; second, author of political fable; third, first of his kind and holder of "an Indulgence" (187); and last, guide dear to all seekers of asylum and one fit to lead "well to seaward" (76). The justice of this reading is supported through Stoker's *Notes*, which suggest "Quincey P. Adams" as the name for one of the principals (91).

Helsing, "having something of angels' eyes" (165), pledged that the activities of the Brotherhood should in no way be incompatible with the Christian faith or gentlemanly honor (182); they are not, though the Church of Rome seems to be portrayed as a "worthless wretch who stole" the golden cross, even if "She knew not altogether what she did" (150). The Professor's pronouncements endow the Brotherhood with Rosicrucian, mystic, and Gnostic overtones: "There are always mysteries in life" (171), "mysteries which men can only guess at, which age by age they may solve only in part" (183); "we see around us every day the growth of new beliefs, which think themselves new; and which are yet but the old, which pretend to be young — like the fine ladies at the opera" (171). Even scientist Seward's proclamation that "Transcendentalism is a beacon to the angels, even if it be a will-o'-the-wisp to man" (293) expresses Thomas Taylor-influenced religious themes that propose a return to ancient rites of renewal previously placed at the center of the Vampire Tale.

The old-beliefs-growing-as-new however give form to *Dracula*'s subject: "We seem to be drifting into unknown places and unknown ways; into a whole world of dark and dreadful things. Godalming is shutting the furnace door" (310). A new era may be dawning in which Hell's fires are less all-consuming and forgiveness is possible. Adam has sacrificed himself and died with clean hands — "unstained" (326) is the word Mina chooses. Even the Vampire, released from its body, knows peace and felicity.

When Dracula was beheaded, Mina commented: "I shall be glad as long as I live that even in that moment of final dissolution, there was in the face a look of peace, such as I never could have imagined might have rested there" (325). In the case of Lucy: "One and all we felt that the holy calm that lay like sunshine over the wasted face and form was only an earthly token and symbol of the calm that was to reign forever" (192). Of the three lamiae, Helsing confessed: "It was butcher work; had I not been nerved by thoughts of other dead, and of the living over whom hung such a pall of fear, I could not have gone on.... God be thanked, my nerve did stand. Had I not seen the repose in the first face, and the gladness that stole over it just ere the final dissolution came, as realization that the soul had been won, I could not have gone further with my butchery" (320).

In every case, true death sparks a "holy ray of light" (198) that is felicity. The false Lucy is executed so that the true Lucy may shine. Stoker's symmetry has resolved the conflict between good and evil, day and night, and it is especially the New Woman that serves as polestar for learning forgiveness. "She is one of God's women, fashioned by His own hand to show us men and other women that there is a heaven where we can enter, and that its light can be here on earth" (169). The elect not only save themselves, but the damned. As the sweeping away of Mr. Hawkins and Lord Godalming by the "scytheman" (216) gave birth to New Men, the harvest of the Un-Dead makes of Mina a New Woman. Feet planted on the Earth, silhouetted against a darkening night sky that glitters with its brilliant inhabitants, crushed serpent, Little Dragon, at her feet, Mina presents an Isian or Marian figure and returns the narrative to its beginning and the rosary.

Jonathan, who had asked Mina "to share [his] ignorance" (100), is compelled by his wife to share knowledge, gnosis. The Professor instructs the notary's wife: "You must be scribe and write him all down, so that when the others return from their work you can give it to them; then they shall know as we do" (297). The final sacramental transformation reserved for the Harkers occurs when the orphans become themselves parents. Lady Love is transformed into The Mother, and the knowing syzygy has answered Sister Agatha's request to come together "in the name of God and Saint Mary and Saint Joseph" and has brought forth a new generation to take the place of the old. In the end, Mr. Hawkins' place is occupied by Abraham; he who had lost a son (157) has found a progeny through orphans Jonathan and Mina.

The Children of Night

> "It struck me as curious that the moment she became conscious she pressed the garlic flowers close to her. It was certainly odd that whenever she got into that lethargic state, with the stertorous breathing, she put the flowers from her; but that when she waked she clutched them close. There was no possibility of making any mistake about this, for in the long hours that followed, she had many spells of sleeping and waking and repeated both actions many times" [145].

Stoker claimed, perhaps facetiously, that dream-life — nightmare — inspired *Dracula*, attributing the novel's genesis to ill-digested dressed crab. He apparently envisioned the Count scurrying, crab-like, down precipitous castle walls. Perhaps being introduced to the Count in dream-life helped frame the novel, for its conceit is fuelled by somnambulism, hypnotism, and opiates. Although dragged-about babes are always to be seen, despite the roughness of their treatment, fast asleep, and though sleep-induction seems to be one of the Count's many charms, it is exclusively within the realm of Dreams that he holds absolute sway and is able to enter into his victim's life-flow, siphon off their anima, and effect his own renewal.

The godfather of the Romantic Vampire Tale, John William Polidori, submits that dreams are "for the convenience of souls having converse with dead or distant friends" (tr. qtd. Macdonald 39). As a romantic, he embraced the age-old view of the dream as a window on an "otherworld" of ancestors, shades, and divinities; as a Doctor of Medicine, his dissertation *Disputatio Medica Inauguralis quaedam de Morbo, Oneirodynia Dicto, Complectens* determines with a shrug that "the actions of the soul, and of external bodies, on the organic body are so obscure, that it seems we shall never know the cause of things. For when in chemistry and even in mechanics we are ignorant of many and great things, how are we to believe that we shall come near to grasping the principles of vegetable life, much less those of animal life and of the soul?" (tr. qtd. Macdonald 39). Dreams, it would seem, are native to the soul and intrinsic to soul-life.

Had Polidori, author of *Ximenes, or, the Modern Abraham* and *Ernestus Brechtold, or, the Modern Œdipus,* been granted the possibility of subtitling his *Vampyre,* he may well have connected it to *the Modern Dionysus,* that masked divinity of theatre and aesthetics, disguised lord of the underworld, dark groom of Persephone, whose characteristics he assigns to Lord Ruthven. Abraham Stoker, having had occasion to subtitle *Dracula,* subtly suggests "The Modern Morpheus" (97) for his own novel, a name stamped from a mythological die that is particularly germane to Count Dracula. It is immaterial whether the Count assumes Morpheus's characteristics or the latter mimics the former's traits: Morpheus inhabits the novel. As Oscar warned in Nodier's melodrama, it is through dreams that the Vampire overcomes his victim, a warning the count himself sternly reiterates, promising that bad dreams await "those who sleep unwisely" (38).

Establishing Morpheus as antithetical to Light, Stoker introduces him by name in having Seward pledge "not to dishonour Lucy by mixing the two" (97). In rejecting Morpheus, Seward adds: "If need be, tonight shall be sleepless" (97). God of dreams, shape-shifting actor able to imitate in walk, voice, and gesture any human form, Morpheus is, according to Cicero, the son of Night (Nocte) and Darkness (Erebo). (Fomenting genealogical obscurity, Ovid presents Morpheus, Icelos and Phantasus, respectively imitators of humans, beasts, and inanimate objects, as the sons of Hypnos.) Although Morpheus has countless siblings among the great brood of "children of the Night," that is, of Night herself, only his relationship with twin brothers Hypnos (Sleep) and Thanatos (Death) directly concerns Stoker, who pointedly salutes the twins in excerpting Thomas Hood's paean to their honor, "The Death-bed": "We thought her dying whilst she slept, And sleeping when she died" (147).

Victorian graveyard statuary represents Sleep as a dozing cherub whose gracefully splayed fingers and outstretched arm rest lightly on an overturned antique lamp. Through this device, Sleep — in whose empty grasp the invisible becomes visible while the ordinarily visible is not to be seen — is figured upsetting the norms of everyday life. The extinguished, overturned lamp also speaks to the forgetfulness that comes with sleep, the drowsing cherub seemingly having lost control over his own plump hand. The fact that such sculptures nearly always appear in cemeteries evidences the indissoluble association joining Sleep to Death, for the overturned lamp was previously lit by the flame of Life. The twins are so alike that the Victorian preferred substituting one for the other, no doubt with the idea of establishing the graveyard as a place of eternal rest and encouraging thoughts of an otherworldly awakening.

Since it is Sleep that affords Morpheus opportunity to hold sway and inevitably provoke a kind of death, *Dracula*, though chronicling the mercurial activities of Morpheus, is concerned first and foremost with accomplices Hypnos and Thanatos, for it is Hypnos who opens the way for Morpheus, Thanatos who appears in his wake. *Dracula* is thus a story about sleeping and guarding against sleep in order to prevent dream-laden Sleep from becoming Death. "Oh, but I am tired! If it were not that I had made my diary a duty I should not open it tonight!" (86) is a typical diarist's plaint that underscores the dogged commitment of the scribes. Seward's dictum "Cannot eat, cannot rest, so diary instead" (61) contrasts physical need with epistemological imperative. The record the writers dutifully assemble is obsessively concerned with sleeping, the travails that come from losing consciousness, and the superhuman burden assumed by those charged with maintaining watch — eloquently articulated in the occulted addendum to *The Demeter*'s captain's log.

The diarists catalogue where and under what conditions sleep occurs, and enumerate the extravagant efforts undertaken to prevent its onset and to defend against unwanted dreams — i.e., the steady stream of flowers from the Netherlands whose flow is compared to "the waters of [the] Lethe" (120), and the sacred symbols of the celestial Lord that are engraved upon persons, places, things, and even the Earth herself. The journalists also chronicle their chagrin and frustration when undesired lapses of consciousness allow Morpheus to sneak past their guard, enter into a sleeper's spirit, and gain dominion over volition.

Morpheus is said to set off at dusk from his mansion in the form of a bat. It is also claimed that once Hypnos has gained the upper hand over a human soul, putting it to sleep, Morpheus soundlessly glides into the spirit of the unprotected sleeper on the wings of the butterfly, like the wings Renfield references in his discussion of "the aerial powers of the psychic faculties" (235). These various rumors of transforming wings are strongly reminiscent of Mélusinian legends, the Welch night-hag Gwrach-y-Rhybyn, and Dumas' claim that ghouls put their victims "to sleep with the whisper of their great wings" (428) in order to suck their handsome youth's life's blood in a deadly embrace. Only in bringing sleep about with the fluttering of wings, are the Ghoul and Vampire able to purloin their victim's *anima mundi,* that is, the soul — blood and soul being symbolic equivalents since the blood contains and circulates the *anima*. The soul, like the Paraclete, is pictured as a winged thing.

Renfield's further comment that "the ancients did well when they typified the soul as a butterfly!" (235) is therefore piercingly to the point. Morpheus's stealing the sleeper's soul away enables his further predatory flights of fancy through the use of the wings of the newly stolen soul. Stoker's Count, however, always setting out for conquest, is only, though repeatedly, represented as "a big bat" (213), a changeless, liminal creature, a flying mammal known for its nocturnal habits, its penchant for living upside-down, and, in three of its species, an appetite for blood. Polidori's Persephone-like Ianthe, Ruthven's original victim, truly was characterized as a butterfly, "a Kashmere butterfly" (270)—a gentle, benign creature celebrated for representing spiritual metamorphosis. She was doomed to forever flutter about certain Attic precincts. Through these winged representational idioms, the poetic image of the Vampire collides with Freudian dogma, the shock of their impact solidifying the clichés of horror. To Freud disciple Ernest Jones, "the appearance of the Vampire in animal form, particularly in that of a butterfly or snake—two of the commonest Oriental representatives of the father, is one of the many characteristic features of this origin [in incest yearnings], as again is the fact that [the Vampire's] activities are altogether characterized by every possible infantile perversion" (130).

It is difficult not to regret the stridency of the Freudians' incest fixation. While Stoker may have been aware of Freud's gestating theories during *Dracula*'s writing through his attendance of the Society for Psychical Research lecture series (Belford 212–13) and attendant interest in Freud mentor Jean-Martin Charcot, Freud exerted no apparent influence on the novel's content. It is thus odd that, though *Die Traumdeutung* only appeared several years after *Dracula*'s publication, Freud has provided the sense-producing filter that has most consistently been applied to Stoker's novel, so much so that the Freudian "latent content" has come to mask *Dracula*'s veritable deep text.

Dismissing Polidori's thesis, Freud subjects the dream processes of Romantic expression to "scientific" examination to conclude that dreams arise from unrealized wishes. Through dreams, he elaborates a theory of mind that furnishes an overarching explanation to human intellectual and cultural life, claiming to uncover socio-neural phenomena whose simple exposition could make baffling dreams and the intellectual processes that produced them intelligible to their authors. Dreams, like magic inverted, are rhetorical entities dependent on metaphor and metonymy, working through narrative techniques of condensation, displacement, figuration—the poet's, and Stoker's, very tools. Freud, however, considering the dreamer as a social creature, concerns himself more with the editorial and publishing aspects of dreams—their auto-representation to the self—than with their poetics *sensu stricto*, leading him to integrate into his theory anthropological notions of taboo, norms of social and moral behavior, and, borrowing from Charcot, the interplay of conscious and unconscious functions of mind. In Freud's wish-fulfilment scheme, the greater the taboo associated with dreamt wishes, the more aggressively "the dream-work," the mind's obscuring poetic function, disguises the wishes represented, legibility operating in inverse proportion to acceptability by the conscious self; *manifest* content masks *latent* content, with the latter speaking to the motivating cause of the representation. The incest taboo, the primordial social constraint, is the mighty psycho-sexual source feeding the great subterranean river of the unconscious's wishes, whose currents periodically bubbles to the surface through dreams.

The temptation to dispose of the complexities of *Dracula,* an admittedly enigmatic, profound, and often disturbing work, with a ready-made cognitive template is understandable. Freudian analysis seems particularly apt in light of Stoker's insistent concentration on tensions between conscious and unconscious selves, such as the alternation observed in Lucy, who accepts and then rejects bouquets of garlic according to her fluctuating state of consciousness.

Fundamental differences between Freud's notion of consciousness and Stoker's, however, are critical. The Freudian self, a two-tiered mind that is termed "psyche" but does not mean "soul," is constituted a bit like the American government, with components of a tripartite structure — ego, id, superego — dynamically vying for power and dominance. Consciousness for Freud is ruled by the self's rational, cognitive elements, the ego and superego. For Stoker, consciousness is simply wilful self–awareness, a recollection of finalities and beginnings: the dust of mortality and the Light of the divine. Freud's and Stoker's views of the unconscious contrast even more sharply. In Freudian usage, the unconscious allows the consciously-censored id freer rein to indulge repressed wishes, exercise sublimated drives, indulge traumatic memories; in Stoker's, it is simply the surrender, even the unwitting surrender, of volition, thus losing sight of ends and beginnings due to the distractions of what is termed the moving world, that is, the forgetting of God. It is also rational, "unconscious cerebration" (69, 237), "brother" (70) to conscious thought, playing a major role in logical problem-solving and cognitive elaboration. Mental activities that are consciously undertaken in Freudian terms can be perfectly unconscious in Stoker's, and vice versa.

Freud's psyche, the mind, and Stoker's, the soul, are incongruous, incompatible. The same must be said for *Dracula*: Freud's *Dracula* is not Stoker's. This is not to disparage the brilliant Viennese analyst and theoretician, to challenge the Vienna Psychoanalytic Society, or to seek some other psychoanalytic filter; it is merely to liberate *Dracula* and return it to the frame that Polidori suggests and Stoker embraces. As Freud's colleague Carl Gustave Jung writes:

> If we assume with [Freud] that the incest motif is the source of all modern man's psychological problems as well as of alchemical symbolism, this gets us nowhere as regards the *meaning* of the symbols. On the contrary, we have landed ourselves in a blind alley, for we shall only be able to say that all symbolism, present and future, derives from the primal incest. That is what Freud actually thought, for he once said to me: "I only wonder what neurotics will do in the future when it is generally known what their symbols mean" [14: 302].

The one work on dreams appearing in the *Notes* (Rosenbach #66), a work by Robert Gray ill-referenced by Stoker under the name of its publisher, Rivington (235), considered dreams, very much within the Polidorian soul-life context, as being oracular, visionary, or requiring hermeneutical interpretation. Gray considers famous examples of profane and sacred dreams as they were recorded in well-known texts — from antiquity, citing classical and Biblical sources, to more recent dreams of well-known figures such as Lorenzo di Medici. Gray dedicates several pages to Ovid's account of Morpheus (94–96), and a chapter to "Inspired Dreams which Contributed to the Confirmation and Advancement of the Gospel." Cicero's Morpheus is granted consideration in a second tome whose most interesting aspect may be the final chapter title, "The Use of Fictitious Dreams in Literature." The *Notes* show that Stoker found little of interest in Gray, and no doubt continued his research through other means.

Despite Stoker's classical use of dreams, the fact that the Count is identified as the Vampire and that he reveals himself to his victims exclusively through dreams makes *Dracula* understandably and irresistibly attractive to Freudians. Applying psychoanalytic principle to the Vampire–inhabited terrain of Nightmare and advancing Freud's theory one step further, Ernest Jones perceives Nightmare as a psychic guillotine, an angst-infested reverie serving to vent the id's taboo desires in order to assure their continued repression. While such a frame seems to contain *Dracula* perfectly (does not the Vampire lose his head in the end?), closer examination shows Stoker intends *Dracula*'s occulted content to triumph in the rosy light of the illuminating moment of judgment. The ambitions of Stoker's text flatly contradict Freud's hypothesis.

Complicating this situation, however, is the history of the Vampire construct itself. Knowing that folklore's vampire only troubles his intimate and familial relations, Stoker duly indulges the incest paradigm, as father-figure Abraham humorously concedes: "Then this so sweet maid is a polyandrist, and me ... am bigamist" (158). Indeed Stoker does everything possible to indulge yet dismissively expose the flimsiness of the garden variety incest trope, with Helsing's burning candle, angled "so that he could read the coffin plates, and so holding it that the sperm dropped in white patches which congealed as they touched the metal" (176), rendering a parody of sepulchral Sleep. To drive the point home, all tools become phallic: "Another search in his bag, and he took out a turnscrew" (176). From turnscrew to the wooden stakes, the phallic tools flirt with parody. The Professor's further comment, "And so the circle goes on ever widening" (190), manifestly refers to the contagious aspect of the metaphysical malady he is trying to stamp out, while latently projecting a spreading incestuous tsunami. Lucy even wonders, "Why can't they let a girl marry three men, or as many as want her, and save all this trouble?" before adding "But this is heresy, and I must not say it" (60). *Dracula* is a sacred, but not a sanctimonious text; its interest in incest, however, is not where the Freudian finds it.

Jones's great work *On the Nightmare* is nevertheless relevant for its survey of literature on the nightmare phenomenon, some portion of which may have actually influenced Stoker. Jones assembles symptomatic descriptions of the condition as reported by medical doctors who suffered from it; for instance, the 1753 "Observations on the Incubus, or night-mare" of Dr. John Bond:

> The Nightmare generally seizes people sleeping on their backs, and often begins with frightful dreams, which are soon succeeded by a difficult respiration, a violent oppression on the breast, and a total privation of voluntary motion. In this agony they sigh, groan, utter indistinct sounds, and remain in the jaws of death [Jones 16].

According to Dr. Woldemar Cubasch, "some kind of Being, most often a shaggy animal, or else a hideous human form presses on the sleeper's breast, or pinions his throat and tries to strangle him. The terror increases with the suffocation, every effort at defence is impossible, since all his limbs are paralyzed as though by magical power" (Jones 24). This terror is imbued with an erotic content however: "With women, the Bogey ... does not suddenly throw himself on his victim, but often enters the room gently and just as gently climbs on to the couch, so as to become a love partner of the sleeper" (Jones 47). Dr. Johann Boerner elaborates: "Sometimes voluptuous feelings are coupled with those of *Angst*; especially with women, who often believe that the night-fiend has copulated with them" (Jones 50).

Dr. Jules Delassus insists that one who senses the approach of Incubus or Succubus is seized with an intense angst. The throat tightens, initiating a feeling of suffocation, all the while the mucous membranes are caressed in voluptuous titillation, as if an extraordinarily expert lover were enveloping you, penetrating you, melting within you. The orgasm is wild; the nervous expenditure, terrible (Jones 47). Nightmare's terrifying and erotic elements are inseparable. In a dictionary entry, Dr. Auguste Motet asserts that the most difficult aspect for the dreamer incapable of stopping the transformational creature from enforcing its will is the feeling of impotence (Jones 19). For many, including Dr. Robert Macnish, whose ideas will be considered in more detail, the *angst* that accompanies the impression of impotence is far worse still.

Jones concludes that "resemblances between the beliefs relating to *Devil, Witch, Incubus*, and Night-bogey (*Alp*) and Night-hag (*Mahre*) are so intimate that they may be said to present merely different aspects of the same theme" (232). "The Vampire superstition is evidently closely allied to that of the

Incubus and *Succubus*" (125). "The main differences are that hate and guilt play a far larger part in the Vampire than in the Incubus belief" (130). "The very fact that the Vampire is a *revenant* is decisive here, for we have already traced this conception to the incest complex" (127). While the apparent certitude of these opinions tends to place them beyond reach of judicious appeal, examination of Jones's sources shows that nearly all are exclusively concerned with Incubi and Succubi, hence eroticized nightmare. In Stoker's work there is need for some other context, some other asylum for the Count, because, in *Dracula*, instead of the dream being something produced by the unconscious it is itself a means of producing unconsciousness, that is, a means of accessing some Otherworld that is both underworldly and celestial, and in which the abandonment of volition can quickly become fatal.

The question of how to bring worlds visible and obscure into disbelief-suspensive contact must have presented Stoker with a significant strategic challenge. Some mechanism, some effective interface between realms, was required to sustain his fiction so that "there seems to be through it all some thread of continuity" (Stoker 161). While Belford suggests that the tarot may have been considered as that mechanism (214), ancient Morpheus and his clan offered a far more appropriate option. Pythagorean and phrenologist Robert Macnish, who begins his 1838 *A Philosophy of Sleep* with the assertion that "Sleep is the intermediate state between wakefulness and Death" (1), drafts a virtual road map to effecting Morpheus's integration into Stoker's "wide world." Macnish's description of nightmare is particularly apropos: "The whole mind, during the paroxysm, is wrought up to a pitch of unutterable despair; a spell is laid upon the faculties, which freezes them in to inaction; and the wretched victim feels as if pent alive in his coffin" (123).

Nightmare, described as having "a connection with physical disorder, ranging along the gloomy confines of terror, holding communication with hell and the grave, and throwing a discolouring shade over human life" (2–3), seems wilfully autonomous, the dreamer being, as one under a spell, a pure victim of gratuitous terror. Dr. Macnish, author of "The Metempsychosis" and other quite successful, light, occult-themed fiction, paints a picture evocative of Fuseli's most celebrated image:

> Sometimes he is involved in the coils of a horrid, slimy monster, whose eyes have the phosphorescent glare of the sepulchre, and whose breath is poisonous ... he is hissed at by serpents, tortured by demons, stunned by the hollow voices and cold touch of apparitions ... the unearthly shrieks and gibberish of hags, witches, and fiends float around him.... At one moment he may have the consciousness of a malignant demon being at his side.... Or, he may have the idea of a monstrous hag squatted upon his breast ... an incarnation of the evil spirit ... or he is entombed alive in a sepulchre, beside the mouldering dead [122–25].

Not limited to a consideration of incubi, *A Philosophy of Sleep* opens out onto a far vaster mindscape that constitutes a ready-made guide to the realm of sleep and its variegated states of consciousness, offering chapters on among other topics, "Night-Mare," "Spectral Illusions," "Sleep-Walking," "Sleep-Talking," "Trance," "Induction of Sleep through Opiates," "Day-Mare," "Prophetic Dreams," "Reverie" and "Abstraction" (vii-viii). Stoker, following in Macnish's shadow, pursues all these phenomena. While Macnish notes that the somnambulist "may safely return, even over the most dangerous precipices ... to his bed" (188) and advises "that sleep-walking is sometimes hereditary" (164), Stoker writes that "Mrs Westenra has got an idea that sleep-walkers always go out on roofs of houses and along the edge of cliffs.... Poor dear, she is naturally anxious about Lucy, and she tells me that her husband, Lucy's father, had the same habit; that he would get up in the night and dress himself and go out, if he were not stopped" (72). While Macnish maintains that "somnambulism as well as lunacy, sometimes bestows supernatural strength upon the individual" (173), Stoker has Renfield declare, "I had heard that madmen have unnatural strength" (245). Ultimately, Macnish authors Helsing's suspect formula: "Decomposition is the only infallible mark that existence is at an end, and that the grave has triumphed" (237). He goes so far as to describe the glazed eyes and shrinking visage of the already dead, useful to contrast with the Un-Dead resting in their coffins. Macnish, whose uncompromising scepticism of premonitory dreams in the modern world complements Dom Augustin Calmet's views on the likelihood of the existence of vampires, compresses the human life cycle into a philosophy of sleep that unites the physic and psychic under the auspices of a benevolent God in a manner bound to appeal to Stoker.

Freud's obscure cave of the unconscious, abode of the primordial psychological being, is hollowed out of emotional bedrock during pre–verbal times. Along its labyrinthine ways uncharted passages link dreams, the realm of individual imaginings, and myth, the realm of the archetypal image. As dream-life reflects myth, dream time approaches mythic time, the cyclical, spiraling realm of continuity and repetition that reaches back to the timeless moment before the beginning. The two conjointly define a locus where Stoker and Freud can momentarily pause and join in admiration for the work of social anthropologist J. G. Frazer before parting ways. For it is here that the psychoanalytical, focusing on projected assumptions of a libidinous human economy anchored in "infantile perversions," assigns the archetypal to the individual, alienating myth's sense and purpose by denying or ignoring myth's communal, spiritual origins; it is here where Freud's psyche, the mind, and Stoker's psyche, the soul, irreversibly diverge. The Freudian seeks to offer scientific help to those with problems of the mind; Stoker is concerned with depicting the sacred and discoursing on the problems of the soul. Jung will eventually make an awkward attempt to bridge the divide, but in 1897 the chasm is dauntingly real.

Anthropology views the mythic soul rising from two possible sources, the shadow and the breath. The first yields the underworldly chthonic soul; the second, the celestial. From a psychoanalytical perspective, the shadow-soul (a projected though insubstantial image) is proper to the dream, yet the Count, while dependent in chthonian fashion on "sleeping" in his consecrated native soil, casts no shadow, returns no reflection. This, according to Stoker's notes, is among the first of the Count's attributes to be established, shadow being, after all, useless to those inhabiting darkness. It is the breath soul that is at play in *Dracula*. The breath soul is moreover encoded in the finality of the Vampire. To prevent the reanimation of Lucy's corpse, Helsing "took ... a little gold crucifix, and placed it over the mouth" (149). To be spiritually released from the binds of the material, the Vampire's head must be severed, mouth filled with garlic, etc.; only when the breath has been surrendered does the Vampire find felicitous, true death.

Rather than being an immaterial spirit or shade, Stoker's corporeal Un-Dead hungers for spirits, souls, and yearns to consume them; it is *not* the blood that is the life, but the soul. Seward suggests as much to Renfield, asking "But ... how are we to get the life without getting the soul also?" (237), thereby presenting the Count's John the Baptist with a wrenching and unanticipated moral dilemma that results in his conversion to a less sanguine faith. The Professor, expert on "obscure diseases" (105), leaves no doubt, in explaining to Mina the peril of dying in her unclean state, that vampirism's danger is to the soul, not the body. This also clarifies why the Vampire's victims would be described as feeling "down in the spirit" (107), or would report of themselves that "sleep has not refreshed me, for today I feel terribly weak and spiritless" (228)—the spirit having been drawn off overnight. To appreciate the oral, celestial soul beyond brute "psycho-sexual instinct" an authentically Gothic representation is instructive and perhaps illuminating of the Vampire's habit of searching out its victim's throat. Lucy, describing her primary symptom, writes, "my throat pains me. It must be something wrong with my lungs, for I don't seem ever to get air enough" (104).

A chapel in the western transept of the Abbatial church of Mont-Saint-Michel contains a polychromed 15th–century alabaster relief produced in Nottingham, England, narrating the Betrayal, Passion, Crucifixion, Burial, and Resurrection in five frames, based principally on the Gospels of Luke and John. The central panel of this retable, representing Christ on the Cross, is substantially larger than the others. At its center, Jesus is stretched upon His Cross atop Golgatha; His head, fallen limp, rests on His shoulder—as the

Saint-Michel Retable. © Centre des monuments nationaux, Paris, Etienne Revault

central image of the central panel, it is key to the artwork's symmetric conceptual and spatial organization. Two thieves, one to Jesus' left, the other His right, are dying. To the left of the Cross, Jesus' right hand side, His Mother Mary, His aunt Anne, Mary wife of Cleophus, Mary Magdalene, and others bear witness; to His left, Roman soldiers wile away their time. The thieves are being punished for crimes of property; Jesus, for a crime of words: In not denying His purported divinity to the Roman consul, He has blasphemed.

Something fabulously original animates the iconography of the Crucifixion scene: Babes are being born from the open mouths of the dying thieves. Each thief— head forced back, mouth agape — is, in giving up his own corporal existence, bringing forth a new being, a spiritual life: a soul. In this fantastic metaphor, the mouth becomes a vaginal construct; the lungs and larynx, the womb of the spirit. Above each thief, delivering the newborns like midwives, an angel hovers: Saint Michel draws the infant/soul from the thief who dies on the right-hand side of Jesus; Lucifer pulls on the body of the new life that emerges from the mouth of the thief who expires on the left (right side of panel). Saint Michel claims the soul of the thief who, according to Luke, indicated in words that he accepted the divinity of Jesus; Lucifer, that of the thief who mocked Him.

It is curious that the Gospel of John states so clearly that in the beginning was the Word, while the first book of Moses, Genesis, describes the beginning so differently. John seems more concerned with volition and the realization of the promises of the Old Testament, Genesis with the construction of a material reality, with corporeality. Genesis claims that God created the

The taking of the souls: detail, *Mont-Saint-Michel Retable.* © Centre des monuments nationaux, Paris, Etienne Revault

universe out of a void, dividing element from element in a dialectical process, identifying binary components of light and dark, solid and liquid, separating one thing from the other by the assignation of names. This universe of Moses is created through performative language: God said, "Let there be light; *and there was light*" (1:3). Remarkably, *Genesis* then reports that God observed the material effect of his proclamation: "And God saw the light, that it was good: and God divided the light from the darkness. And God called the light Day, and the darkness he called Night" (1:5). Thus in a substantial sense, the Word *was* the beginning. The identification of separate aspects of existence, the merging of a phenomenon with the idea of the phenomenon is achieved through the attachment of a name to a thing. John, clearly referring to the account of Genesis, proclaims that in Him (meaning God, hence the Word) was life; "and the life was the light of men. And the light shineth in darkness; and the darkness comprehended it not" (1:5). The Word, formed of the breath, is constitutive of the soul. As Sir Oracle observed and insisted, it is the words that are attached to the deceased that will be critical on Judgment Day.

Moses and John, pivotal authors of the Old and New Testaments, return to mythic time in their introductory statements, a moment not simply preceding history, but creation. It is a time that repeats cyclically, even as the Betrayal, Passion, Crucifixion, Burial, and Resurrection of the *Mont-Saint-Michel Retable* are revivified each time the act of transubstantiation, the miraculous investment of Christ into the unleavened bread of Communion, occurs before it.

Morpheus first appears in a sacred text whose portrayal of the beginning is reminiscent of Genesis's bifurcating process of material creation: Hesiod's *Theogony*. The fertile divine persona it introduces come into being through a mitotic, procreative process:

> Verily at the first Chaos came to be, but next wide-bosomed Earth, the ever-sure foundations of all the deathless ones who hold the peaks of snowy Olympus, and dim Tartarus in the depth of the wide-pathed Earth, and Eros (Love), fairest among the deathless gods, who unnerves the limbs and overcomes the mind and wise counsels of all gods and all men within them. From Chaos came forth Erebus and black Night; but of Night were born Aether and Day, whom she conceived and bare from union in love with Erebus [¶116–138].

And from these latter did Morpheus and his kind derive. The Chaos that birthed Night and Erebus is akin to the *Néant* that claimed Ruthven, but what, it must be asked, and Stoker insists on it, came before the "Chaos came to be"? The divine realm of the soul.

As will be seen, philosophy rather than theology will help Stoker probe the question of unbegottenness, for the dialectical divisions of the Old Testament are no more the crux of The Book of Stoker than the genealogy of Hesiod's *Theogony*, though both contribute to its sacred discourse. Morpheus and dream-life, Genesis and Exodus are harnessed to facilitate art. Intersecting, ecliptic mythological discourses and pagan temporal ordering offered Stoker great integrative possibilities, and, one might suspect, speak to a syncretic mode of seeing mankind's spiritual quest that pleased him. Drawing on the antique and the prophetic while maintaining a disciplined focus on the topical, technological, and contemporary, Stoker integrates the pagan and Christian with no more conflict than Lazarus encountered when summoning guides at the inn. Antique gods, Children of Night, interact with humans as "Watchers" of mythic time once did. In *Dracula*, however, the scribing Harkers work to petition God in the name of mankind. Stoker's creative and spiritual vision foresees nothing less than the establishment of a New Jerusalem by a New Woman and New Man who conjointly form an aware and knowing syzygy within an eternal divine.

To clearly perceive the functioning of Stoker's Vampire as a haunter of dreams, an invader scaling the broken battlements of consciousness, it is instructive to look closely and discover traces of Morpheus's presence within the novel's earliest énoncés:

> I did not sleep well, though my bed was comfortable enough, for I had all sorts of queer dreams. There was a dog howling all night under my window,

> which may have had something to do with it.... Towards morning I slept and was wakened by the continuous knocking at my door, so I must have been sleeping [10].

Sleep and dreams are encountered prior to any direct encounter with the Count, whose subtle introduction, beyond the barking of dogs and visitations by queer dreams, is given form in his only textual contribution to the cento.

> My FRIEND,—Welcome to the Carpathians. I am anxiously expecting you. Sleep well tonight [12].

A secondary focus on the Word and on writing arises soon thereafter, positioning the preserved, conscious, written word as antithetical to the unconscious-yet-vividly-experienced dream, an opposition that is fiercely sustained throughout the novel, whether expressed by Mina who notes, "No sleep now, so I may as well write" (87), or by Dracula, executing his scorched word policy, burning "the manuscript" (249) as he flees his tormentors. These contrasting poles are fixed by Jonathan as natural at the beginning:

> I am not sleepy, and, as I am not to be called till I awake, naturally I write till sleep comes. There are many odd things to put down [13].

These comments anticipate the physical imposition of the octagonal room that separates the Count's library and Jonathan's sleeping chamber. Among the many "odd things" needing to be put down, Jonathan writes of having experienced "a queer sting on the tongue" (13), and as hearing "a lot of words often repeated, queer words" (13) from people of many nations seated on a "word-bearer." Before separating from Jonathan, society hands him a rosary, "gifts ... of an odd and varied kind ... given in simple good faith, and a kindly word, and a blessing, and that strange mixture of fear-meaning movements which I had seen outside the hotel at Bistritz—the sign of the cross and the guard against the evil eye" (16), along with a warning from the driver:

> "No, no," he said; "you must not walk here; the dogs are too fierce"; and then he added, with what he evidently meant for grim pleasantry—for he looked round to catch the approving smile of the rest—"and you may have enough of such matters before you go to sleep" [16].

Ultimately, "bad dreams for those who sleep unwisely" (38) and "the good practice" (112) of writing, those embodiments of unconscious and conscious representation respectively, prove to enjoy a conflictive yet ultimately symbiotic relationship. To understand, and following Ernest Jones's methodology, it should be fruitful to extract and consider from the collected statements that make up *Dracula*'s numerous individual reports on the invasion of their dreams, noting their coincidence.

The first to encounter Morpheus is Jonathan:

> Something made me start up, a low, piteous howling of dogs somewhere far below in the valley, which was hidden from my sight. Louder it seemed to ring in my ears, and the floating moats of dust to take new shapes to the sound as they danced in the moonlight. I felt myself struggling to awake to some call of my instincts. Nay, my very soul was struggling, and my half-remembered sensibilities were striving to answer the call. I was becoming hypnotised! Quicker and quicker danced the dust. The moonbeams seemed to quiver as they went by me into the mass of gloom beyond. More and more they gathered till they seemed to take dim phantom shapes. And then I started, broad awake and in full possession of my senses, and ran screaming from the place. The phantom shapes, which were becoming gradually materialised from the moonbeams, were those three ghostly women to whom I was doomed [48].

Lucy, Morpheus's next acquaintance, reluctant to believe that he had indeed come to know her, stridently disbelieves, confounding the conscious and unconscious. "I didn't quite dream," she insists, in that "it all seemed to be real" (94). She felt a fear-driven impulse to attain the bench of Sir Oracle, without knowing why or of what she should have been afraid. She had, but a few days earlier, daydreamed of taking her fiancé "up to the seat on the churchyard cliff and showing him the beauty of Whitby" (72). Now she, the Beauty of Whitby, imagines that she must have gone there while sleepwalking, though she recalls,

> I heard a lot of dogs howling—the whole town seemed as if it must be full of dogs all howling at once, as I went up the steps. Then I had a vague memory of something long and dark with red eyes, just as we saw in the sunset, and something very sweet and very bitter all around me at once. And then I seemed sinking into deep green water, and there was a singing in my ears, as I have heard there is to drowning men, and then everything seemed passing away from me [94].

The most startling portion of her report, however, concerns her soul: "My soul seemed to go out from my body and float about the air. I seem to remember that once the West Lighthouse was right under me, and then there was a sort of agonizing feeling, as if I were in an earthquake, and I came back and found you shaking my body. I saw you do it before I felt you" (94). In other words, she returned from some otherworld to her body and found it being shaken. As Macnish warns, the somnambulist may "be insensible not only to a slight touch, but a severe shaking of the limbs" (188).

When after a similar ordeal she once again returned to "consciousness" she was aware that an indeterminate amount of time had passed during which she was exterior to herself. Still, "dogs all round the neighbourhood were howling, and in our shrubbery, seemingly just outside, a nightingale was singing. I was dazed and stupid with pain and terror and weakness, but the sound of the nightingale seemed like the voice of my dead mother come back to comfort me" (132). Like Jonathan, Lucy too is drawn in and amazed by a queer phenomenon, the appearance of a vortex of materialization: "The air seems full of specks, floating and circling in the draught from the window, and the lights burn blue and dim" (132).

Dr. Seward, man of science, refused to acquiesce to Morpheus. He nevertheless witnessed the nightmare spectacle of the graveyard where the deceptively cherubic Sleep most particularly holds sway at midnight. "Never did bough creak so mysteriously, and never did the far-away howling of dogs send such a woeful presage through the night," he records. As he waited in the night, "a long spell of silence" (187) produced a "big, aching, void" (187) only filled by a signal from the Professor. Looking

> far down the avenue of yews we saw a white figure advance, a dim white figure, which held something dark at its breast. The figure stopped, and at the moment a ray of moonlight fell upon the masses of driving clouds, and showed in startling prominence a dark-haired woman, dressed in the cerements of the grave. We could not see the face, for it was bent down over what we saw to be a fair-haired child. There was a pause and a sharp little cry, such as a child gives in sleep, or a dog as it lies before the fire and dreams [187].

Mina was pointedly linked to Morpheus in having her initiation rite interrupted. When asked to recall the particulars of one encounter with Morpheus, she replied, "I can't quite remember how I fell asleep last night. I remember hearing the sudden barking of the dogs and a lot of queer sounds, like praying on a very tumultuous scale, from Mr Renfield's room.... And then there was silence over everything, silence so profound that it startled me, and I got up and looked out of the window" (227). What she saw and heard was an absence of anything to see or hear, for everything was "dark and silent, the black shadows thrown by the moonlight seeming full of a silent mystery of their own. Not a thing seemed to be stirring, but all to be grim and fixed as death or fate, so that a thin streak of white mist, that crept with almost imperceptible slowness across the grass towards the house, seemed to have a sentience and a vitality of its own" (227). Death and fate having mated, a lifeless vitality—a seeming consciousness—stealthily advanced towards her abode, that being, as always, her bodily living self.

Somehow the curious serpentine mist brought not only a reassuring comfort but a growing languorous lethargy that forced Mina to take to her bed again. "I lay a while, but could not quite sleep, so I got out and looked out of the window again. The mist was spreading, and was now close up to the house, so that I could see it lying thick against the wall, as though it were stealing up to the windows" (227). Renfield's cries kept growing louder as the mist approached his window. Mina claims that though she was unable to understand his words, his tone communicated "some passionate entreaty" (227) that approached the desperate and left her so distraught by the commotion beneath her that she retreated under the covers with her fingers in her ears, attempting to deny her very role as a Harker. The next thing she recalled was awakening, even though the last thing she remembered prior to waking was not being sleepy. "I think that it took me an effort and a little time to realize where I was, and that it was Jonathan who was bending over me. My dream was very peculiar, and was almost typical of the way that waking thoughts become merged in, or continued in, dreams" (227).

Mina, too, perceives whirling forms, but with several significant differences from the spiraling "simoom in the desert" (131) that Jonathan, Lucy, and the Professor report. First, she establishes a parallel between her inner, conscious self, and an external quasi-unconscious world: "Things began to whirl through my brain just as the cloudy column was now whirling in the room, and through it all came the scriptural words 'a pillar of cloud by day and of fire by night' Was it indeed such spiritual guidance that was coming to me in my sleep?" (227), she asks herself, exercising her critical capacities. Then, accenting the un–Freudian nature of consciousness in *Dracula*, Mina's oneiric ordeal causes her to lose consciousness even as she sleeps and dreams. She recalls Jonathan's ordeal at Castle Dracula: "Suddenly the horror burst upon me that it was thus that Jonathan had seen those awful women growing into reality through the whirling mist in the moonlight, and in my dream I must have fainted, for all became black darkness" (227). Finally, having described the loss of consciousness in a dream, she ends her session with the Professor as if emerging from an exercise in hypnosis, retracing her return to consciousness. "The last conscious effort which imagination made was to show me a livid white face bending over me out of the mist. I must be careful of such dreams, for they would unseat one's reason if there were too much of them" (227–28).

Mina, having entered a spiritual desert, is being divinely led, day and night. This lesson of Exodus, journal of the trials of those being led from one state into another, promises that faith will indicate her way: "So we came down this road; when we meet other ways — not always were we sure that they were roads at all ... the horses know and they only. I give rein to them, and they go on so patient" (314).

Renfield, whose ambivalent role has already been discussed, was not hostile to the Count. He reports his accession to him in familiar terms: "Then the dogs howled, away beyond the dark trees in His house. He beckoned me to the window" (244). This "beckoning" is evidently an image of the mist. The collation of the various reports has Mina, above, retreating to her bed as Renfield, below, rises from his. "I got up and looked out," reports Renfield,

> and He raised his hands, and seemed to call out without using any words. A dark mass spread over the grass, coming on like the shape of a flame of fire. And then He moved the mist to the right and left, and I could see that there were thousands of rats with their eyes blazing red, like His only smaller. He held up his hand, and they all stopped, and I thought he seemed to be saying, "All these lives will I give you, ay, and many more and greater, through countless ages, if you will fall down and worship me!" And then a red cloud, like the colour of blood, seemed to close over my eyes, and before I knew what I was doing, I found myself opening the sash and saying to Him, "Come in, Lord and Master!" [244–45].

The use of capitals indicates the divine role ascribed to Morpheus by the Lunatic.

The barking dogs, sonic commotion and clamoring tongues, the rustling trees, and the plunging sensation are constants that to each individual seem so unlike a dream that they feel compelled to note the confounding, disorienting impression. Through dream life, they have tumbled into liquid, mythic depths. Two clashing realms that work to negate each other are reflected in the imagery: the "wide world" we inhabit and the mysterious mansion of Sleep in which dwells Morpheus. Edith Hamilton, paraphrasing Ovid's *Metamorphoses XI*, describes that noble dwelling to which Morpheus drags back souls as

> near the black country of the Cimmerians, in a deep valley where the sun never shines and dusky twilight wraps all things in shadows. No cock crows there; no watchdog breaks the silence; no branches rustle in the breeze; no clamour of tongues disturbs the peace. The only sound comes from the gently flowing stream of Lethe, the river of forgetfulness, where the waters murmuring entice to sleep. Before the door poppies bloom, and other drowsy herbs [107].

In Dryden and Garth's verse translation:

> Near the Cymmerians, in his dark abode,
> Deep in a cavern, dwells the drowsy God;
> Whose gloomy mansion nor the rising sun,
> Nor setting, visits, nor the lightsome noon;
> But lazy vapours round the region fly,
> Perpetual twilight, and a doubtful sky:
> No crowing cock does there his wings display,
> Nor with his horny bill provoke the day;
> Nor watchful dogs, nor the more wakeful geese,
> Disturb with nightly noise the sacred peace;
> Nor beast of Nature, nor the tame are nigh,
> Nor trees with tempests rock'd, nor human cry;
> But safe repose without an air of breath
> Dwells here, and a dumb quiet next to death [Ovid XI].

Within the various dream testimonies, the barking dogs, cacophonous prayers and trembling branches depict the moment of Morpheus's arrival in an alien land where "Sleep has no place it can call its own" (272). The dogs, like that of Swale's silent friend, are alarmed — as is all nature — due to the Count's presence. Rather than being commanded by the Count, they, "the best and truest of friends" (216), betray him by sounding the alert. When Helsing, seeking to administer an "injection of morphia" (119) into plot, speaks of "the waters of Lethe" and "Lotus flowers" (120), he — rummaging within Ovid's account of Morpheus — consciously dispatches his patient to the land of Hypnos. Entwined within his hybrid text mixing mythology, classical poetry, and Platonic dialogue, Stoker encloses more contemporaneous musings: Keats's "Nightingale" singing to redeem Mrs. Westenra's immortal soul, summer's departed days, and the terrible terrain where dream dreamt and life lived have become indistinguishable. Stoker's dream-like, interweaving organization is typical of both the Vampire Tale and of scripture, in which the New Testament reiterates much of the Old while transforming it through a new significance.

Reaching beyond the merely organic in assembling Morpheus's extended clan, Stoker atomizes sleep into finer components than those dozen phenomena Macnish marshals into his philosophy, representing: dizziness, fainting, stupor, drowsiness, fatigue, sleep deprivation, insomnia, falling asleep both voluntarily and involuntarily, sleep, nightmare, paralysis and petrifaction, somnambulism, sleep-talking, premonition, prophecy, somniphobia, narcotic sedation, trance, hypnosis, hallucination, insanity, astral projection, telepathy, materialisation, forgetfulness, obliviousness, amnesia, death, anamnesis, awakening, and felicity — conditions that frequently accumulate into multi–faceted metaphysical experiences. While their combined effects occasionally give rise to a sleep that is purely physical, it is more frequently richly psychic. Lucy's experience, perhaps based on the *Republic*'s Platonic parable of Er, includes an episode of astral projection that accentuates Stoker's East–West–East motif, as she passes from East Cliff to West Lighthouse and back again, Stoker — always concerned with symmetry and solar movement, makes great effort to inform his reader of a light that had just been installed on East Cliff.

When describing their states of consciousness during their respective initiations, the Harkers make similar statements, both describing their encounters with the Vampire as something seen despite closed eyelids. Mina reports: "I closed my eyes, but could see through my eyelids" (227); Jonathan: "I was afraid to raise my eyelids, but looked out and saw perfectly under the lashes" (42). Jonathan also describes a thrall he experienced, which, perceived as a form of hypnosis, he battled to resist: "I felt myself struggling to awake to some call of my instincts. Nay, my very soul was struggling, and my half-remembered sensibilities were striving to answer the call. I was becoming hypnotised!" (48). In contrast, Mina actively seeks out hypnosis: "I have an idea.... He must hypnotize me before the dawn, and then I shall be able to speak" (271) (though how she knows of the Professor's interest in Charcot remains a mystery). Whereas Mina's hypnosis opens telepathic links to the Count, Jonathan's fear of the hypnotic-as-forgetfulness opens a connection to a central aspect of theme, *forgetfulness* being instrumental to *theme* the way Mina's telepathic link with the Count is to *plot*.

In Jonathan's written statement, he amends his initial phrase, revising his thought to contradict himself. He writes first of awakening an instinct. Then, correcting that, insists that it was in fact not instinct, that canny animal intelligence, but his "very soul" that was called on to battle the forces of Hypnos, volition summoning 'half-remembered sensibilities'; sensibilities half-, and no doubt nearly entirely-forgotten. What Thanatos is to the material, Hypnos is to the spiritual, a force of corporal domination and psychic relaxation which causes forgetfulness. Even Mina, though willingly submitting to hypnosis, insists, "I don't like this lapsing into forgetfulness" (156).

In the logic of myth, to forget is to endanger the soul and the accomplishment of life's sacred mission: the return of the soul, enriched, renewed, to the point before the beginning, the moment before Hesiod and Moses begin their accounts of creation. In the aftermath of their encounters with Morpheus, *Dracula*'s characters are unable to remember what has happened to them, recalling only their fear and accompanying angst. Forgetfulness characterizes them all, consigning those who have dreamt unwisely to a repast of Lotus blossoms washed down with the waters of the Lethe. Those assigned to watch over the dreamers are forbidden sleep in order to protect the dreams of those they guard, a chore that is in and of itself a nightmare; as the Professor, eerily sounding like the Count, warns his student, "Remember, she is your charge. If you leave her, and harm befall, you shall not sleep easy hereafter!" (116).

Omnipresent Nightmare finds *Dracula*'s protagonists reporting classic symptoms: "I was powerless to act, my feet, and my hands, and my brain were weighted, so that nothing could proceed at the usual pace" (227); "For an instant my heart stood still, and I would have screamed out, only that I was paralysed" (251); "it seemed to me as if my feet were weighted with lead, and as though every joint in my body were rusty" (88). Nightmare is notably omnipresent until the Count takes flight, with amnesiac sleepers reluctant or incapable of recalling their guillotine dreams. "More bad dreams. I wish I could remember them" (103), is Lucy's halfhearted regret. Jonathan, according to Mina, "does not remember anything that has happened to him for a long time past. At least, he wants me to believe so, and I shall never ask" (99). Seward observes that even Mrs Harker seems to lose sight of her trouble for whole spells" (280). At last, Renfield, "working in the interval" and encouraged to "tell us your dream" (243), confronts truth: "I must not deceive myself. It was no dream, but all a grim reality" (243). Through this announcement, Renfield marks the turning point of plot.

Dracula's entire population of Britons, with the exception of oracular Swales, is swept up by the glamour of what is repeatedly called either "the wide world" (62, 100, 152, 184, etc.), or, variously, "the moving world" (215), "the world ... at movement" (256), "world of life" (100), and even "the brute world" (223), and thus in their distraction forget themselves. The Professor from the Low Countries, too, momentarily (if only occasionally) forgets himself: "But presently I forget all of watching; and when I sudden remember that I watch, I find her lying quiet, but awake, and looking at me with so bright eyes" (315). The others forget themselves blindly.

The young men, captivated by Lucy, world of light and light of the world, become lovers and so enamored of the moment as to be forgetful of the Otherworld to which their own soul-life belongs, so enmeshed in the web of linear, historic time that they lose sight of the ultimate cyclic force of returning that inevitably defines their adventure. Those disappointed in love, attempting to lose themselves through other means — through work on Seward's part, adventure on Quincey's — fail to recall themselves in their melancholy. This is how and why, as Mircea Eliade remarks, "'forgetfulness is assimilated to death" (115), meaning spiritual death, the extinction of the soul. The soul of Stoker's *Dracula* is the Platonic soul, recalled by the Vampire due to its loss and an undying, Un-Dead hunger to recover it. Socrates' turning analysis of the moving world in the *Phaedrus* seems to have been particularly influential upon Stoker, contrasting the volitional, self-moving being with the Vampire-dominated soulless body:

> The soul through all her being is immortal, for that which is ever in motion is immortal; but that which moves another and is moved by another, in ceasing to move ceases also to live. Only the self-moving, never leaving self, never ceases to move, and is the fountain and beginning of motion to all that moves besides. Now, the beginning is unbegotten, for that which is begotten has a beginning; but the beginning is begotten of nothing, for if it were begotten of something, then the begotten would not come from a beginning. But if unbegotten, it must also be indestructible; for if beginning were destroyed, there could be no beginning out of anything, nor anything out of a beginning; and all things must have a beginning. And therefore the self-moving is the beginning of motion; and this can neither be destroyed nor begotten, else the whole heavens and all creation would collapse and stand still, and never again have motion or birth. But if the self-moving is proved to be immortal, he who affirms that self-motion is the very idea and essence of the soul will not be put to confusion.

> For the body which is moved from without is soulless; but that which is moved from within has a soul, for such is the nature of the soul. But if this be true, must not the soul be the self–moving, and therefore of necessity unbegotten and immortal? [*Phaedrus*].

The activity of the scribe, writing, established as the antidote to sleeping, allows dreamers to overcome forgetfulness. It is both an act of remembrance and recollection, and an investment in transcending the momentary. Through the witness and the witnessing of dreamers, awakening is achieved. Stepping away from rigid scepticism on letters as merely productive of the show of wisdom without the substantative reality, and assuming a more forthrightly Gnostic stance, the Professor instructs his former student Seward: "Remember, my friend, that knowledge is stronger than memory, and we should not trust the weaker" (112). He counsels to commit all observations great and small to writing, sustaining the Platonic belief that the living word of knowledge has a soul whose image can be contained, however imperfectly, by the written word.

The Professor, having listened to Mina's analysis of the Vampire's consciousness and diagnosis of his fatal conceptual flaws, somewhat mystifyingly announces: "'Dos pou sto,' said Archimedes. 'Give me a fulcrum, and I shall move the world!'" (296). This comment — promising to move away from passivity, from being hypnotized by the moving world, towards activity, that is, towards being the engaged force that sets the world to moving — seems to mark *Dracula*'s epistemological turning point, for the text suddenly becomes clogged with such un–scientific terms as "child-brain" (264), "man-brain" (294), "child-thought" (295), "man-thought" (295), and "half-thought" (295). The Professor has understood that the archaic fallen angel is unaware of the new context of the transformed contemporary world. In terms of Watchers, and by analogy Harkers, that new context was born in Bethlehem to come to maturity in Jerusalem with the Crucifixion and Resurrection. The Dutchman proposes to move the world forward in overcoming superior force through the application of knowledge, gnosis. Yet the question of what the Professor intends to leverage remains not entirely clear, leaving the reader to surmise that he intends to exploit the Count's cognitive limitations to effect the Vampire's destruction. What the Professor celebrates no doubt is his knowledge of the Count's ignorance and the Count's ignorance of his knowledge: Such it would seem is his lever.

Mina distils the Professor's arguments, noting that the strategies of Evil, rooted in things of the earth, the material, and of present time, are forever the same, though the spirit of volitional freemen progresses and evolves due to the self–moving soul. Thus the Vampire, having no soul of its own, is incapable of advancing, for what "advancing" truly means in the dream-logic, mythologic of *Dracula*, is "returning," returning to God and to the unbegotten state existing beyond matter and beyond time, that timeless moment before cosmic infancy.

For John the Evangelist, the Word is key to the recovery of a glimpse of what was before the beginning. For Hesiod, the ineffable and eternal is accessed through the story told by the Muses, daughters of omniscient Mnemosyne, who sing of the castration of the Father of fathers and Kronos's beginning of Time, the declination of the gods, and birth of the Children of Night. Jean-Pierre Vernant, considering the ontological function of myth, regardless its tradition, writes: "The past thus revealed is much more than the antecedent of the present; it is its source. In going back to it, recollection does not seek to situate events in a temporal frame but to reach the depths of being, to discover the original, the primordial reality from which the cosmos issued and which makes it possible to understand becoming as a whole"* (qtd. in Eliade 120). Yet for the volitional being, having forgotten the self-moving soul, having been distracted by the fogs and mists of the world whose reality is the ultimate source of illusion, is it not possible that in the universe of *Dracula* the fulcrum that has appeared to set the world in motion anew, by creating New Woman and New Man, is the Count? That is, in terms of plot, the Professor leverages the Count's epistemological limitations against the Vampire; but in thematic terms, Stoker leverages the Count to move his protagonists towards the sacred and their own purification.

The Count's role is thus to awaken his victims profoundly, first by subjecting them to forgetfulness and then by horrifyingly calling them to themselves when the spiritual *enjeu* becomes clearly defined. To Jonathan and Mina he is as much a spiritual guide as the Professor, albeit one who leads with the stick rather than the carrot. He is moreover a being that defies the image in that he lacks the *Imago Dei*. Returning to Plato's "Phaedrus," Socrates maintains that

> every soul of man has in the way of nature beheld true being; this was the condition of her passing into the form of man. But all souls do not easily recall the things of the other world; they may have seen them for a short time only, or they may have been unfortunate in their earthly lot, and, having had their hearts turned to unrighteousness through some corrupting influence, they may have lost the memory of the holy things which once they saw. Few only retain an adequate remembrance of them; and they, when they behold here any image of that other world, are rapt in amazement; but they are ignorant of what this rapture means, because they do not clearly perceive. For there is no light of justice or temperance or any of the higher ideas which are precious to souls in the earthly copies of them: they are seen through a glass dimly; and there are few who, going to the images, behold in them the realities, and these only with difficulty [*Phaedrus*].

The Count establishes the dangers of the mortal world when, upon his

*From article "Aspects mythiques de la mémoire en Grèce," in *Journal de Psychologie* (1959), p. 7.

sudden appearance, Jonathan is surprised by what he has failed to see reflected in his shaving mirror, as if that which the looking glass contained was identical to the real. His surprise and disorientation cause him to cut himself and his life's blood to flow. The Count seizes Jonathan's shaving glass, saying: "'And this is the wretched thing that has done the mischief. It is a foul bauble of man's vanity. Away with it!' And opening the heavy window with one wrench of his terrible hand, he flung out the glass, which was shattered into a thousand pieces on the stones of the courtyard far below" (31). The sense of the Count's warning is of course not understood by Jonathan, but it should be clear that Stoker truly is asserting that man's vanity deceives him into believing the illusory to be the real, confounding the image and the substance, even when it is the substance of the insubstantial.

Stoker leads his reader into the forgetfulness of plot with a frantic coach ride, the driver determined to have his horses seize from Space what he would redeem from Time and steal away from the evening when all evil things in the world hold sway. As Jonathan catches occasional glimpses of "God's seat" through the trees, and spring blossoms brighten the fading day, he notices wayside shrines. "By the roadside were many crosses, and as we swept by, my companions all crossed themselves. Here and there was a peasant man or woman kneeling before a shrine, who did not even turn round as we approached, but seemed in the self-surrender of devotion to have neither eyes nor ears for the outer world" (15). The devout may not be distracted by the outer world that rushes by in full movement, but for the rest of us, approaching evil may serve to intensify spiritual awareness, forcing us to realize that we existed within Mythic Time before being born to the historic, that our existence therein shall endure when History has been dissolved and atomized, and that our psyche entails more than the organic mind.

Without awakening, sleep gives way to death, Hypnos becoming Thanatos. In The Theology of *Dracula*, as we have been uncovering it, anamnesis, the recalling and awakening, is the ultimate spiritual act; it is the Living Office of the Dead, dealt with repeatedly in scripture, for gnosis comes from being alert, conscious, and aware. As Mina exclaims when she comes to Jonathan and finds him asleep: "He is waking!" (99).

In awakening, we are recalled to ourselves as spiritual beings and brought into a useful relationship with the knowledge we have gained. Repeated Platonic references mark Stoker's *Dracula*, this magnum opus that calls so fully on Stoker's life experience, from his clerical duties in Dublin's Court of Petty Sessions, to his role as president of "The Phil," Trinity University's philosophical society. It is *Phaedrus* that is most often suggested; when, of Renfield it is said, "He did not care for any of the things of mere earth; he was in the clouds and looked down on all the weaknesses and wants of us poor mortals"

Contemporary shrine along the Sacred Way. © Rarignac

(235), Phaedrus seems clearly indicated, as it is through the various discourses on madness. "All men are mad in some way or the other; and inasmuch as you deal discreetly with your madmen, so deal with God's madmen, too—the rest of the world" (111). As the Professor tries to explain with his King Laugh speech, as Renfield serves to illustrate in his very being, true awareness is madness:

> the fourth and last kind of madness, which is imputed to him who, when he sees the beauty of earth, is transported with the recollection of the true beauty; he would like to fly away, but he cannot; he is like a bird fluttering and looking upward and careless of the world below; and he is therefore thought to be mad. And I have shown this of all inspirations to be the noblest and highest and the offspring of the highest to him who has or shares in it, and that he who loves the beautiful is called a lover because he partakes of it. ... There was a time when with the rest of the happy band they saw beauty shining in brightness,—we philosophers following in the train of Zeus, others in company with other gods; and then we beheld the beatific vision and were initiated into a mystery which may be truly called most blessed, celebrated by us in our state of innocence, before we had any experience of evils to come, when we were admitted to the sight of apparitions innocent and simple and calm and happy, which we beheld shining in pure light, pure ourselves and not yet enshrined in that living tomb which we carry about, now that we are imprisoned in the body, like an oyster in his shell. Let me linger over the memory of scenes which have passed away [The *Phaedrus*].

We are imprisoned in the body, like an oyster in his shell. Let us linger over the memory of scenes which have passed away!

Kingdom Come

> "The girl is dead. Why mutilate her poor body without need? And if there is no necessity for a post-mortem and nothing to gain by it — no good to her, to us, to science, to human knowledge — why do it? Without such it is monstrous" [149].

On the eve of *Dracula*'s publication Bram Stoker took time to draft a note to former British Prime Minister William Gladstone in which he pledged that there was "nothing base in the book" about to appear, then added, "and ... I hope it is not irreverent" (letter of 24 May 1897, British Library Mss. 44525, 221–22, reproduced in *Journal of Dracula Studies* 1 [1999]:48). As there is no reason to doubt that Stoker made these comments earnestly and with perfect sincerity, it is ironic that *Dracula* in all its incarnations is forever recalled by enthusiasts and detractors alike as a scandalous and sordid tale of questionable interest and poor taste, featuring perversion, depravity, sexism, intolerance, xenophobia, incest, and boundless variations on moral deviance couched in melodramatic language and coated with a thickly applied glaze of genteel sentimentality of perfectly Victorian fabrication and quasi-parodic magnitude.

While it may be difficult to square Stoker's pledge with representations of deathless beings that nourish themselves on the blood of innocent human life, the most perverse feature of *Dracula* may be the elevated position that academia has of late bestowed upon it, the novel's attainment of respectability and canonical status being largely due to the very reasons for which it had for generations been shunned.

Dracula's ruby-lipped embrace by a cadre of new women and men pursuing new orientations in the humanities, a field of endeavor for identity-affirming critical approaches that set practitioners busily unpacking dedicated theoretical objects from Stoker's textual cornucopia to thrive on notions of "excess" and "transgression" (particularly politico–sexual excess and transgression), "effaced" boundaries (particularly politico-sexual boundaries), and boundless configurations of "Otherness," is frankly comic in its irony, since these projects necessarily grate against the author's stated intent, which — classical and cathartic in the deepest sense — is to purify. Stoker's own intense concern with the Other was uniquely invested in the dichotomous nature of being in all its dimensions and definitions, "some dual life that is not as the common" (179). Determined to produce a sacred text, ill at ease with the usage he, in the weaving of his narrative, had made of superstition, yet realizing that a work founded upon a superstition could hardly avoid some commerce in it, Stoker found solace in his belief that the book was "calculated to cleanse the mind by pity and terror" (Stoker-Gladstone letter). In monstrous fashion, and perhaps at the root of *Dracula*'s confusing aesthetic position, he took an Aristotelian end and assigned it to a thoroughly Platonic undertaking.

Sylvia Starshine, considering the rushed theatrical adaptation that Stoker made of *Dracula* for its unique and pro-forma 18 May 1897 Lyceum performance as *The Un-Dead*, notes the importance of the Platonic by signaling Stoker's concern with the position of the Professor: "Stoker was a busy man with a demanding job, and it soon becomes obvious that the initial creative intent to dramatise the novel properly soon gave way to the imperative of moving the plot along. There is also a favouring in the amount of stage time given to Van Helsing, suggesting that Stoker was rather preoccupied with the good doctor's ideas and thoughts" (xii). The Professor is so thoroughly Stoker's principal Platonic conduit that he appears to have been summoned from the most hellishly infernal regions of the Low Countries exclusively to profess a mystic's view through the all-enveloping parable of the Vampire and original demonstrations of the force of the Eucharistic Host. Yet while the Professor does not immediately respond to his student's "Why do it?" interrogation on Lucy's post-mortem, the response he eventually provides shows that *Dracula*'s *raison d'être* is in fact to contribute to human knowledge, gnosis; the Professor so signals with a question of his own: "Do you know all the mystery of life and death?" (171).

Stoker's spiritual investment in *Dracula* seems so transparently central to the work that, were it not for the fact that it has hardly ever been considered, it would seem almost pointless to call attention to it. However it may be read and whatever it might represent to today's identity-centric critical reader or become for tomorrow's scholar, Stoker's *Dracula* is not a book about homosexuality. It is not about syphilis or STDs. It is not about incest, though the author indicates an awareness of the potential to read its knotted relations through that prism. It is about colonialism only in the most remote and abstract way, in that it is about a wide world where all cultures and societies exert influence on all others as they attempt to return through myth and rite to the primordial moment and that which always preceded it. It is about the world and the empire not of this world. While absolutely concerned with the Alpha and the Omega, it is scarcely a piece of proselytization for some exotic religious movement, though it definitely embraces a syncretic from-Renfield-to-Professor-expressed vision of being. A sacred work of art, yes, but not from any one clear tradition that would guide exegetic efforts like a compass.

While many have speculated upon Stoker's connection to the late 19th, early 20th-century magical order recalled as the Golden Dawn, no evidence has been produced to support any firm linkage — perhaps Douglas Menville's unsubstantiated contention "that Stoker was probably a member of a splinter group of the famous occult society, the Hermetic Order of the Golden Dawn" (qtd. by Hennelly) is justifiable, though it seems most likely Mr. Stoker formed a group of one. He has, at any rate, created a complex theological statement that — put to parchment with the sharp edge of a shovel, then locked within boxes, entombed, enclosed and immured — truly requires intensive unpacking. In its mission, it fully interacts with Stoker's own Victorian period and social milieu, replete with a *clin d'oeil* directed at "Ellen Terry" (160), but surely the author considered, even in writing to former Prime Minister Gladstone, that he was addressing the historically atemporal with a parabolic discourse on the ineffable.

In light of the immensity of his ambitions, and resigning himself to the reach of the possible, Stoker contented himself with the simple project of representing evil as *baffled*: "It would be impossible to describe the expression of hate and baffled malignity — of anger and hellish rage — which came over the Count's face" (267); "Never did I see such baffled malice on a face; and never, I trust, shall such ever be seen again by mortal eyes" (188). *The Demeter's* captain sets the course: "But I shall baffle this fiend or monster, for I shall tie my hands to the wheel when my strength begins to fail, and along with them I shall tie that which He — It! — dare not touch; and then, come good wind or foul, I shall save my soul, and my honour as a captain" (84).

The *Notes* show that as his text evolved from an ill-defined story of a "Young man" and an "Old man" (Rosenbach # 35, *Notes* 17) into the epic that finally reached the public in 1897, Stoker was guided by an idea that materialized from dust and mist; he was very willing to jettison or modify certain of his earliest ideas while ferociously refusing to let go of others. Structure and polarity seem to be more rigidly fixed entities, the detail of contents far more fluid.

As an example of an idea modified, Stoker considered, early on, affixing the name "Abraham Aaronson" to the solicitor he eventually christens Peter Hawkins. He wished Abraham Aaronson to be identified as a member of "the Incorporated Law Society," an organization Stoker sought to feature from

Dracula's genesis. Reference to Exodus, Mosaic law, eloquent pleading, magical accomplishment, and the golden calf— that is, law, magic, transgression, idolatry — seem intended through the Aaronson appellation. "Abraham," was readily available to serve whatever character was to be cast as the founding pillar of a new faith and humanitarian age, a father figure, and alter ego of Stoker himself; thus the name "Abraham" along with much of solicitor Aaronson's symbolic function, were attributed to Helsing, with a fainter echo being heard in the person of seaman Abramoff, one of a number of ill-fated sailors with prophetic or apostolic names that set off on *The Demeter*, that vessel with a religious but anonymous captain.

Retained ideas are plentiful. Stoker, from the very beginning, envisages the Count claiming Jonathan as his own man with the transformed Nodier-like phrase "This man belongs to me" (*Notes* 17, 29, 39). He places great stock in having a Texan and a "Silent Man" among his cast of characters; in incorporating consecrated grounds and zoological gardens into his roster of dramatical loci; in endowing a lordly Un-Dead with certain uncanny powers and compensatory limitations based on the interplay of light and darkness; and in featuring, as in previous vampire texts, a promise that he terms "The Vow." Rather than giving the "Silent Man" to the Count as a servant, as initially planned, Stoker winds up assigning him and an eloquent dog to Mr. Swales as boon companions. Page 8 of the *Notes*, Rosenbach #2 (29), setting out a relatively complete outline of the novel's structure and a primitive *ébauche* of its prospective contents, instructs, "Texan to go to Transylvania," remarking later, "On the track — Texan in Transylvania." The outline concludes, but a phrase manifestly added later is penciled in at the bottom of its last page, "Bring in the Texan"; from these words a vertical line emanates and rises before trailing off, assigning the idea to an indeterminate place somewhere in the latter part of the concluding Book IV. Despite numerous discarded incarnations, the Texan, evidently intended to trigger a cataclysmic ending, survives and dies in the person of Quincey Morris.

Elizabeth Miller, in "The *Dracula* We Might Have Read: What Stoker Cut from His Manuscript," duly observes that Stoker's *Notes* reveal that an explosive ending, with Castle Dracula being struck by lightning, shaken by an erupting volcano, and rattled by earthquake as a "Texan" fires away with a "maxim gun" (*Notes* 117), was at one point intended, Stoker ending his novel with the *néant* first imagined by Charles Nodier. A typewritten draft in the possession of a collector includes the apocalyptic scene along with an editor's notation for cutting it: a boxed section of text barred vertically. Both Peter Haining and Barbara Belford have written on this suppressed ending, and Elizabeth Miller ("*Dracula 2*: The Sequel?") has assayed their arguments:

> The published novel contains this sentence: "The Castle of Dracula now stood out against the red sky" .... According to the typescript, that line was originally to have been followed by this passage, which was deleted before publication:
>
> > —As we looked there came a terrible convulsion of the earth so that we seemed to rock to and fro and fell to our knees. At the same moment with a roar which seemed to shake the very heavens the whole castle and the rock and even the hill on which it stood seemed to rise into the air and scatter in fragments while a mighty cloud of black and yellow smoke volume on volume in rolling grandeur was shot upwards with inconceivable rapidity.
> >
> > —Then there was a stillness in nature as the echoes of that thunderous report seemed to come as with the hollow boom of a thunder-clap—the long reverberating roll which seems as though the floors of heaven shook. Then down in a mighty ruin falling whence they rose came the fragments that had been tossed skywards in the cataclysm.
> >
> > —From where we stood it seemed as though the one fierce volcano burst had satisfied the need of nature and that the castle and the structure of the hill had sunk again into the void. We were so appalled with the suddenness and the grandeur that we forgot to think of ourselves [qtd. in Belford 267].

Offering facsimile pages of a typewritten text with handwritten emendations (266–67), Belford claims that this cataclysmic finale made it through into the typesetter's proof before being deleted in extremis, and wonders whether the change was implemented to set the scene for a sequel.

Should Stoker have been intent on authoring sequels, *Dracula*'s every conceivable ending could offer the potential for new beginnings. In a text filled with examples of the atomized Vampire materializing from dust, fog, and mist, the disintegration of an Un-Dead's body or a granite fortress hardly guarantees that along its dust-to-dust continuum no further materialization will occur. Such an outcome, however, would impose an absurdist's viewpoint on an author believing in God, the possibility of human perfectibility and the promise of material progress. While the facsimile appears to be made from a working draft in an indeterminate state of development, the modifications to the text seem likely due to no commercial consideration but to Stoker's own evolving understanding of the theological rock on which his text reposed. Not generated as a commodity but as a prayer, *Dracula*'s creation necessarily involved true inspiration—the work, taking on a life of its own, contributed to its own development.

The novel's intended final destination is retained in its beginning, as it traces the progress of that coach flying over a paradisiacal land beyond the forests.

> There was everywhere a bewildering mass of fruit blossom—apple, plum,

> pear, cherry; and as we drove by I could see the green grass under the trees spangled with the fallen petals. In and out among these green hills of what they call here the "Mittel Land" ran the road, losing itself as it swept round the grassy curve, or was shut out by the straggling ends of pine woods, which here and there ran down the hillside like tongues of flame. The road was rugged, but still we seemed to fly over it with a feverish haste. I could not understand then what the haste meant, but the driver was evidently bent on losing no time in reaching Borgo Prund [14].

Jonathan Harker, accompanied by people of many nations, sun setting directly behind them, charges eastward. "Beyond the green swelling hills of the Mittel Land rose mighty slopes of forest up to the lofty steeps of the Carpathians themselves" (15). A passenger cried out, "'Look! Isten szek!'—'God's seat!'—and he crossed himself reverently. As we wound on our endless way, and the sun sank lower and lower behind us, the shadows of the evening began to creep round us" (15). At mid-spring they traverse the Mittel Land, a place of greenery, fruitfulness, and sharply differentiated seasons. Flower petals replace snowflakes, but the road is not yet at its summertime state of repair. The road, described as an "endless way," has of course a finality as yet unseen, and it shall inevitably lead the reader thither.

Mittel Land, or Midgard as it is called elsewhere, signifying middle garden or middle enclosure and referring to the world of our quotidian reality, is a cosmologically loaded term. Derived from Norse saga, it is present in all Teutonic as well as in many Celtic peoples' mythologies and has been inserted into popular virtual mythologies of modernity's manufacture through the myth-raiding efforts of writers of fantasy fiction. Midgard, according to *The Prose Edda*, was formed by Odin and his brothers out of the brow of the giant Ymer; they then formed man and woman out of two trees. In the Old English *Beowulf* the world we inhabit, embodied as "middangeard," originates in a fraternal mythos.

Having used the term Mittel Land, Stoker is nearly required to provide an apocalyptic debouchment, in that its use establishes contrast with other realms of being and inevitably leads towards the dissolution of this world at the moment of judgment. "Ragnarök" is the Eddic name for the end conflict. The wolf, chained to the mountain of Odin, devourer of Sun and Moon, is to be the great god's bane. Once the Sun has turned black, hammer-bearing Thor kills the great serpent Jormungandr. The world and Yggdrasil tremble and the earth sinks into the sea. Aspects of the Christian apocalypse were eventually incorporated into Ragnarök in various traditions to live on in folklore. This template accommodates the unmoored ship careening through great storms and many other details that do figure prominently in *Dracula*. One suspects that additional elements woven into Stoker's nexus derived from variations crafted to fill the formal requirements of Wagnerian opera. In a chapter on the occult, though primarily concerned with Stoker's vacations, Belford reports that the Stokers "attended the Wagner cycle in Bayreuth" (220), and one can hear in Lord Godalming of Ring a queer resonance with Wagner's *Götterdämmerung*.

Mark M. Hennelly, Jr., reading Stoker plainly, perceives this very image: "The four horsemen (Harker, Morris, Godalming, and Seward) climactically 'rid[e] at break-neck speed' from north and south in order to seize Dracula's four-sided cart (cf. quatre) and unseal his coffin before sunset ... suggesting the liminal value of the apocalyptic Seventh Seal, as well as dramatizing a *fin de siècle* version of *Götterdämmerung* (from 'Betwixt Sunset and Sunrise')." His article "Gnostic Quest and Victorian Wasteland," dating to the threshold moment of *Dracula*'s 1970s academic canonization, considers the evident prognostic-ations of Helsing—or "Hell-sing" (22), as Hennelly puts it—as a generic marker. Concerned primarily with considering *Dracula* against a backdrop of Victorian societal and literary currents, Hennelly nonetheless notes a "consistently-stressed analogy between vampirism and Christianity" (18) established through three contentious parallels: zoophagy and transubstantiation, chthonic versus celestial rituals; and sublimated theomachy through conflicting symbolic and iconographic displays. Prior to focusing on exogenous literary questions, Hennelly asserts that the engagement of a gnostic quest, indeed a complex of competing gnostic quests, sustains the novel. In "Betwixt Sunset and Sunrise" the notion of "gnostic quest" is pursued as Hennelly offers a study of liminality in *Dracula*, its impact on and expression through the threshold status of its neophytes as they gain in knowledge.

The observation that a race for gnosis animates the novel opens an efficient avenue of approach to the enigmatic novel's core. Such a quest sends the Professor to Exeter to appear at the Harkers' door, integrates the Harkers into the circle of the Purfleet Brotherhood, and ultimately justifies the compilation of the text itself, the text embodying the fruit of a collective "gnostic quest." This quest lends an essential dimension to the great chase from Charing Cross to Castle Dracula, taking over plot to such an extent that the Professor's posse, obsessively focused on liminality, spends anxious days waiting around the Black Sea hypnotizing Mina and interrogating petty officials when they might have less stressfully gone directly to the castle, sanitized the sacred earth of the Vampire's final resting place and patiently awaited the Count's return.

Like the dragon who displays the attributes of all animal classes—bird, serpent, fish, amphibian, carnivorous beast—yet conforms to none, the Vampire is a classification-defeating entity. It *apparently* exists in a liminal zone in which taboo is dissolved, boundaries are eradicated, definition, hence order, is defied and the sacred defiled, but *Dracula*'s little dragon may be more of a red herring than anything else. What the Professor's posse is most stridently concerned with sounding through the liminal-dwelling Vampire and all epistemological means available, is the unknowable realm of the True-Dead, otherworld of the spirit; that is, they are interested in performing an epistemological post–mortem. Their extravagant pursuit — not even discovering what it's like to be a bat — merely ends up tracking a package.

The false gnosis of the apparent liminal and monstrous distracts from a True Gnostic quest and cathartic odyssey towards Sophia and the Son of Man. And it is this, this interior-penetrating Gnostic quest, that likely motivated Stoker to write the book in the first place. In drafting his magnum opus, in wrestling with the theological considerations it contains, Stoker gained spiritual insight. No longer dependent on a scheme borrowed from Teutonic and Neolithic mythologies, he was freed to abandon a Ragnarök-dictated ending for something finally quieter, simpler, truer, newer — spectacular volcanic eruptions becoming vulgar and superfluous.

To expropriate Ernest Jones's phraseology, the very fact that the Vampire is Un-Dead is decisive here, for this concept is necessarily linked to liminality. It is therefore to be expected that Stoker will meticulously mark the crossing of thresholds, limit the Count by the extremes of the tides and apparent solar movements, and, conversely, have Mina feel her autonomy buttressed by those same forces. Mme. Blatovsky's Victorian age Theosophical dogma rested on "the absolute universality of that law of periodicity, of flux and reflux, ebb and flow, which physical science has observed and recorded in all departments of nature. An alternation such as that of Day and Night, Life and Death, Sleeping and Waking, is a fact so common, so perfectly universal and without exception, that it is easy to comprehend that in it we see one of the absolutely fundamental laws of the universe" (4).

Trinitarian tensions between Sun, Moon, and Earth author these phenomena that are experienced as binary universals. *Dracula*'s assemblage of characters is specifically limited, or not, by the forces of sun and moon and notions of residence, attachments to Earth. Liminality, rather than a specific status-obscuring condition impacting particular persons, actions, gestures, situations, forms a central, enveloping theme that seeps into and saturates the fiction's every aspect. Notably, it marks the plot's temporal extremities and dramatic limits as particularly significant — indeed so significant as to require textual addenda as special markers —, for on the other side of the threshold of the novel's plot lies the unexplored silence of Winter's half-year of darkness and the final chilling destination of every character. The novel, rather than testing, pushing, or challenging boundaries, as it seemingly does, works to reinforce and delineate boundaries and their finalities while amalgamating everything seen, from May to November, and unseen from, November to May, into a great circular ring that melds time and space. It accomplishes this not through repression but through dissolution, atomization. Even in planning the novel, Stoker portrayed the Count as falsely liminal: "Dracula visits asylum. Stumbles on threshold" (Rosenbach #16 *Notes* 55). Yet, in truth, if the Count is falsely liminal it is because, and only because, in the logic of myth he is also truly liminal. To dispose of the problem, under Stoker's pen thresholds are conveniently converted to "joinings" (227).

Rather than engaging the simple gnostic quest of the detective story or spy novel genres, Stoker dispatches his protagonists into the field "armed against ghostly as well as carnal attack" (258), "against evil things, spiritual as well as physical" (282), and sustains them through Hebraic scripture and Christian and Gnostic symbology. When Abraham proclaims, "And then begins our great quest" (193), he rallies a freshly matured generation to set out upon a veritable crusade. Providing Arthurian images of a search for the Holy Grail and True Cross, young Lord Godalming's given name, Arthur Holmwood, expresses the quest's religious nature. They set off chivalrously pledging themselves to Madam Mina.

The Professor's theory, Stoker's, is that the Kingdom is within and accessible to those who actively strive to defeat evil. The novel's end comes as a moment of confrontation, judgment, and victory, less an occasion of divine retribution than an instance of the triumph of human volition and the capacity of a community of dedicated souls to reject evil and do good. The vicinity of Castle Dracula, God's seat, becomes the seat of judgment for Jonathan, Mina, the Professor, Quincey, Seward, the Count, Weird Sisters, and Art, Lord Godalming; the Professor defines Judgment Day as the occasion on which God "most suredly shall ... redress all wrongs of the earth and of His children that He has placed thereon" (259).

The previously considered 15th-century crucifixion scene of the alabaster altarpiece at Mont-Saint-Michel constitutes a judgment scene transposed. At the crest of a hill the royal judge, crown formed of thorns, having himself been subjected to trial and punishment, is, rather than seated on a throne, stretched out upon a cross. At a somewhat lower level, on the cross to the left of Jesus, a faithless thief is condemned to damnation; to his right another crucified thief, having been pardoned, has his soul led towards heaven by Saint Michael. Matthew writes: "Then the king will say to those on his right hand, 'Come, blessed of my Father, take possession of the kingdom prepared for you from the foundation of the world'" (25:31). Roman soldiers gathered to the right of the cross, to the left hand of Jesus, are separated from the faithful standing to the right. Soldiers, squatting on the ground, engrossed in a game of chance disputing the mantle of the dying man, will be forgiven by Jesus as ignorant and unknowing. The three Marys and the courageous faithful are shown facing the crucified Christ on the side where the believing thief has died. The faithful are positioned on the right-hand side of Jesus, the soldiers and temporal authorities are with the blasphemous thief to his left. This is how the Judgment, like the Crucifixion, is to be conducted, the moving-world stopped and arrayed in perfect symmetry. Indeed, the Crucifixion accomplishes this effect by revolutionizing the history of man.

A flow of successive liminal moments, felt on earth as the movement of the sun and moon, are produced by the sweep of a great cosmic pendulum fixed by the terrestrial perceptive eye; sense and finalities, on the other hand, are determined by the pivot of justice's scale, the balance of Themis. Scale and pendulum require a fixed central point of equilibrium. Due to the novel's title and a fascination with his glamor, the popular imagination places the Count at the novel's center, resulting in meaning being consigned to the dark season and thus going unseen. If the novel's title was intended to be indicative of a principal character, that singular, indexical, transformational entity ensconced at plot's center, it should read *Wilhelmina*. She is *Dracula*'s true personification of liminality, ready to shift as a bascule in one direction or another, and, with polestars in her eyes, its stable and guiding center. When she identifies the Count as "the Thing" (202, 322), an object rather than a subject, it is not without larger significance. When she graciously maintains, "It was my privilege to be your friend and guide" (101), she could be addressing us all.

Dracula's plot largely concerns itself with gaining knowledge of the journey of the dead, physically expressed in the shipment of a half-century of wooden cases, geometric sarcophagi, later reduced to a single coffin. A man named Smollet supplies information on the progress of this odyssey and provides an early key to tracking it. "He remembered all about the incident of the boxes, and from a wonderful dog's-eared notebook, which he produced from some mysterious receptacle about the seat of his trousers, and which had hieroglyphical entries in thick half-obliterated pencil, he gave me the destinations" (229). This evocation of half-obliterated hieroglyphics that retrace the journey of the dead connects the quest to a 3000-year-old Egyptian image. "Spells for Setting Forth by Day," recalled as *The Egyptian Book of the Dead*, was translated in large part from the scroll *The Papyrus of Ani*, purchased and housed at the British Library in 1888. Stoker owned a copy of the book. Accompanying its hieroglyphs, a vignette depicts Psychostasia, that is, the weighing of his heart or soul. The scroll of Hunefer, a section of which is reproduced below, contains remarkably similar images. Not unlike the *Mont-Saint-Michel Retable* in composition, the image shows the scale of divine justice as the gods evaluate the life of Hunefer as his soul sets forth at harvest time. Above the weighing floor a panel of gods form a jury, half manifest the

***The Weighing of the Heart*, from Book of the Dead of Hunefer. ©The Trustees of the British Museum.**

ankh or *crux ansata*, graphically echoing the cruciform of the scale; half do not. The scale, its centrality, symmetry and geometry are striking.

To the right of the scale in the image, we see Toth with the head of an Ibis, stylus in hand, ready to assume his role as scribe, recording angel. Anubis fixes the pointer of the scale while a monstrous beast with the head of a jackal, soul-eating Amemit the Devourer, awaits the verdict. Hunefer's heart is posed on the left-side basket; on the right is placed the unit of divine justice: an ostrich feather belonging to the goddess Ma'at. The departed, Hunefer, is seen twice, or rather in two different states of being. On the left of the image, an ankh-bearing, jackal-headed divine leads him to his trial; to the right of the scale, Horus awaits to present Hunefer to Osiris who, in a further portion of the vignette not reproduced here, is seen on his throne, Isis standing behind him and a third avatar of Hunefer, his hair now whitened, kneeling before him.

Returning to the persistent rumors tying Stoker to the Golden Dawn, Mina Mathers, wife of Samuel Liddel "MacGregor" Mathers, the order's chief of the 1890s, echoed the phrase of the Tyrolean seer of Nodier's *roman*, and maintained that the Hermetic Order based their rites "on the ancient mysteries, chiefly those of Egypt, Chaldea and Greece" (Gilbert 117). More generally, Victorian armchair anthropologists, mythographers, theosophists, and occultists consistently pursued the notion of a world-binding universal theology, a myth-led Neolithic belief system, finding unique expressions within

The Papyrus of Hunefer cruciform scale. © Rarignac

each tribal order, but bridging the globe through shared common macro-structures. We find that notion expressed by Jacob Grimm, J. G. Frazer, Sabine Baring-Gould, and other writers with whom Stoker was familiar. As the keeper Thomas Bilder establishes equivalency between jackals, hyenas and wolves ("I gives the wolves and the jackals and the hyenas in all our section their tea afore I begins to arsk them questions" [123]), Stoker, concentrating largely on Teutonic myths, Transylvanian superstitions, Roman Catholic liturgy and iconography, and Gnostic rites, is more apt to work with the lycanthropic than jackal-headed figures, but the image of the cross-as-scale and the composition so similar to the *Mont-Saint-Michel Retable* seem to illustrate the structural basis of Stoker's four-part novel and speak to his myth-inspired plot.

Life, possessed of an inescapable symmetry and balance expressed through the tides and daily and seasonal solar cycles, provides Stoker with his grand metaphor and underlying structure. The general palindromic A-B-C — C-B-A scheme is easy to perceive: A mid–spring coach ride leads a neophyte (male) to Castle Dracula; the youth is soon initiated within; an infant and its mother are sacrificed. A ship sails west with the Vampire aboard; at its (white) destination one young woman is initiated (destroyed); a mother and her child are sacrificed. The Office of the Dead is read for the previously initiated girl; a vampire is destroyed (initiated). Another young woman is initiated (nearly destroyed); the Office of the Dead is read for the second girl. A ship sails east with the Vampire aboard to its destination (black). A mid–autumn coach ride leads an initiate (female) to Castle Dracula; vampires are destroyed (initiated). The initiate is perfected.

While beyond "that interesting place" (11) "to the dark side of twilight" (11) the "moving world" may offer the illusion of definitive states of being—darkling night, luminous day—life is mostly lived as a passing along a chain of liminal moments, times of uncertain status succeeding each other like beads on a rosary; we are seemingly poised at the verge of change without end until, at last, death intervenes. Celestial and earthly balance, symmetries wrought by compensatory shifting elements, percuss through men on planes "carnal" (190, 252), the body which imprisons the soul, and *spiritual*, represented as consisting of soul, mind, mood, strength, and volition, until death rives the duality and the soul is freed.

A moment near the autumnal equinox finds numerous grief-crippled protagonists experiencing a spiritual low tide, and lacking robustness in their will to persevere. Jonathan's nature is "so injured that the very essence of its strength is gone" (143); Seward, "too miserable, too low-spirited, too sick of the world and all that is in it, including life itself, that [he] would not care if [he] heard this moment the flapping of the wings of the angel of death" (144); and Arthur asking himself, "What shall I do? The whole of life seems gone from me all at once, and there is nothing in the wide world for me to live for" (152). Feelings of hopelessness and fatalism pervade the season "to the dark side of" equinox, and "it all seems like a horrible tragedy, with fate pressing on relentlessly to some destined end. Everything that one does seems, no matter how right it may be, to bring on the very thing which is most to be deplored" (226). Seward, reflecting on despair and the obligation to maintain faith in life regardless of the tribulations faced, dictates: "To me it seems only yesterday that my whole life ended with my new hope, and that truly I began a new record. So it will be until the Great Recorder sums me up and closes my ledger account with a balance to profit or loss" (71). Faith dictates that man go forward with courage, "for none of us can tell what, or when, or how, the end may be" (285).

In the complex universe of *Dracula* it is often an inversion, negation, or transformation rather than identical elements that are placed in the balance, heavy heart being tested against lightness's very image, negative elements offsetting positive, light compensating dark: "We shall tonight play sane wits against mad ones" (102), as Seward, figuring his accounts, puts it. Due to the influence of the master actor Morpheus, people, places and things are or aren't what they seem, existing in a true state and a false one, making it difficult, as Jonathan discovers, to maintain a reasonable sense of certitude. Meaning is often dream-coded, clear statements being issued with the intent of signifying the reverse of their literal sense.

Not only does Stoker transparently negate values — acknowledging, for instance, his debt to Wilkie Collins by having *The Westminster Gazette* quote a headline hawking "The Woman in Black" (159) — he portrays a world in which things become doubly reversed yet not quite restored to their original condition. Yet from prefatory statement to closing "Note," from the sequence of actions to the intersecting personalities that accomplish them, a meticulous balance is in all ways maintained as Stoker piles element after element in the baskets of his cruciform scale. This promotes a deliberate homogenizing effect from the earliest pages. For instance, the cunning Count perniciously impersonates his prisoner by wearing Jonathan's clothes to Bistritz, the center of human habitation closest to his dwelling place, where he is able to post letters, to abduct babies, and, while he's at it, to inculpate Jonathan. The second skin of clothing sufficiently approaches the living and the Un-Dead in appearance to cause an aggrieved mother to mistake one for the other just as Léonti had mistaken Aubray for Ruthwen.

Flushed-face, Apollonian Jonathan may indeed be more like the black-as-night habited Count than is immediately apparent. When Jonathan penetrates the Count's inner-sanctum, he notes, "The only thing I found was a heap of gold in one corner — gold of all kinds, Roman, and British, and Austrian, and Hungarian, and Greek and Turkish money, covered with a film of dust as though it had lain long in the ground" (50); when he slashes through the Count's black clothing at Piccadilly, "a stream of gold fell out" (266). It is said these incidents make of the Count a money bag, but the gold, like the incongruous straw hat he wears on Doolittle Warf, reveals that the Count has within a hidden solar aspect. Light-bearer Lucifer, a luminous spirit visible only at dawn and dusk, fallen in Enochian shame, contributes much to constructing the Count, for "he is the devil in callous" (209). For imprisoned Jonathan, awash in darkness, the sun is an agent of God, indeed the Paraclete: "When the sun grew so high this morning that it struck the top of the great gateway opposite my window, the high spot which it touched seemed to me as if the dove from the ark had lighted there" (49). Stoker introduces this worshipper of light as he approaches his hotel, the Golden Krone — indexing a gold coin — where he is soon to be drinking "Golden Mediasch" and curiously dining on a dish taking its name from the fact that it isn't what it seems: "Robber Steak" (13).

Occasionally, Stoker attains equilibrium through displacement, as can be seen through the device of Renfield's kitten. Renfield requested from Seward "a kitten, a nice little, sleek, playful kitten, that I can play with, and teach, and feed — and feed — and feed!" (70) which was denied him. Renfield not only wants to feed it three times, he thrice repeats his always denied request. Later, when Renfield escapes from the asylum to attack the carters hauling away the Count's great cases from neighboring Carfax, the asylum's personnel belatedly arrive to subdue the lunatic and stop his assault of the movers. The doctor in charge reports that Renfield "struggled with the three of us, pulling us to and fro as if we were kittens" (142). Still, Renfield's prime task is to serve as the Count's herald and messenger, thus the image of the kitten reappears in a description of Mina's initiatory ordeal, which bore "a terrible resemblance to a child forcing a kitten's nose into a saucer of milk to compel it to drink" (247).

An example of contrasted equivalence resides in certain letters that comprise the text itself: Jonathan's ersatz letters sent by the Count to Mina are compensated by Mina's heartfelt-but-never-received missives to Lucy, eventually studied in post–mortem by the Professor. The Professor, of whom it is noted that Seward, Arthur, and Lucy "must accept his wishes," and the Count, who asserts that "it was understood that my needs only were to be consulted" (37), are sufficiently alike to balance the narrative vessel and more. The Professor readily acknowledges their common traits: "Our old fox is wily; oh! so wily and we must follow with wile. I too am wily and I think his mind in a little while" (273). The Professor's coming has him leave the Netherlands "to do what [he] can of good," whereas the Count's going signifies that "the earth is free from a monster of the netherworld" (224). As earlier mentioned, Abraham is figured as progenitor of a new sacred order of men, yet the Professor sees the Count as potentially "the father or furtherer of a new order of beings, whose road must lead through Death, not Life" (263).

While the Count, with his wolves, mountain, and leiter-wagon or leiterwaggen, is figured in a Teutonic mode as Woden or Odin, the grandfatherly Professor, shown as a driver of wagons, wielder of a great hammer, is, in that idiom, Thor-like. The "leiter-wagon — the ordinary peasant's cart, with its long, snake-like vertebra, calculated to suit the inequalities of the road" (15) — is described as one more curiosity in Jonathan's travelogue, but the association of the Count with these and similar carts will be incessant; the Count, as noted, even does business with a man named Carter. That the English involved in hunting the Count down ubiquitously speak of "leiter-wagons" rather than the more familiar "cart" or "hay cart" is certainly not by accident, for the "leiter-wagon" is associated with Odin. It will be through his continual use of wagons that the Count's movements are monitored. It further explains why he appears on Doolittle's Warf in a cart and wearing a straw hat.

Something like solar-lunar interplay is offered in feminine guise through the persons of Lucy and Mina, but their sympathetic relationship, as they admire and assist each other, reverses the enmity existing between Jonathan and the Count. Luminous Lucy virtuously claims, "I must imitate Mina"

(103), a compliment the Professor carries forth, telling Mina that Lucy wrote "in imitation of [her]" (164), and Mina unambiguously and affectionately sums up her relationship with Lucy with the declaration, "She and I were like sisters" (209).

Beyond giving their hearts and blood to the same woman, Lucy's beaux, hunting partners Quincey and Art, are so closely associated with each other that they appear in each other's place, one speaking for the other. The major difference between them seems to be that in their pursuits of game Art takes charge of animals and Quincey of armaments and strategic planning. That they separate from each other for their final hunt — one going by water, the other by land — seems strange, incongruous, but their separation is required to maintain balance. While all the male protagonists are hailed as noble, aristocratic Lord Godalming and Count Dracula share the distinction of being exceptionally landed, men of property, of the earth, even if the Transylvanian boyar be more literally so.

The Count, described as "more prisoner than the slave of the galley, than the madman in his cell" (211), is further linked to both Jonathan and Renfield. These latter two, beyond their quite evident shared experience of being held against their will, manifest other countervailing traits: Jonathan has "had brain fever, and that is to be mad" (99–100), while the fleeting, intermittent insanity of Renfield renders him a true "lunatic"; both are repeatedly depicted scribbling indecipherable records into their notebooks. They also contrast. As happened in the accident with a mirror and razor while Jonathan was shaving, a letting of blood occurs when Renfield invades Seward's office and rushes at him with a dinner knife, cutting him. Whereas the Count was forced to control his appetites by the power of the rosary, Renfield threw himself down onto the floor to lap up the spilt blood, chanting, "The blood is the life!" (130). In the end, however, Renfield, Lazarus-like, joins Jonathan in opposing the Count; a concern for the soul has him cast his unhappy lot with the Brotherhood, no doubt bringing salvation upon himself.

The association of zoophagous Renfield with the vampiric Count is established more pointedly and with greater effort at making the linkage evident: Referring to the Professor, Seward notes: "He thinks that in the meantime I should see Renfield, as hitherto he has been a sort of index to the coming and going of the Count" (199). Seward expresses similar sentiments in rationalizing his own mistrust of Renfield's sanity: "He seems so mixed up with the Count in an indexy kind of way" (219). Seward, having heard Renfield seek reassurance from the Count — "You will not pass me by, will You, dear Master, in Your distribution of things?" — perceives mercantile greed in Renfield, commenting: "He thinks of the loaves and fishes even when he believes he is in a Real Presence" (98). Seward, as is often the case, may have misread the situation. Renfield's plea sounds more likely a transformation of the Lord's Prayer (Matthew 6:9–13).

In linking his inmate of the asylum to the inmate of the grave, Stoker goes so far as to have Renfield complete a half-rendered portrait of the Count. At Castle Dracula, Jonathan "saw ... the Count's head coming out from the window" (39), specifying, "I did not see the face, but I knew the man by the neck and the movement of his back and arms." At the asylum, Renfield's guard "ran back and saw [Renfield's] feet disappear through the window" (97), Renfield, like the Count, evidently going head-first out the window. Stoker thus provides interior and exterior perspectives of a single, birth-like action, of blood-obsessed men escaping their asylums to assault the world. Jonathan confesses that his "very feelings changed to repulsion and terror when I saw the whole man slowly emerge from the window and begin to crawl down the castle wall over that dreadful abyss, face down, with his cloak spreading out around him like great wings" (39). Renfield, too, is repeatedly represented as winged; the *Notes* first envisage him as a fly man who has been tied down ("fly patient — bound down" [*Notes* 29]).

Having encountered all kinds of half-human beings, including a gypsy "like a Centaur" (323), and been introduced to the law firm of "Wholeman, Sons" (150), Drs. Seward and Helsing forthrightly merge into a unitary form, the Professor urging, "Let us not be two, but one, that so we work to a good end" (150). Seward, losing autonomous critical abilities, asks: "Are you mad that speak such things, or am I mad that listen to them?" (184) Soon others join them: "Simultaneously we each took one of the old man's hands and bent over and kissed it. Then without a word we all knelt down together, and, all holding hands, swore to be true to each other" (259). All these seemingly conflicting personalities, from the Count to the Harkers, are energetically amalgamated, independently of their having transfused Lucy or not, to form a singular personality incorporating conflicting tendencies, good and evil.

Not only identity, but ideas flow like water, with eddies, whirlpools and counter–currents mixing and redistributing fungible contents, streams of symbolic transaction meandering in serpentine fashion.

The testimonies of the captain of *The Demeter* (Petrovsky missing, Abramoff disappeared, etc.) and Captain Donelson of *The Czarina Catherine* serve to balance the text, both in their relative positions across the temporal span of plot, and in the novel's typical virtuous-vicious, positive-negative, asymmetrically-symmetric manner: All hands died on *The Demeter*, none on *The Czarina Catherine*. It is curious, moreover, to find a man named Donelson setting off from Doolittle Warf as skipper of the Russian *Czarina Catherine*, since Donelson is the name of the American diplomat, nephew of Andrew Jackson, responsible for negotiating the treaty of annexation of Texas that

Renfield admiringly referenced upon his introduction to Quincey. Mythical torch-bearing "Demeter" brings light to the world through her role in the Eleusinian Mysteries; Catherine the Great, native Pomeranian who was christened Sophie by her Lutheran parents, became known as the Enlightener or Illuminator, and brought Russian dominance and the spark of the Orthodox faith to the Black Sea region through her victories over the Ottoman Turks. Sophie, flowing from the Greek for "Wisdom," became Catherine (also from Greek and, as with catharsis and Cathar, signifying "Pure") upon her conversion to the Orthodox faith. Voltaire celebrated the empress as "the Star of the North," the immutable, thereby aligning her with Mina and contrasting her with the Count as Lucifer and the morning star—visible only at dawn and dusk. "The Czarina Catherine" is fittingly named for a vessel intended to transport a gnostic quest towards its ultimate ends: Wisdom and Purity.

In Whitby, the Count's agent is Billington of the Crescent; in Romania, a man of the Count's hated "Crescent" (34), in that he appears in a fez. Billington was an important source of information on the Count's movements, since through his billing for the work of Carter and brethren the Count's penetration of England could be traced. Captain Donelson divulges that Count Dracula's agent goes by the name of Immanuel Hildesheim (302), and he had already taken possession of the square box shipped to the Romanian hinterlands by London's urbane Count de Ville. The portrayal of this "Hebrew of rather the Adelphi Theatre type" (302) is often cited as an expression of Victorian, and Stoker's own, anti-Semitism.

Matthew the Evangelist tells us that *Immanuel* signifies "God is with us" (1:23). It twice appears in the Prophecies of Isaiah, first when he foresees the birth to a virgin of a son, to be called Emmanuel, who knows to refuse evil and choose good (7:14), and then when Isaiah envisions Emmanuel spreading his wings across the earth (8:8). Matthew recalls Isaiah to equate Emmanuel and the Messiah, and in his depiction of an angel instructing Joseph to protect the Virgin Mary, with child by the Holy Spirit, and to name the infant to be born "Jesus."

Stoker employs the image of wings, angelic or malefic, spreading over the world of men on several occasions. Seward imagines "for many a long day loneliness will sit over our roofs with brooding wings" (159), declaring, "I would not care if I heard this moment the flapping of the wings of the angel of death" (144), and the Professor launches an idea as "a big swan thought that sail nobly on big wings" (295).

Hildesheim is a place name denoting a town in Lower Saxony—a town Stoker no doubt passed through on his way to Bayreuth—where the Tree of Life (*Irminsul*, variant of *Yggdrasil*) was commemorated through a stone pillar. Perhaps toppled and buried at the time of Christian conversion, this stele was excavated in the 13th century during the construction of Hildesheim's Gothic Ste. Anne's Chapel, part of the cathedral Dom Santa Maria complex, where it was installed as a pillar that also served as a central candelabra—hence a pillar of fire. Though incorporated into the church, the pillar represented a defeated pagan element, the *Irminsul*, whose destruction by Charlemagne is commemorated on Laetarean Sunday.

Immanuel Hildesheim's office is situated on the Burgen-strasse, a Germanic appellation suggesting "The Castles' Road." Hildesheim consigned the box directly to riverboat shipper Petrof Skinsky, who, having disposed of his charge, is soon discovered "inside the wall of St Peter's churchyard" (303), his throat torn open as if by some wild animal. This event of the day on which *The Czarina Catherine* arrives at its Black Sea port provides, on one hand, counterpoint to the ancient mariner Oracle Swales' death at Ste. Mary's churchyard and the killing of the mastiff so savagely ripped apart on the night that *The Demeter* washed up at Whitby; but, on the other hand, it serves to counterbalance in a curious way the account of Petrovsky of *The Demeter*'s crew. Petrovsky, which can be reduced to Petr, or Peter-of-Sky, mirrors Petrof Skinsky, which in turn yields Petr, or Peter-of-Skin-Sky, celestial Peter—particularly significant when it is considered that the latter's body is described as found in St. Peter's churchyard, perhaps intending to evoke the Holy See and the rationale for the claim of Catholicism. Stoker worked so hard to place his Petrovsky and his Petrof Skinsky in positions of equilibrium in his text, one wonders if and how Peter indeed holds the keys to the Kingdom.

The quest is often rendered concrete, made tangible, as a search for a key whose legion referents summarize plot: "I looked for the key, but it was not in the lock, and I could not find it anywhere" (50); "You didn't have any key?" (232); "When the Professor locked the door he gave the key to Arthur" (193); "friend John, where are the skeleton keys?" (220); "She tries the door, and finding it locked, goes about the room searching for the key" (73); "On a table in the hall was a great bunch of keys, with a time-yellowed label on each" (220); "With a little trouble we found the key on the bunch and opened the door" (221); "Dr Van Helsing had taken the key of the hall door from the bunch, and locked the door in orthodox fashion, putting the key into his pocket when he had done" (223); "We now have a rare job on hand—unless we can find the Count's key basket" (235); "But think, in all probability the key of the situation is in that house in Piccadilly" (255); "Now we wish to get into the house, but we have no key; is it not so?" (256); "Then he held the door partly open, steadying it with his knees, whilst he fitted a key to the lock. This he finally handed to Lord Godalming" (261); "He held up a warning hand as he spoke, for we all could hear a key softly inserted in the lock of the hall door" (266).

In initiating the quest for the key, Jonathan reveals much: "I thought he might have the keys on him, but when I went to search I saw the dead eyes, and in them, dead though they were, such a look of hate ... that I fled" (51). "Then a wild desire took me to obtain that key at any risk, and I determined then and there to scale the wall again" (53). "I knew I must search the body for the key.... I searched all over the body, but no sign could I find of the key" (53). The corpse searched is itself the key, it contains the remains of the Count's body but no key, for the soul is no longer to be found within.

The importance of this descent into the underworld is repeatedly stressed, Helsing proclaiming Jonathan "a noble fellow; and let me tell you from experience of men, that one who would do as he did in going down that wall and to that room — ay, and going a second time — is not one to be injured in permanence by a shock" (167). Seward agrees: "That going down to the vault a second time was a remarkable piece of daring" (199). The key present through its absence contains Stoker's apophatic premise: "A key is nothing" (177). As we have heard through the Professor's description of the Count as one less free than a prisoner, the key is indicative of the first frankly Gnostic turn in Stoker's theology: The body constitutes the soul's prison.

Whether or not the true key is ever found, the searched-for key is often associated with gold and material wealth, always with dust. Even more than gold, dust defines the Count's constitution and natural environment: "He come on moonlight rays as elemental dust — as again Jonathan saw those sisters in the castle" (211); "the very moonlight alive with grisly shapes, and every speck of dust that whirls in the wind a devouring monster in embryo" (307). But the Count's activities never disturb dust's accumulation as it, in turn, never registers his activities: "The whole place was thick with dust. The floor was seemingly inches deep, except where there were recent footsteps, in which on holding down my lamp I could see marks of hobnails where the dust was caked. The walls were fluffy and heavy with dust" (220). More comically, it is observed: "There was dust that thick in the place that you might have slep' on it without 'urtin' of yer bones" (201). Dust is merely the sign of the material, realm and essence of the Vampire — "Hardly had my knife severed the head of each, before the whole body began to melt away and crumble into its native dust" (321) — only the soul endures.

It is not merely people, ideas, actions, and symbols that, full of contrasts and poetry, are made to speak in Stoker's text, but, as was seen with the topographically opposed Carpathians and the Thames tidal flats, and the "chess game" (223) polarity of Whitby and the Black Sea, the landscape and the elements are equally eloquent of matters that are immaterial but oh so pertinent. One senses, for instance, that Whitby's "black mass of Kettleness" (75), presented with the evocation of a Turner painting or a Whistler nocturne, seeks to evoke Ceridwen's mythic cauldron of pagan traditions. The Dailygraph clipping that describes the storm presaging The Demeter's shipwreck reports that "some of the gossips who frequent the East Cliff churchyard, and from that commanding eminence watch the wide sweep of sea visible to the north and east, called attention to a sudden show of "'Mares'-tails' high in the sky" (75). Stoker, seizing on a curious figure of speech, no doubt confected this detail in full knowledge that the goddess Demeter, personified as a mare, led initiates in the annual procession to Eleusis; he had already told us that the East Cliff churchyard's commanding eminence is Oracle Swales, the Ancient Mariner. The article's reporting that as The Demeter approached shore "the silence was so marked that the bleating of a sheep inland or the barking of a dog in the town was distinctly heard" (76) seems intended to foretell their sacrifice; the dog personified in the mastiff, the lamb in Lucy.

Sheep constitute a returning image, from Hildeshein's nose to, ironically, the assembled hunters of the lupine Count, whom Stoker characterizes "like sheep in a butcher's." Matthew proclaims that "when the Son of Man shall come in his majesty, and all the angels with him, then he will sit on the throne of his glory; and before him will be gathered all the nations, and he will separate them one from another, as the shepherd separates the sheep from the goats; and he will set the sheep on his right hand, but the goats on the left" (25:31–33) and these will go into everlasting punishment.

Most often the Word is at the origin of Stoker's creation. He seizes on curious names for things, latches onto them for their latent, often overdetermined meanings, and uses them to enrich symbolic discourse, *each* word weighed and weighted, phonetic spellings, Scottish, Geordie, Dutch, Cockney accents, and assorted malapropisms designed to simultaneously encode and obscure meaningful information.

Parabolic discourse is rampant. *The Pall Mall Gazette*'s report on an escaped wolf is far less concerned with communicating information than with providing readers with keys to reading. The parable of discoursing with beasts relates how animal appetites must be satisfied, nature gratified — metaphorically scratched behind the ear — before more abstract and spiritual activities can be undertaken. Thomas Bilder, an inmate of the zoo who lives with his wife in an enclosure behind the elephant house, in claiming to serve tea to wolves, jackals, and hyenas before questioning them, joins together as a unified genus beasts of the Egyptian deserts and the Nordic forests. Referred to as "the worthy Thomas" (128), he and his wife, like Mina, unable to "resist the temptation of mystifying him a bit" (164), enjoy pulling the leg of the interviewer. Thomas believes that the wolf will become hungry, try to steal meat from a butcher's shop, though he "shouldn't be surprised if the census is one baby the less" (128). To conclude the interview, the Norwegian wolf, Berserker, returns to be received "like a sort of vulpine prodigal son" (129), being fed "a piece of meat that satisfied, in quantity at any rate, the elementary conditions of the fatted calf" (129).

The Pauline Epistle to the Hebrews 3:3, asserting Jesus's superiority to Moses, claims "the worthy builder," rather than "the worthy Thomas," is more honored than the house he builds. But Thomas the Apostle, the Gnostic evangelist known as the Twin, is recalled as a master builder and preacher, bringing the gospel to Syria, Persia, and the Indian subcontinent. Engaged by an Indian maharaja to build a palace, Thomas is said to have distributed the raj's money to the poor, explaining to the king that he was constructing a heavenly abode. It is Thomas who determined to accompany Jesus to raise Lazarus, even should it cost his own life. This incident, during which Jesus remarks, "Are there not twelve hours in the day? If a man walks in the day, he does not stumble, because he sees the light of this world. But if he walks in the night, he stumbles, because the light is not in him" (John 11:9–10), figures predominantly in Maquet and Dumas' *Le Vampire.* Thomas, who doubted Christ's resurrection, was nonetheless, alone among the apostles, chosen to witness the Virgin Mary's Assumption.

The large "man in an office of wood so small that the man looked bigger than the office" (275) on Doolittle's Warf, whose treasure is kept in a tiny bag hidden in an obscure part of his person, seems to be inserted as a comment (perhaps on the overlords of theatrical box offices) on similarities between the situations of the living and the dead. Renfield, in alluding to the author of the Monroe Doctrine, references the noted anti–Masonic politician John Quincy Adams, son and eventual successor of the 2nd American president, secretary of state to President Monroe, and the doctrine's author; in transforming "Quincy" to "Quincey," Stoker enlarges his field of referents to include Thomas de Quincey, author of a text invoking the significance of the Ruthven family name, the debunking "Inquiry on the Origins of The Masons and Rosicruicians." Stoker is likely cautioning the reader to not be too taken in by allusions to rosy crosses or by plot similarities to the *Fama Fraternitas,* for he is perhaps offering a new doctrinal statement for a New World in which hemispheric concerns, separating day and night, are dissolved.

Smollett, contract shipper and hauler at times known as Jack and at others as Joseph, is hailed as "a decent, intelligent fellow, distinctly a good, reliable type of workman, and with a headpiece of his own. He remembered all about the incident of the boxes ... from a wonderful dog's-eared notebook" (229). As with the reference to "the Woman in Black" offered in tribute to Wilkie Collins, Smollet seems destined to recall Tobias Smollet and his *Count Fathom* of 1753, a novel recounting the adventures of a young Hungarian rascal who invades England as Count Fathom on a wild mission of unholy adventure, has empty cases shipped to his dwelling to deceive neighbors into thinking him a man of property, and whose story ends in the mystical initiation of a quasi-divine couple of near orphans, the forgiveness of the serpent, and universal felicity. Stoker's Smollet, through his accented phonetic spelling, also serves to teach scribe Jonathan to read in a new, less traditional manner in his search for "the depite" (230).

Stoker in his gnostic quest could, along with Jonathan, say that his Church of England heart was comforted by surprisingly powerful Catholic iconography, liturgy, and theology. Yet the Pauline view of the role of woman in the Roman church, too, seems difficult to reconcile with Stoker's. The numerous, deliberate sexist touches Stoker's male characters promulgate are intended to argue for woman's equality, even if, it is true, an equality limited to the context of the sacred syzygy. Thus, Jonathan's initiation, undergone as "a 'nine days' wonder" (80), calculated from the moment he accepted the Count's invitation to enter his castle *proprio motu*, was identical to Mina's from the time she accepted the Professor's request to admit him as a visitor. The links and parallels between the Professor and the Count become perfectly articulated therein, and their metonymical roles as drivers on the road to the castle, Telesterion, the Count with Jonathan, the Professor with Mina, crystallize their unitary role: The function that one performs in the initiation of one member of the syzygy, the other assumes with that member's mate. Only the significance of the "castle" changes. Menfolk may indulge well-intentioned sexism, but it always serves merely to compound their problems, as Mina, sequestered, reminds them by recalling: "There was in the room the same thin white mist that I had before noticed. But I forget now if you know of this; you will find it in my diary which I shall show you later" (251).

Stoker's discourse on phrenology and brains — reptilian, mammalian, child-like, man-like, woman-like, the Professor's status as an expert on brain evolution and Seward's role as director of an asylum for the mentally disturbed stimulate, it is true, certain epistemologically-rooted questions. It is worth noting, however, that in Mina's case, her "man's brain" (295) is both highly feminine, memorizing schedules, and maternal. "I have an idea," she announces. "I suppose it must have come in the night, and matured without my knowing it.... Go quick, dearest; the time is getting close" (271). In urging Jonathan to react with haste and to go get the doctor, she makes it seem as if her idea were a baby come to term. The reader reaching that phrase undoubtedly recalls that the last thing to come upon Mina in the night was the Count performing the bridal chamber anti-sacrament. Appropriately, her idea is to exploit the link then established between the Count and herself through the use of hypnosis.

Should, as the Professor contends, the Count have intended to perpetuate a thriving vampire colony in London, he was demonstrably a slacker. Although *Dracula* fuels its progress through the shedding of cadavers, curiously few are attributable to vampirism, even in Transylvania. To render a Renfield-like accounting: Jonathan's diary informs us directly or indirectly of two outside-of-plot infant deaths; it also reports on witnessing a mother being fed to wolves, upon the Count's command, rather than being reserved to provide nourishment for vampires; it further meditates on the journal author's dire plight, though he nonetheless survives and thrives. Despite numerous allusions to Coleridge's "Rime of the Ancient Mariner," for all we know, mysterious circumstances and hysteria drive the eight-member crew of the schooner *Demeter* to throw themselves overboard, leaving her captain, lashed to the wheel, alone to die of unknown causes. Ancient Mariner Oracle Swales is discovered dead, his neck broken, on the stone bench, though it seemed to Mina that he died from having seen Death's approach. His death is not considered suspicious. About the time of Swales' demise, a large, half-breed mastiff was killed at Whitby, its throat ripped apart and belly torn open. Lucy is soon thereafter attacked and bled over an extended period of time, eventually dying of blood loss suffered in satisfying the Count's appetite. Mrs. Westenra, Lord Godalming, and Peter Hawkins die without being attacked, though Mrs. Westenra's death was hastened by fright upon seeing the Count's lupine emissary. Numerous flies, spiders, and birds were ingested by Renfield, who sacrifices himself to oppose the Count's will. A maritime shipper in Bukovina had his throat ripped apart, as if by a wild animal, and Quincey died of a knife wound near Castle Dracula.

On the other side of the ledger, Lucy, three "Weird Sisters," and the Count are executed or true-killed by various members of the Brotherhood. The books are thus quite balanced. The Count seems clearly homicidal, but the most curious conclusion we can reach is that Stoker wished to represent him, through his victims, as effete and sterile: He is only dangerous to potential brides and to seamen, that is, Swales, the men of *The Demeter* and, perhaps, *The Czarina Catherine*, and the Bukovinian shipper. Taking Mosaic Seward, seen as Seaward, as an inverted paradigm, the seamen left mysteriously dead due to coincidental contact with the Count intend to speak of "semen." *Dracula* is not about an exchange of bodily fluids, but the depravation of ethereal "soul."

The novel's conceit depends upon materializing the immaterial, and stigmata, signs of suffering, allow for recognition, reversal, and catharsis, particularly as it concerns the removal of Mina's Eucharistic scar on one hand, and the disappearance of Lucy's twin stigmata preceding her death on the other. The *Phaedrus* uncannily helps connect the image of the winged soul being drawn from the larynx of the dying thieves and the scars observed on the throats of the Vampire's victims. Plato claims that when the soul is connected with the divine it sprouts wings. "But when she is parted from her beloved and her moisture fails, then the orifices of the passage out of which the wing shoots dry up and close, and intercept the germ of the wing; which, being shut up with the emotion, throbbing as with the pulsations of an artery, pricks the aperture which is nearest, until at length the entire soul is pierced and maddened and pained."

If, for those who become infected by the Vampire, "there comes with the change the curse of immortality; they cannot die, but must go on age after age adding new victims and multiplying the evils of the world; for all that die from the preying of the Un-Dead become themselves Un-Dead" (190), then, as previously observed, the Count's London gambit was a signal failure. Although Jonathan, upon his happenstance London crossing of the Count's path, wondrously exclaims the Count "has got younger, and how?" (168), the Vampire had, at that point, only been rejuvenated through his relations with Lucy. Where, too, was the Walachian voivode's tributary population of Transylvanian vampires; where were the teeming masses of incestuous Un-Dead? The polygamous Count, depicted dutifully stealing babies with a well-used sack, apparently unable to rely on the "Weird Sisters" to help with housework during Jonathan's stay, was hardly promiscuous. The occasion of Jonathan's initiation concludes with an acrimonious exchange between the Un-Dead on the subject of love — past and present, though lacking a sense of futurity — the Count claiming his companions knew from prior experience that he indeed could love and had knowledge of love: "you yourselves can tell it from the past. Is it not so?" (43). It seems that these feminine figures had at one time been courted by the Count. Despite eroticization, these womanish beings are sterile lamiae, Lilith-like thieves of the lifeblood of infants. The Count's wives, rather than enjoying a productive life within a sacred union, are condemned to purloining the fruits of the wombs of others to indulge their murderous appetites.

When a true mother, spying Jonathan at his window, believes she recognizes the kidnapper of her child, she throws herself "on her knees, and raising up her hands," cries out from her prayerful position: "Monster, give me my child" (48). In response, "high overhead, probably on the tower, ... the voice of the Count ... in his harsh metallic whisper" (48) calls out to his tributary wolves, which pour in upon the distressed mother "like a pent-up dam when liberated" (49). The grieving woman meets her death in stony silence. To preserve compositional equilibrium and pave the way to Mina's initiation, Stoker sacrifices a mother and child in England: Mrs. Westenra and Lucy, mother once again dying because the Count has summoned his wolf. "For a second or two she sat up, pointing at the wolf, and there was a strange and horrible gurgling in her throat; then she fell over, as if struck with lightning, and her head hit my forehead and made me dizzy for a moment or two" (131).

The mother disposed of, child unconscious, the Count drained Lucy of her illuminating soul. "The funeral was arranged for the next succeeding day, so that Lucy and her mother might be buried together" (147). The daughter was mourned not as a young woman about to be married but as "that poor lily girl" (163), "that poor dear child Lucy Westenra. 'God! God! God!' he said. 'What have we done, what has this poor thing done, that we are so sore beset? Is there fate amongst us still, sent down from the pagan world of old, that such things must be, and in such way? This poor mother, all unknowing, and all for the best as she think, does such thing as lose her daughter body and soul.... Oh how we are beset!'" (124), is the Professor's despairing cry of confusion.

In England the Count attempts to form sacrilegious syzygies with women from a specific milieu; as Ruthven had only been interested by Aubrey's sister, the Count is exclusively interested in possessing a pair of women connected to Jonathan, inserting himself into Jonathan's place, donning his clothes so to speak. In proclaiming "the man belongs to me," the Count lays claim to his wife and her bosom companion as well. All phenomenological evidence presented through the text indicates that the Un-Dead otherwise only crave the blood of the innocent. A regular parade of suckling babes is represented along with the sufferance and incidental sacrifice of grieving mothers. The Count hunts for infants to provide for the Weird Sisters, but abandons consort Lucy to fend for herself.

In her short career the false Lucy snared numerous tots, piercing their flesh with her transformed dentition; the children described are pre-verbal infants clinging at her breast. Seward recalled the graveyard scene in a recording on a wax cylinder, as the Professor "pointed, and far down the avenue of yews we saw a white figure advance—a dim white figure, which held something dark at its breast" (187). "With a careless motion, she flung to the ground, callous as a devil, the child that up to now she had clutched strenuously to her breast, growling over it as a dog growls over a bone" (188). *The Westminster Gazette* of 25 September reports on a series of child abductions, observing, that when recovered, examination reveals "the children ... have been slightly torn or wounded in the throat" (160). "In all these cases the children were too young to give any properly intelligible account of themselves, but the consensus of their excuses is that they had been with a 'bloofer lady'" (159), *belle dame sans merci*. One child explained that the "'bloofer lady' had asked him to come for a walk, the others had picked up the phrase and used it as occasion served" (160). The latter part of the 19th and beginning of the

20th centuries record several occurrences of children claiming to have seen a beautiful lady who appears with various instructions. The Virgin Mary was reported to have appeared at LaSalette (1846), at Lourdes (1858), at Knock (1879) and at Fatima as Our Lady of the Rosary (1917), and millions of people, including members of the press, believed in and communally witnessed certain of these apparitions.

A perversion of the Holy Mother, stealing infants on the public ways, Lucy is debased through her unholy alliance with the Count. Lucy as false mother, throwing the infant down on the ground, contrasts to the true mother at Castle Dracula's courtyard, selflessly sacrificing her own life in the name of her child. The status of true and false mothers in *Dracula* seems attributable to marriage rites. Even in a text where all things and people flow into one another, the most important acts of union were those contrasting events occurring in the Convent of St. Joseph and Ste. Mary, and in the Harker's bedroom of the Purfleet asylum, where, it seems, Stoker's portrayal of the Count's sacrilegious rite is an attempt at presenting a "black" reversal of the Valentinian sacrament of the bridal chamber.

Unknown for over a millennium, this Gnostic rite has for recent generations been an object of inquiry and speculation; doubtless little more about this rite is known today than at Stoker's time, a half-century before the *Nag Hammadi*'s unearthing. Likely intended to help a sacred couple achieve mystical union — that is, spiritual and physical union as a single body and soul, and dissolution into the godhead — its logic was trinitarian. The presence of two individuals is brought into relation with a Third, ordinarily imperceptible being, made palpable due through ritual investment and preparation. The principle is comparable to the bipolar ebb and flow of the oceans and periods of day and night that are due to the interaction of three heavenly bodies, yet whose triangular commerce is only made evident to mankind during lunar or solar eclipses. If the third presence in the bridal chamber should be the Holy Spirit, the probable intent is nonetheless the hierogamous generation of a Christ-like progeny. In the case of the Count's moonlit violation of volition, with the groom in a stupor and the bride bound by the wrists, the third presence, literally diabolic, was ungodly and dry of seed; the intent is to doom the spouses to stealing new life in order to stifle it. Across the parable of the Vampire that is *Dracula*, the central role of binary phenomena, earlier attributed to trinitarian tensions between Sun, Moon and Earth, in generating the story is an abstraction of the relationship existing between solar Jonathan, lunar Mina, and the chthonic Count.

The Count is understandably interpreted as antichristic, the Cross of Jesus being posited as his countervailing force. Accordingly, the Count's death should mark the novel's finality. The entire last segment of the novel reinforces that proposition, melodramatic suspense prolonging the hunt from Piccadilly to Transylvania. At last, in the shadow of Castle Dracula, the end seems near at hand. "Look! Look! Look! See, two horsemen follow fast, coming up from the south. It must be Quincey and John" (322). "At the same time I knew that Jonathan was not far off; looking around I saw on the north side of the coming party two other men, riding at break-neck speed. One of them I knew was Jonathan" (322).

In their pincer movement, the horsemen trace the transversal arms of the cross whose principal axis runs along the West-East direction that their journey towards the Orient had drawn beneath the heavens. The travelers, pilgrims of a sort, have constructed in the moving world an open cathedral beneath the vaulting heavens. Like with a Celtic cross, at its center a double ring has been traced: a "Holy circle" (326), demarcated by the Professor, and a defensive "ring of Szgany" (323) surrounding the Count that "Mr Morris had had to use force to pass through" (323). At the very intersection, an overturned wooden case containing earth forms an altar where the sacrifice of man, the transformation of mankind and an unorthodox exercise in transubstantiation will be performed. As Quincey breaks through the circle, he is pierced through his side, blood spurting from his wound. He nonetheless aids Jonathan in cutting down the Count, stabbing him through the heart as Jonathan severs his head. With the Vampire turned to dust, "the dying man" (326) is left centered on the cross. In this passion, the mythologies of the North, East, South, and West meld in enduring faith in the symbol of the cross.

> For my own part, I see no difficulty in believing that it formed a portion of the primeval religion, traces of which exist over the whole world, among every people; that trust in the Cross was a part of the ancient faith which taught men to believe in a Trinity, in a War in Heaven, a Paradise from which man fell, a Flood, and a Babel; a faith which was deeply impressed with a conviction that a Virgin should conceive and bear a son, that the Dragon's head should be bruised and that through Shedding of blood should come Remission. The use of the cross, as a symbol of life and regeneration through water, is as widely spread over the world as the belief in the ark of Noah. May be, the shadow of the Cross was cast further back into the night of ages, and fell on a wider range of country than we are aware of.
>
> It is more than a coincidence that Osiris by the cross should give life eternal to the Spirits of the Just; that with the cross Thorr should smite the head of the Great Serpent, and bring to life those who were slain; that beneath the cross the Muysca mothers should lay their babes, trusting by that sign to secure them from the power of evil spirits; that with that symbol to protect them, the ancient people of Northern Italy should lay them down in the dust [Baring-Gould 384–85].

The Professor's principal representational attribute is a black bag containing "the ghastly paraphernalia of our beneficial trade" (112), extended to include sacred implements and The Sacral. On the day of Lucy's initiation into the order of the True dead, he is seen carrying a second, larger satchel, which contains a wooden stake and a mighty hammer. To compensate for his suffering, the Professor allows Art to wield Helsing's mighty hammer. As Helsing read the prayer for the dead, Godalming struck the stake with the hammer. "He looked like a figure of Thor as his untrembling arm rose and fell, driving deeper and deeper the mercy-bearing stake" (192). The stake, element of a sacred tree, perhaps related to the cross, may bear mercy to its receiver, but its force resides in the hammer and the arm that wields it. As Stoker makes clear, it is Thor's hammer, the godly instrument Baring-Gould confounds with the cross, that communicates merciful death and separates the soul from its prison. It is this hammer that reappears at the conclusion: The Professor, having made the castle holy, remarks: "The blacksmith hammer which I took in the carriage from Veresti was useful" (319).

At the ends of the world, as the season of light yields to antithesis, the Count and the sun disappear. At that instant Quincey, pointing at Mina, cries out, "Look! Look!" (326) In drawing attention towards Mina, away from the dust that had been the Count, the dying man marks the novel's indexical moment. Living, but having arrived at the threshold of death's asylum, Adamic Quincey rejoices, having, at life's liminal moment, attained gnosis. Mina, standing in the East, is figured against a deepening sky, celestial objects sparkling around her head. A rosy light reveals her to be immaculate. "The Syzygy" concludes that Mina was finally represented in the guise of a feminine divine: "Feet planted on the Earth, silhouetted against a darkening night sky that glitters with its brilliant inhabitants, crushed serpent, Little Dragon, at her feet, Mina presents an Isian or Marian figure and returns the narrative to its beginning and the rosary" that Jonathan accepted for the sake of his mother as the novel began. In Stoker's next breath, he tells of Mina, who had worn a sky blue ribbon around her neck as she prepared to wed, becoming a true mother.

Initially portrayed as a giddy young woman, playfully mischievous at times, she has changed and in so doing she has transformed others. At first her vision was parochial and somewhat selfish: "I suppose one ought to pity anything so hunted as is the Count," she, unable to do so, would concede. "That is just it: this Thing is not human — not even beast. To read Dr Seward's account of poor Lucy's death, and what followed, is enough to dry up the springs of pity in one's heart" (202). Indeed, the Count with his "cruel mouth" and sharp nose is depicted as incapable of love, and, since "the heart of him is not" (209), he is doomed to fail in his weighing of the heart. Through her newly gained knowledge of good and evil, Mina, however, extends her own heart to him and becomes *this Thing's* great champion, intervening to beg mercy for him, pleading that the world and the divine pity him. "The poor soul who has wrought all this misery is the saddest case of all. Just think what will be his joy when he too is destroyed in his worser part that his better part may have spiritual immortality. You must be pitiful to him too, though it may not hold your hands from his destruction" (269). As there was a false Lucy, fallen like Lucifer, and a true Lucy, the true Count Dracula, though long-cloaked in darkness, is now possessed of a solar sacred nature.

Whether or not Stoker was a Golden Dawn adept, *Dracula*, reaching its conclusion in the rosy dusk, unquestionably casts a critical eye on secret societies and brotherhoods to confirm the New Woman's position as a privileged agent of the Holy Spirit. The rosy light speaks not as much to the rosy cross as to the roses cradled in Our Lady's arm, Mina being shown as her special flower, "branch of wild rose" (212). Whether Dracula is or is not both evil and an aspect of God, or God's double, working to awaken us from our spiritual forgetfulness, or the antichrist that the engagement of Christian symbol and sacrament to baffle the Count would seem to indicate, would seem to make little difference; these possible significations tend to dissolve and crumble into dust along with the Vampire's body. Through the complex ritual that is plot, Mina is transformed, in appearance and function, to become transformative herself.

While Mina is evocative of the Blessed Virgin, she is identified as "but mortal" (273), able to recollect the taste of "the original apple" (164), fruit of the Tree of Knowledge of Good and Evil. On her way through the bountiful fields of Mittel Land, Mina has been more than sated on the fruits of the Yggdrasil that she was made to taste. Mina, represented as an habitué of places evoking Ste. Mary, Mina who consulted the Oracle at Ste. Mary's churchyard and married at the Convent of St. Joseph and Ste. Mary, is shown somehow elevated beyond the sphere of normal human beings, '"one of God's women, fashioned by His own hand to show us men and other women that there is a heaven where we can enter, and that its light can be here on this earth" (168), one of those "whose lives and whose truths may make good lesson for the children that are to be" (166). The Holy Mother is humbly represented as her servant; it is she who shows the Professor into Mina's life: "Mary opened the door, and announced "Dr Van Helsing" (163). In introducing himself the Professor makes a startling claim: "Madam Mina, it is on account of the dead I come" (163).

Through Mina's intervention, the dead are served and the living protected. When we have become purified, undergone catharsis, and attained Sophia, becoming one with the great emanation, darkness will no longer obscure and cover truth.

The Professor had prepared his Anglican friends to traverse the sacred threshold in commending their spirits into God's care in the tongue of the Romans: "*In manus tuas, Domine*!" (220). If the Count had previously stumbled at the threshold of this world and the next, Jonathan and Quincey had now helped him transcend it. Upon the Count's dissolution, the season of darkness envelops the earth; like man, divided into carnal and spiritual, earthly time and space separate into day and night, summer and winter. Although the no-longer-visible Count may perhaps rematerialize in a whirlwind of dust, that now seems curiously unimportant. Stoker nonetheless troubles this placid resolution by interjecting the issue of the transmigration of the soul. On the anniversary of Quincey's death the following year, a baby is born to Mina and Jonathan. The blessed child, Son of the New Man and New Woman, is habitually called "Quincey." He seems as likely to be the reincarnation of the Count as the Texan, indeed more likely, since Dracula, little dragon, embodies the skin-shedding capacity of reincarnation.

If it takes but nine days to be initiated into the unholy soul-stealing union of the Vampire, it takes nine contemporary (eight classical) months to be initiated into the divine soul accorded man. The new generation that is young Quincey, revealed as he reaches the age of reason, was conceived at the antipodes of the anniversary of *The Demeter*'s grounding. Perhaps this contains Stoker's last symmetric touch. While material *mater*, The Mother, Demeter, brought forth the chthonic lord, the God-chosen mother brings forth a spiritual New Man, answering the Professor's prayer: "Oh! If such an one was to come from God, and not the Devil, what a force for good might he not be in this old world of ours" (279).

Through the *Phaedrus* Plato has Socrates ask:

> Would a husbandman, who is a man of sense, take the seeds, which he values and which he wishes to bear fruit, and in sober seriousness plant them during the heat of summer, in some garden of Adonis, that he may rejoice when he sees them in eight days appearing in beauty? at least he would do so, if at all, only for the sake of amusement and pastime. But when he is in earnest he sows in fitting soil, and practises husbandry, and is satisfied if in eight months the seeds which he has sown arrive at perfection?

Stoker has answered.

The Overturned Lamp

> "'That poor creature that we all love has had put into her veins ... the blood of four strong men.... Then, coming close ... he spoke in a fierce half-whisper: 'What took it out?' (138) I shook my head. 'That,' I said, 'is the crux'" [138].

If, indeed, "the blood is the life!" (130) then *Dracula* is but a pale and moribund entity—"bloodless" (105) is the term Dr. Seward employs in diagnosing the condition. Prior to the mortal injury suffered by Quincey Morris in the very last of *Dracula*'s hundreds of pages, very little blood at all had been shed—only a small shaving accident, a superficial wound caused by a dinner knife, slight trickles of coagulated blood visible at the corners of unwashed mouths, and a precious few "gouts of fresh blood" (53) spilling over to punctuate the text here and there. Rather than indulging bloodlust, the entire novel meditates upon blood's apparent lack, its inexplicable absence, and the ill-phrased question: "And how the blood lost or waste?" (170), meaning: "Where did the blood go?"

Not only are there great quantities of missing blood that have vanished from Lucy's body without a trace, but prior to Quincey's self-sacrifice, death only touched the reader through Lucy's seemingly long, frantically pathetic struggle. All other deaths occur distantly, outside of plot, with the exception of the attack that claims Lucy's mother. Mrs. Westenra, however, had "got her death warrant" previous to the Count's arrival—"her doctor" having already "told her that within a few months, at most, she must die, for her heart [was] weakening" (91). By the end of August, still weeks before her ultimate demise, Art was preparing the way, warning, "Her doom is spoken—disease of the heart" (104), with all concurring that "any shock could prove fatal" (112). Hers was a bloodless and mercifully quick death, she expired "as if struck by lightning" (131).

This is typical of *Dracula* as an anaemic vessel; the few vampiric assaults that the novel does depict, rarely violent, merely involve a surrender of will, as disoriented victims yield themselves *à contrecoeur* to the clever and seductive wishes of Morpheus. Indeed it is the ideas of the crimes committed in *Dracula* that shocked generations, not their portrayal.

Renfield's motto, "The Blood is the Life!" is in fact a logician's well-formed phrase, uttered to establish identity between "blood" and "life," the oddly-applied definite article "The" expansively assuring universality. The question of "Where did the blood go?" thus becomes identical to the question of "Where did the life go?" More to the point the question "Where did the Life go?" is, in the logic of *Dracula*, simply another way of asking "From where did the Life come?" for it has been determined that it comes from and goes to the same state of pre-mythic unbegottenness. The vehicle Stoker employs to pose and incarnate this transformational question is Lucy Westenra.

While much of the novel concerns itself with the daily rotation of the Earth, its annual revolution around the sun, and the movements across its surface of wooden cases intended to accommodate the Count's body, the thoroughly parochial comings and goings of the Un-Dead body of Lucy lend unique substance to the mysteries at hand. When the Professor blocked the Westenra crypt's thresholds or "joinings" (227) with the Body and Blood of Christ he established that "there was no exodus" (186). This was hardly an innocent turn of phrase on the Professor's part.

Exodus is the story of human deliverance from a state of captivity and enslavement to a promised land through God's direct intervention. It is also the story of people becoming lost, losing faith, worshipping idols before discovering their error and regaining and retaining true faith — trusting to the true God to enable them to reach that which is His goal for them, as ratified through a sacred covenant. In a more abstract sense — and explicitly through Jesus' 40 days of fasting in the desert and implicitly through a host of scriptural links — Exodus is the Christian story, a story of individual pilgrimage, retracing a journey from the moving world to the moment that fills the empty-because-inexistent space/time–time/space of pre-creation that fully continues after time's exhaustion. It speaks about being held captive by the moment's temporal ruler, about crossing the desert of Sin, worshipping the golden calf, knowing thirst without the possibility of quenching it, knowing hunger and despairing of it, and then, through faith, of being nourished with unleavened bread through the hand of God, the Eucharistic Host's unleavened bread making specific reference to the manna of the desert and the Passover bread. This journey towards knowledge of God, Gnosis, is necessarily contributory to the sacred discourse of *Dracula*.

The grave normally represents the body's Promised Land rather than its place of bondage, yet, in the case of Lucy, the sacred has imprisoned the profaning body, the false Lucy—she who in life had been light, with hair like "sunny ripples" (146), has become a "dark-haired" (187) "foul [thing] of the night" (209). The organic shell that Socrates defined as the soul's prison is now itself imprisoned within the more durably material construct of the tomb by the Divine Presence made material. This illuminates Stoker's insistence on the necessity of consecrating to God what is already sacred to man, and provides a key to his complex construct of true and false entities that share a nominal identity. His job as a novelist is to move us from one towards another, East to West, in order to return again, East-West-East, with new knowledge and understanding—hence the importance of Lucy.

While it is Lucy who first connects us to Exodus through the Professor's reference, the novel's pages abound with many others. One particularly striking and clear example comes through Mina thinking herself led by divine signs in her oneiric ordeals: "It got thicker and thicker, till it seemed as if it became concentrated into a sort of pillar or cloud in the room, through the top of which I could see the light of the gas shining like a red eye. Things began to whirl through my brain just as the cloudy column was now whirling in the room, and through it all came the scriptural words 'a pillar of cloud by day and of fire by night.' Was it indeed some such spiritual guidance that was coming to me in my sleep?" (227). Plot eventually shows the wisdom of Mina's question and justifies her investment of faith.

Internalizing the lessons of Exodus, Stoker often works to remind us that the reflected gleam of the golden calf blasphemously generates a travesty of God's luminous brilliance. Gold, at a pagan, poetic level, exposes the hidden Apollonian nature of the Count, but at another, purely human and Christian, it is shown as a blinding hence corrupting agent. Posited as emerging from within the earth on a night when all evil has its way, it is consistently advertised as a substance falsely idolized by men: "His arguments were pointed with specie—we doing the punctuation—and with a little bargaining he told us what he knew" (302). From early on, Stoker issues frequent reminders of money's function as a corrosive agent: "Backsheesh again" (81), they begin. "Thank God! This is the country where bribery can do anything, and we are well supplied with money.... Judge Moneybag will settle this case, I think!" (290).

Those who power and animate the moving world, the shippers and haulers, constantly owe their devotion only to the golden calf: "So off we go to Doolittle's Wharf, and there we find a man in an office of wood so small that the man looked bigger than the office ... when Quincey give him something from his pocket which crackle as he roll it up, and put it in a so small bag which he have hid deep in his clothing, he still better fellow and humble servant to us" (275). '"Well, guv'nor, you've treated me very 'an'som'—I had given him half a sovereign—'an' I'll tell yer all I know'" (229). "I told him that if he could get me the address it would be worth another half-sovereign to him" (229). "A half-crown tip put the deputy's knowledge at my disposal" (231).

The imperial yet temporal nature of metonymic half-crowns and half-sovereigns is insistent, even leading to a "half-consent" (290), as if trying to call attention to the divide separating that which is Caesar's from that which is God's. The half-sovereign also comments on the absence of the divine in men's calculation of worth, wealth, and value. Only once is the sovereign portrayed whole, entire, unified: "Through the sound of the shivering glass I could hear the 'ting' of the gold, as some of the sovereigns fell on the flagging" (267). The Count, stooping to scoop them off the ground where they had fallen, will raise the sovereign from the earth to the heavens as he leads his hunters to the heights of "God's seat" on the day of judgment, temporal antipode to the evening when gold manifests itself through the appearance of bluish flames and all evil things hold sway.

For the lower classes—"movers with thirst and needing bribe" (143)—drink is established as equivalent to money in its powers of corruption, in its ability to loosen tongues, and in its capacity to inspire a particularly legalese mode of euphemistic expression: "The boxes were 'main and mortal heavy,' and that shifting them was dry work. One of them added that it was hard lines that there wasn't any gentleman 'such-like as yourself squire,' to show some sort of appreciation of their efforts in a liquid form; another put in a rider that the thirst then generated was such that even the time which had elapsed had not completely allayed it. Needless to add, I took care before leaving to lift, for ever and adequately, this source of reproach" (201). "The opportunities of acquiring an abnormal thirst had been here limited; a noble use of them had, however, been made, and again I was compelled to deal with the result in an *ex post facto* manner" (201). "Here again I found the tally agreeing exactly; the carriers' men were able to supplement the paucity of the written words with a few details. These were, I shortly found connected almost solely with the dusty nature of the job, and of the consequent thirst engendered in the operators. On my affording an opportunity, through the medium of the currency of the realm, of the allaying, at a later period, this beneficent evil" (201), information was forthcoming.

For these workmen of mercantile forthrightness, Stoker's metaphor joining money, thirst, dust, and labor, is deliberately very mixed. Their toils in the dust of mortality recall the fate of the Count's victims, Lucy and Mina—who "had both a fight for it with the dusty miller" (86), and the final disposition of all men, the Count included. The chronic thirst of these laborers emphasizes how our efforts in this mortally dusty place do bring about an enduring thirst that brute men little know how to satisfy. And while it is Lucy who recalls "something very sweet and very bitter all around me at once" (94), it is the Professor who attempts to console us and to give us strength to persevere by returning three times to the desert thirst of Exodus 15: "We ... will have to pass through the bitter water before we reach the sweet" (154); "a hundred thousand times more do I know that he must pass through the bitter waters to reach the sweet" (180); "You are now in the bitter waters, my child. By this time tomorrow you will, please God, have passed them, and have drunk of the sweet waters" (189). In his frequent trinitarian mode, the threefold repetition always points out one of Stoker's more ardently dispatched messages "Oh, about number three — I needn't tell you of number three, need I?" (61) he teases.

Indeed, every occasion of triple-telling always proves to be significant, though on one occasion somewhat puzzling. Stoker thrice draws attention to the Professor's curious habit of making the passive element active and the active passive in his rendering of common dictums: "You must not let your sight pass from her" (116); "The dilemma had me between his horns" (319); "The milk that is spilt cries not out afterwards" (208). It seems that the only explanation for these deliberately odd transformed figures of speech is that Stoker wishes to call his reader's attention to the aspects of his work that are not seen turning as the rumbling coach careens on by, but that remain intent and steady, the axle rather than the wheel — the immutable. We are called to more fully consider the function of apparently passive elements, most especially, it would seem, Lucy.

Stoker's most obvious embodiments of three-ness are given form in a lamia triune and in the three suitors of light that become part of the Brotherhood. He introduces the human trio as they are caught up in the most corporal and lively aspects of life, providing them with a spiritual subtext as they present themselves, one after the other, to Lucy Westenra at Hillingham, all asking for her hand on the same day. The occasion is rendered brighter through contrast: Lucy's light and joyous courtship occurs nearly concurrent to Jonathan's somber encounter with Castle Dracula's lamiae. Considering Stoker's typical word games, the Westenra's estate, Hillingham, likely intends to situate its residents in a place of high sexual attractiveness to the male, Hi(gh) lingham, or Lingham Hill, where all the suitors, lost in love and given to forgetfulness, come, blood risen to high noon, to propose a union through marriage to the young beauty.

Lucy describes each suitor's charm — curly-haired Art, penetrating Seward, and good-natured Quincey — to Mina in a letter. She paints Quincey, a man who depicts her anticipated kiss recollected as a flame to "keep off the darkness" (60), as amusing her with American slang. She says he reserves it for intimates, but when he feels he has licence to indulge his love of colloquial color, rather than just reciting a collection of pat lines, he invents curious phrases that seem tailor-made for each given occasion, and seems to hold in reserve an endless store of sayings for any and every situation imaginable. This apparently explains the down-home folksiness of his proposal of marriage: "Miss Lucy, I know I ain't good enough to regulate the fixin's of your little shoes, but I guess if you wait till you find a man that is you will go join them seven young women with the lamps when you quit. Won't you just hitch up alongside of me and let us go down the long road together, driving in double harness?" (59).*

The image of life as a journey is one he returns to upon her refusal of his marriage proposal, resigning himself to that "pretty lonely walk between this and Kingdom Come" (60). Quincey's metaphor is Stoker's, with the moving world manifest in London flies, and transcontinental trains, and steamboats, and cargo ships, and charging coaches orbited by lunar predators—"We sped onwards through the gloom, with the howling of the wolves around us, as though they were following in a moving circle" (19)—that make clear the cosmic scope of his vision. Yet the rest of Quincey's declaration of love is quite original in its mixing of referents.

Quincey's "slang" associates Lucy with the Vestals, keepers of the sacred flame, protectresses of pagan Rome, and maidens whose blood could not be spilt. In the same phrase he references John the Baptist's proclamation that he was unworthy to loose the sandals of Jesus. Matthew 3:11 has the Baptist join the image of flame to the concept of baptism. "I indeed baptize you with water, for repentance. But he who is coming after me is mightier than I, whose sandals I am not worthy to bear. He will baptise you with the Holy Spirit and with fire." John 1:26–27 has the Baptist simply say: "I baptize with water; but in the midst of you there has stood one whom you do not know. He it is who is to come after me, who has been set above me, the strap of whose sandal I am not worthy to loose."

Mark 1:7–8 quotes the Baptist as saying, "One mightier than I is coming after me, the strap of whose sandals I am not worthy to stoop down and loose. I have baptized you with water, but he will baptize you with the Holy Sprit." Matthew seems to attach his imagery to the Mysteries of Eleusis as well, for he immediately adds: "His winnowing fan is his hand, and he will thoroughly clean out his threshing floor and will gather his wheat into the barn; but the

*Lucy concludes her thoughts on Quincey's verbal stream by noting that she sympathises "with poor Desdemona when she had such a dangerous stream poured in her ear, even by a black man" (59). The claim there is racism in this phrase, Stoker's or Lucy's, put into the mouth of a man from the southern United States, is not only asinine, but typical of the worthless quality of much of the learned commentary on *Dracula*. In this phrase we find Stoker 1) attempting to clarify more strongly the significance of Quincey Morris—i.e., *More is*: The man subjecting Desdemona's ear to a flow of words, Othello, is not a black man; he is a "Moor." Quincey Moor-is Is-more than Quincey; he is Adam. Stoker 2) also wants to link greedy-eared Desdemona and Lucy, who is at heart and by nature a "Harker."

chaff he will burn up with unquenchable fire" (3:12). This image of the winnowing of souls, common to post–Neolithic cults, is consonant with the weighing floor image of Hunefer's book of the dead, "The Weighing of the Heart." *Dracula*'s divine winnowing hand has been shown personified in the Brotherhood, composed largely of Lucy's beaux. In harvesting evil and exercising forgiveness, it fills the storehouse with felicitous goodness.

The suitors, even those rejected by Lucy, return to Hillingham three months later, their blood, despite Lucy's metaphysical infection, still at high tide. Stoker assures that their donations to Lucy's blood-starved heart will still — first, foremost, and forthrightly — be eroticized. To begin, Arthur contributes his "so bright" (114) blood, "blood so pure" (114); the next day Lucy, figuring Love as a stallion, claims that he "feels very, very close.... I seem to feel his presence warm about me. I suppose it is that sickness and weakness are selfish things and turn our inner eyes and sympathy on ourselves, whilst health and strength give Love rein and in thought and feeling he can wander where he wills. I know where my thoughts are. If Arthur only knew!" (117). Next, it is Seward's turn to contribute fluids. His investment prompts the comment: "'You are looking pale yourself. You want a wife to nurse and look after you a bit; that you do!' As she spoke, Lucy turned crimson, though it was only momentarily, for her poor wasted veins could not stand for long such an unwonted drain to the head" (120).

When the Professor transfuses his blood, Lucy again feels the beauty of the new day, but recalls her ordeal: "I have a dim half-remembrance of long, anxious times of waiting and fearing; darkness in which there was not even the pain of hope to make present distress more poignant; and then long spells of oblivion, and the rising back to life as a diver coming up through a great press of water" (124), the latter phrase recalling and completing her description of her baptism in vampirism at Whitby. Finally, it is Quincey who transfers his haematological quintessence to Lucy. "His very heart was bleeding, and it took all the manhood of him — and there was a royal lot of it, too — to keep him from breaking down" (138). Lucy's passion was nearly at an end. Quincey, who, like Lucy, described himself as a "tough nut to crack" (66, 68), is destined to be her eternal soulmate as they mystically move in double-harness to preserve Mina, for, in this case, the Vestal's blood, though not spilt, shall indeed cry out afterwards.

Stoker's interest in introducing and mixing classical pagan and biblical references appears to be, as usual, multiple. Should luminous Lucy be a guardian of a sacred flame (for she never does marry) it is in keeping with her celestial identity. Her association with John the Baptist serves to justify a term the Professor applies to Mina's Bridal Chamber anti-sacrament: "the Vampire's baptism of blood" (280). Lucy serves as a true Baptist to Mina, as Renfield serves as a false baptist to the Count. Mina was not baptized with water but, as Matthew quotes the Baptist as saying, "with the Holy Spirit and with fire" (3:11): with the Holy Spirit during her eventual passage across "the 'Mittel Land'" (14) in "the straggling ends of pine woods, which here and there ran down the hillsides like tongues of flame" (13); and with fire in being branded with the Eucharist, Jonathan even asserting that they "all went through the flames" (326). As John the Baptist not only baptized Jesus but foreran him by being in essence accused of and martyred for the crime of the Word for which Jesus would later be crucified, Lucy will precurse Mina to reveal the nature of the Vampire's unholy rites.

The imagery of sandals and of going before, of preceeding Mina, is intimated from the moment of the Count's arrival on English shores. On the occasion of Lucy's initiation, an alarmed Mina hastened to bring Lucy back from her graveyard tryst. Reaching the suicide bench, Mina wraps Lucy, clothed only in her nightdress, in a shawl and puts her own shoes on Lucy's feet before awakening her. Reaching a gravel path, now polluted Lucy offers Mina the shoes that she might walk in them. Mina ostensibly refuses, but then covers her bare feet in mud, as if standing in the chthonic and unclean place of Lucy, "so that as we went home no one, in case we should meet any one, should notice my bare feet" (89), and she remarks, "We got home without meeting a soul" (89). The blood brotherhood formed to save Lucy's body will become a sacred brotherhood in a struggle to safeguard Mina's soul. Again, Lucy is largely responsible for alerting her one-time suitors to the spiritual dangers abroad. Driving the point home, they must kill her dead body to save her living soul.

False Lucy is killed to bring forth true Lucy. False Count Dracula — "man-that-was" (212) become "the semblance of man" (39) — is killed to give rise to the true Count. By all rights, the novel should represent the killing of a false god in order to release the true God, since it is this ritual scenario, for millennia enacted annually through dying-god rites in post-Neolithic cultures, that was appropriated to give the Vampire Tale form. Adamic Quincey's self-sacrifice on the virtual cross, undertaken to accomplish the birth of the half-sovereign, partially-divine New Man, hardly qualifies as the death of a false god.

Another violent death approaching plot is Renfield's, who returns the story to earlier renditions of the Vampire Tale in which the old chthonic god is killed in order to resurrect as the new chthonic god. But Renfield's mission, to serve as one who makes ready the way before the Count, was unrealized. Once he begins to weigh the heart as soul, his own and others, and to consider that it is the soul inviolate and not the blood that engenders life eternal, Renfield abandons the Count and saves Mina. Renfield's death therefore tells a human story of personal redemption and selflessness, but nothing more. Beyond these martyrs, *Dracula*'s dead are vampires, seamen, infants, and mothers.

Matthew's report on the Baptist saying he is not worthy to loose Jesus' shoe, and then, attaching foot to hand, speaking of the winnowing hand of Jesus, clearly intends to engage the Mysteries, notably Demeter's sacred implement, the winnowing fan. The Professor's "ear of corn" Mysteries speech and other references in the work establish a firm connection between *Dracula* and earlier Platonic recountings of the Dionysian Vampire. Lucy, rather than retaining a ghostly form and being doomed, Ianthe-like, to eternally haunting Athenian neighborhoods in search of the simple violet, will be dispatched to an eternal and Christian slumber; she accomplishes good through awakening others, through alerting her friends and fiancé to their sacred mission: to facilitate the exodus of the soul. Hearing her plea through the determined efforts of the Professor, the Brotherhood sees to it that she is laid to eternal rest, True Dead, and deposited alongside her True Dead mother.

Through these and other actions, Stoker assigns the role of the false god to be sacrificed to Artemis-Diana in her avatar as Persephone. It is she whose death is to bring forth the True Divine, that is, The Sacred Mother and The Maiden united: the Blessed Virgin. Persephone's elimination will be assured through the dissolution of her lover-son, the Dionysian Vampire, and the extinguishment of the sacral flame of torch-bearing Demeter.

Preceded by mares' tails, *The Demeter* delivered her underworldly progeny in a snug harbor beneath the graves of Romanesque Whitby Abbey, a structure left a ruin by the near descendants of the self-same Goths that under Alaric had pulled Byron's Temple of Ceres down to dust and rubble. The derelict vessel, her crew disappeared, is left beached, an abandoned wreck under a dead man's hand. Her apostate helmsman espouses from beyond life a belief in Jesus Christ and in the mercy of His divine Mother. As the moment of the annual Mysteries celebration approaches in late September, Lucy's mother is stricken as if by a flash of lightning. Her death appears to signal Mystery Night's arrival. The Daughter will soon follow The Mother across the Acheron to forever remain amongst the True Dead.

The pagan winnowing fan has been replaced by the hand of Jesus; the rosy cross and golden dawn have been forsaken for a truer brotherhood maintaining Christian principles, gentlemanly comportment, and a willingness to enter the season of darkness unafraid, its members believing the light is now within them. The Vestals' flame, like that of graveyard Sleep, has been overturned and extinguished so that, even at the price of Rome's fall, a truer light might shine.*

Although *The Demeter* births the Ploutonian figure that initiates Lucy's ordeal, it will be Jesus Christ that resolves her wayward vagabonding. He, too, will bring peace to the Dionysian hunter through the intercession of the

*Curiously, in the 1931 Universal film entitled *Dracula*, the name of the ship conducting the Count to England became *The Vestal.*

Holy Mother and her instrument, the "quite heroic" (86) Mina. In her moment of liberation from evil, at the instance of her becoming immaculate, Mina is revealed bathing in the rosy light of the western light, Lucy Westenra, which lingers to illuminate her visage in its remarkable radiance. Like the Moses of Exodus, whose face after 40 days of divine discourse reflected the divine presence in light, the brilliance of goodness is given expression through the light of Lucy Westenra that lunar Mina reflects. While Mina is the wild rose branch, Lucy, repeatedly described as rosy, is the Blessed Virgin's bouquet. Mina herself reminds the reader of "the roses in [Lucy's] cheeks" (93) that were either "fading from her cheeks" (92) or "coming back already" (93).

While Jonathan's Transylvanian adventure — that circuitous coach ride to the castle, the dusty pile of gold and chains, and numerous other of its curious details — impinges on initiation rites of certain branches of Freemasonry, these are but minor elements in a vast tapestry. Stoker joins the initiatory procession along the Sacred Way to complete and redirect Byron and Polidori's Neoplatonic Vampire Tale, calling most particularly on the "Phaedrus," its Socratic proof of the soul and related images to make his case. Overturning the antique Mysteries, he argues — in a pilgrimage that, having completed the East-West itinerary of Polidori, again returns to the East — for a new Christian covenant.

Until Stoker focused *Dracula* on trinitarian relationships, the Vampire Tale was enclosed within a bipolar universe. The feminine actors in the drama were passive objects lacking original volition. In their annual Apollonian-Dionysian conflict, Polidori's Aubrey would occasionally "baffle" Ruthven, but Aubrey would ultimately be overwhelmed with grief from the loss of both his true love and his only sister to wily Ruthven. Nodier and Planché seemingly stripped Ruthven of his victories by having time run out on his attempts to wed the Apollonian figure's maiden sister, condemning him to Gnostic annihilation, but in fortuitously dispatching evil, they risk dismissing and belittling its compellingly seductive power. Dumas has Ruthven deprive Gilbert of two sisters, one spiritual, the other biological, at a six-month interval and climb out of the Black Sea on a 366th day to claim Gilbert's fiancée in his stead. Ruthven's betrayal by the Ghoul provides Gilbert with the means to defeat the unrepentant Vampire with a consecrated sword. Ruthven's undoing unites Gilbert, his bride, and the spirits of the lost sisters at a felicitous sacred wedding, the Ghoul causing her own death through her act of love.

Stoker maintains the Vampire Tale's template through Apollonian Harker and Dionysian Dracula, but the Apollonian-Dionysian doppelganger is accommodated by and subsumed within an eclipsing triadic solar-lunar-chthonic configuration binding Jonathan to Mina to the Count — Jonathan even being present as one of a *ménage-à-trois* as the Count takes his wife in unholy matrimony. Through the Lucy-Mina doppelganger, the triangular relationship is nearly squared, even tending towards, and ultimately reaching, the ogdoadic through the Brotherhood. By pairing solar Lucy and lunar Mina, Stoker greatly develops, clarifies, and empowers the feminine personality, assigning it a determinant role; women, no longer simple objects of contention, are resolving subjects and centers of power emanation. Although the spiritually devastating effects of the Count's activities are reversed, he scores resounding temporal victories, irreversibly in Lucy's case and nearly so in Mina's.

What is occulted in *Dracula* is always exposed, exoteric dominating the esoteric. The captain of *The Demeter* wrote out his Tale of the Vampire on a scroll that he sealed in a water- and air-tight container conceived to weather a terrible storm so that his word and witness might eventually reach human eyes and understanding. Rather than an addendum to the canon of the ship's log, his scroll was termed an apocryphal gospel. So many of Stoker's positions, as they emerge from his own text, are consistent with the apparent stance of the apocrypha of ancient Gnostics as understood at the moment of modernity. It is mystifying to understand this correspondence, considering that though interest was high in the age of Theosophy, knowledge of Gnosticism was quite limited prior to the unearthing of the cache of documents known as *The Nag Hammadi*. The primary so-called Gnostic works that would have been available to Stoker were limited to Irenaeus of Lyon's polemical *Against Heresies*, published in English in 1885; *The Book of Enoch*, 1887; *The Pistis Sophia*, in Latin 1851 and English 1896; and Charles King's *The Gnostic and their Remains*, 1864, revised 1887; with more fragmentary sources incidentally scattered throughout the writings of late classical writers, such as Hippolytus.

Stoker's "Gnostic" touches include the depiction of the body as a prison; the role of light as a divine marker; the temporal division of understanding, "six months turned to the left, six months turned to the right" (*Pistis Sophia*); the privileged place given to apostles John, Matthew and Thomas; the elevated position of women; the particularly stressed role of Mary; the suggestion of a composite feminine Sophia; and, more abstractly, the name Harker. Jonathan on one occasion actually scribes "Hark!" (54) to convey his listening "blindfold" (203, 305) to the exodus of the self-willed Count, abandoning his castle, as he heads for *The Demeter* and flight to what he believes will be his promised land, England. Mina, too, accentuates hearing: "The sheep and the lambs are bleating in the fields away behind me" (68); before her, dueling orchestras, one playing the sensuously whirling, still-scandal-tainted triple-time of "a harsh waltz," the other, the strident double-time of "the Salvation Army" (68). "Neither of the bands hears the other, but up here I hear and see" (69). In the *Pistis Sophia*, Jesus constantly stresses the word "Hark!" enjoining disciples, "Who hath ears to hear, let him hear!" It is the divine Word, not the image, that contains the Logos.

The objective set out, to demonstrate that *Dracula* was written as a sacred text, has been attained. The Book of Stoker, commenting on an eastward pilgrimage whose record is filled with illuminations "such as we see in old missals" (11), is an epistolary text "'focussing' some account" (69) out of recordings, journal entries, memoranda, logs, and missives whose spiritual nature even the Count can appreciate, as he concedes to Jonathan, "Your letters are sacred to me" (46) (although the Count abhors shorthand as blasphemous). Decrying clerics "printin' lies on paper an' preachin' them out of pulpits" (65), Stoker attempts to offer a contemporary clerk's truer gospel for a newer time. To distil a theology from its many pages would be problematic; like other sacred texts, *Dracula* is not a catechism. Certain of its features are nonetheless remarkable.

The triumph of Ste. Mary and the repeated disparaging of St. Peter seem to signal an acceptance of Catholic rites but a rejection of the Catholic institution, the Vatican, and especially—recalling the gate keeper with his hand out—practices that might be seen as relating to simony. The elevated place accorded woman remains steadfastly within a traditionalist view of the sacred couple as formed by a man and a woman, the syzygy, and idealized in the sacred family of "St. Joseph and Ste. Mary" (96) and the Divine Child. The body, starkly established as a soul-enslaving prison, explains why, along with the dusty gold discovered in the Count's chamber, "there were also chains and ornaments, some jewelled, but all of them old and stained" (50); no matter its ornamental splendor, a chain binds. The presence of pagan evil is seen as a potential pillar of light and goodness, as the *Irmunsul* of Hildesheim's Dom Santa Maria suggests. Forgiveness becomes a universal possibility for all those having slain or having had slain the unclean spirits residing within themselves, sacramental confession having no role in the dynamics of forgiveness. The Professor urges his Christian fellows of the Brotherhood to act on behalf of the Vampire as if for themselves. For should we become afflicted, he warns, to "us for ever are the gates of heaven shut; for who shall open them to us again?" (209). Mina, conceding the Professor's case, argues more generally and with greater purity for the good of forgiveness as an exercise in the divine, especially rallying the "menfolk" to pity the Count. This marks the opening of a new era in which, Jonathan seems to suggest, the flames of hell may be greatly contained.

Life, the life of the blood, is the bitter water; the truly sweet water is the pure eternal soul life which connects to that which comes before and after everything. Stoker says as much: "Sweet it was ... but with a bitter [quality] underlying the sweet, a bitter offensiveness, as one smells in blood" (42). In hungering and plunging with Lucy "like a cormorant" (101) into the depth of these estuarial waters bitter and sweet we have come to encounter Matthew and John the Evangelists, Hesiod, Socrates, and Moses, all intent on resolving the question of what is, was and will be before and after being. But, most particularly, we find Jesus, the unblinking fish, multiplying bounty, who looked at Lucy as she delivered her body to the Count for his profaning baptism.

How was Stoker to produce a sacred text if not through reference to earlier sacred texts, as the Prophets and Evangelists had done before him? The question of what was before the beginning and what endures after the end is the mystery that is sealed in the tomb we set out to resolve. The key is locked within but as it is immaterial Jonathan, despite his desperate intensity, could not at first find it. Mina's attitude is more joyous: "Now I shall learn something pleasant, I am sure; for it will tell me the other side of a true love episode of which I know one side already" (196).

Approaching the same question from a different angle, Jonathan considered the comfort brought to him through the rosary difficult to comprehend, but determined to "examine this matter and try to make up my mind about it. In the meantime I must find out all I can about Count Dracula, as it may help me to understand" (33). Why he joins the two, rosary and vampire, is obscure, but he seems to think that darkness explains light the way death explains life. What he finds out about the Count is quite similar to what he finds out about himself. When he looked in the mirror while shaving, he mistook seeing his own face for not seeing the Count's, yet the Count, in his ways of Morpheus, has been shown sharing identities with most everyone, but particularly with Jonathan — even to the extent that he marries Jonathan's wife.

The Count, described as a guide and conductor in the same manner as the Professor, has also been qualified as hierophantic. Neither the Count nor the Professor constitutes, however, a psychopomp, their mission being not to lead the soul from the body, but to reconcile the living individual to the supremacy of the soul over the body even in the busiest of seasons in the moving world. In this regard, both Dracula and Helsing function as special types of exorcists, one casting the soul out of the body, the other, remedially, the body from itself in order to recover the soul, again plying on the idea of making what is sacred to man sanctified to God.

To seize the nature of the Count's role in *Dracula* is no doubt to return to the 13 persons at the dinner table and Stoker's *Notes*, and perhaps to gain some insight into Stoker's struggle with his Transylvanian boyar and to clarify something of the Gnostic overtones of his work. Present at the Passover feast, foundation of the new Eucharistic age, and Last Supper of Jesus, was the apostle Judas. John claims that Judas was motivated by "Satan" to betray Jesus. Clearly Judas was required to effect the new era of man; his deliverance of Jesus had a tragic quality but gave rise to a joyous moment. Most importantly, this action, the sacrifice of the Paschal lamb, was determined by Jesus himself. Luke relates that there were contentious relations between the apostles that day of the Last Supper, and that Satan would also move Simon Peter to deny knowing Jesus as his master, as indeed came to pass. Mark tells the same story, that before Jesus declares "This is my blood of the new covenant, which is being shed for many" (4:17), he maintained that one amongst the 12 would betray him, and another deny him.

Matthew has again a somewhat different version of the event to relate. Jesus foretells his betrayal by one at the table, and "Judas who betrayed him answered and said, 'Is it I, Rabbi?' He said to him 'Thou hast said it'" (26:25). A conspiratorial shadow envelops this exchange. Judas hails Jesus as "Rabbi," spiritual master, but Jesus turns the acknowledgment around through his reply, provisionally assigning Judas the masterly voice. Without Judas, the realization of Jesus' mission could not have been attained: Judas effects His release from His corporeal form and the revelation of His True Self. Judas may be the stake, but Jesus is the hammer.

The equation of the Count and Judas is explicitly suggested by Jonathan: "The last I saw of Count Dracula was his kissing his hand to me, with a red light of triumph in his eyes, and with a smile that Judas in hell might be proud of" (52). The betrayal of the Count concerns his own spiritual nature; in denying it, in giving himself purely to the material, the Count is inescapably evil in a way that Judas is not, but he serves to remind us of the missing half-crown, the half of everything that goes unseen. Dumas assigned the Ghoul a very Judas-like role, in that she betrayed the Vampire at the cost of her own existence. Stoker confides this part to Renfield. Unlike Dumas' Ruthven, Count Dracula is never given the opportunity for repentance, but it seems unlikely he would ask for forgiveness, making Mina's argument for forgiveness all the more stunning and profoundly Christian.

There is, nonetheless, another aspect of the Count that is intermittently given expression: his role as *Rex mundi*. He is called "the King-Vampire" (320); Jonathan Harker hears him "like a king speaking" (33); Dracula enters London through King's Cross, even if travelling as purely material freight; his victim Lucy is deposited in the "churchyard at Kingstead" (183); he is a king in a two-dimensional bivalent universe where the Professor, matching wits with the Count, can gleefully call, "Check to the King" (135). Like Jonathan at Castle Dracula, Jesus, on the occasion of His passing 40 days and nights in the desert, has only one companion: Satan. Satan would present Jesus with the material, asking Him, for example, to transform rock into bread. Upon His refusal, Satan led Jesus on high, above the temple, where he displayed the material splendor of the earth, promising all to Jesus in exchange for a declaration of subservience. Renfield describes a similar scene in which he was tempted by the Count with millions of lives, in the form of masses of glowing-eyed rodents. Renfield at first succumbs to the Count's temptation, but later redeems his crime by sacrificing himself to save Mina. As he had with Judas, Jesus eventually commands Satan, establishing His mastery: "Begone, Satan! for it is written, 'The Lord thy God shalt thou worship and him only shalt thou serve'" (Matthew 4:10). Perhaps most importantly, the satanic aspect of the Count derives, in Cathar fashion, from his dusty nature: He is purely material. By going through the fire of the material, purification becomes possible.

Stoker told Prime Minister Gladstone that he intended to purify his reader, that his work was conceived as cathartic. Perhaps his plan was to attach a forthright and questing chivalrous romance to the Albigensian Cathari and their theologies, largely consistent with the ideas Stoker presents, and explaining the material Count's portrayal as the worldly king. If so, could Stoker perhaps be relating his text to the Bogomili, a medieval sect native to the Count's historic realm and the probable theological source of the Cathari heresy?

Massimo Introvigne of the Centre for Study of New Religions kindly read certain sections of this text as it was being drafted. His encouraging comments were tempered by a cautionary note concerning *Dracula*'s author: "I would say, based on his non–Dracula writings and bio[graphy], that Stoker was more conventionally Christian than it appears in the text." This is no doubt true. Yet in choosing not to represent the dark season, in joining at its threshold the light of Lucy and Mina's radiant smile, in ending his novel by having his now wholly-sovereign heroine experience true catharsis and bask in the rosy light of the divine, Stoker nonetheless shows himself to be a true and dedicated torch-bearing illuminato. Stoker's sacred text, The Book of Stoker, was designed not only to illuminate, but to spark the inner light within each reader. This is what he told William Gladstone he intended to do, and this is what he did. Only his sacred project can explain and unify the novel's many motifs — from the gold to the dust, from the solar to the lunar, from the beads to the cross, from the spotless forehead to the repeated references to the superstition of the "evil eye" (14, 16, 302, 312), from the corpse to the key — to form a coherent and mighty artistic statement that continues to shine on brightly across time.

> No one lights a lamp and puts it in a cellar or even under the measure, but upon the lamp-stand, that they who enter in may see the light. The lamp of the body is thy eye. If thy eye be sound, thy whole body will be full of light. But if it be evil, thy body also will be full of darkness. Take care, therefore, that the light that is in thee is not darkness. If, then, thy whole body is full of light, having no part in darkness, it will all be illumined, as when a bright lamp illuminates thee [Luke 11:33–36].

> Light of lights, in whom I have had faith, leave me not in the darkness until the end of my time.

> Help me and save me through thy mysteries; incline thine ear unto me and save me [A Prayer of Pistis Sophia].

Coniunctio Oppositorium

> "When are you to be married, and where, and who is to perform the ceremony, and what are you to wear, and is it to be a public or a private wedding? Tell me all about it dear; tell me all about everything, for there is nothing which interests you which will not be dear to me" [141].

The presence of the triumphant, evil-vanquishing Christian cross in *Dracula* does not preclude this ancient symbol from intersecting and interacting with other orders of signification. Considering Stoker's familiarity with Baring-Gould's essays on the cruciform, the circle, Melusina, the shipping of the dead, and the Sangreal, it is telling that Stoker's Christian symbols peacefully coexist with heretical rites, ancient myths, and pagan gods; meaningful that, in interacting in ambiguous comfort with these remnants of the old beliefs, the icons of Christianity dissolve the fatal polarity Goethe established through "The Bride of Corinth." Indeed *Dracula*'s compulsive, geometrically-balanced treatment of temporality, iconography, plot events, protagonist characterization, and geographic location tends — through cross, host, rosary, and other emblems — to index further authorial investment in a web of deliberately layered meanings.

Barbara Belford's suggestion that Stoker considered using tarot imagery gains added sense once the discerned Cathari and Bogomili influences on the particular Christian theology that Stoker advances are taken into account. C. G. Jung, retracing the perpetuation of Gnostic thought in Paracelsus and his followers, finds it "very probable that those heresies which began with the Euchites, Paulicians, Bogomils, and Cathars, and which developed the concept of the Paraclete very much in the spirit of the founder of Christianity, were continued in alchemy, partly unconsciously and partly under a deliberate disguise" (13: 229).

Sister proto-sciences astrology and alchemy share symbolic representational traditions that, mixing the sacred and the profane, may be related to the imagery "found in missals" that Stoker cites as he begins his novel with a journey through the Mittel Land. As seems to be indicated by the name Van Helsing—so resonant with that of the author of *Oriatrike, or Physick refined*, Dr. Van Helmont—Stoker is particularly eager to trade in distinctive appeals to alchemistic imagery and thought. He is also prepared to embody the Holy Spirit in a feminine form, transforming the trinitarian godhead into a quaternity, the Blessed Virgin Mary being assumed not only into heaven, but also into the divine amalgam of the godhead.

The polysemous quality of *Dracula*'s symbolic system both in its individual and collective aspects (micro-and-macrocosmically) its proximity to Rosicrucian texts, alchemistic motifs, and its correspondence, through the triangular relationship linking Jonathan, Mina, and the Count to the allegoric transformative marriage of Sol and Luna unavoidably bring The Book of Stoker into direct contact with, to employ the term Christian Rosenkreutz celebrated in his allegory of the magically Christian Easter-time renaissance, the "*Chymical wedding*." This spring-rites royal union is motivated by the same dynamic as the antique agricultural Mysteries of Eleusis: Death giving rise to Life.

In that regard, and going well beyond issues of temporal structuring, Stoker's magnum opus is more firmly bound to Dumas' "fantastical drama" than has previously been discussed, as is made clear by Renfield's notably improbable declaration that Seward "might as well ask a man to eat molecules with a pair of chop-sticks" (238) as to ask him not to want blood. The frequently cited interplay of polarities, trinities, and quaternities expressed though *Dracula*'s characters, actions, and elemental, ideational and geographical paradox, strongly suggests that Dumas's Mélusine interlude may inform a sub rosa armature that, in supporting the plastic, earthy clay of plot and character, structures the material body of Stoker's Gnostic-flavored novel. In Stoker's quadrille the couples are more difficult to discern than with Dumas, for they are never introduced as simple pairs: Lucy is first shown with her many beaux, Jonathan with the three lamiae and his fiancée Mina, Mina with her several husbands, and the Count with his multiple wives. Yet a close look at the dance of Stoker's cast reveals its own quadrille within a cosmic drama in which the Gnostic bridal chamber sacrament becomes an alchemistic exercise. The union of Sun and Moon is indeed conducted before the assembled members of the Purfleet Brotherhood as if a sacred rite in the Telesterion of Eleusis, bringing to light a son with many names, none of which are ever revealed. To understand this linkage, certain details of the French play must be recalled and juxtaposed with corresponding elements of the Anglo-Irish novel.

In the Dumas-Maquet *Vampire*'s second act at Tormenar, during the scene of Juana's last supper, one traveler proclaims his simple, total and exclusive belief in the tangibly material, advancing, of all things, the wine in his

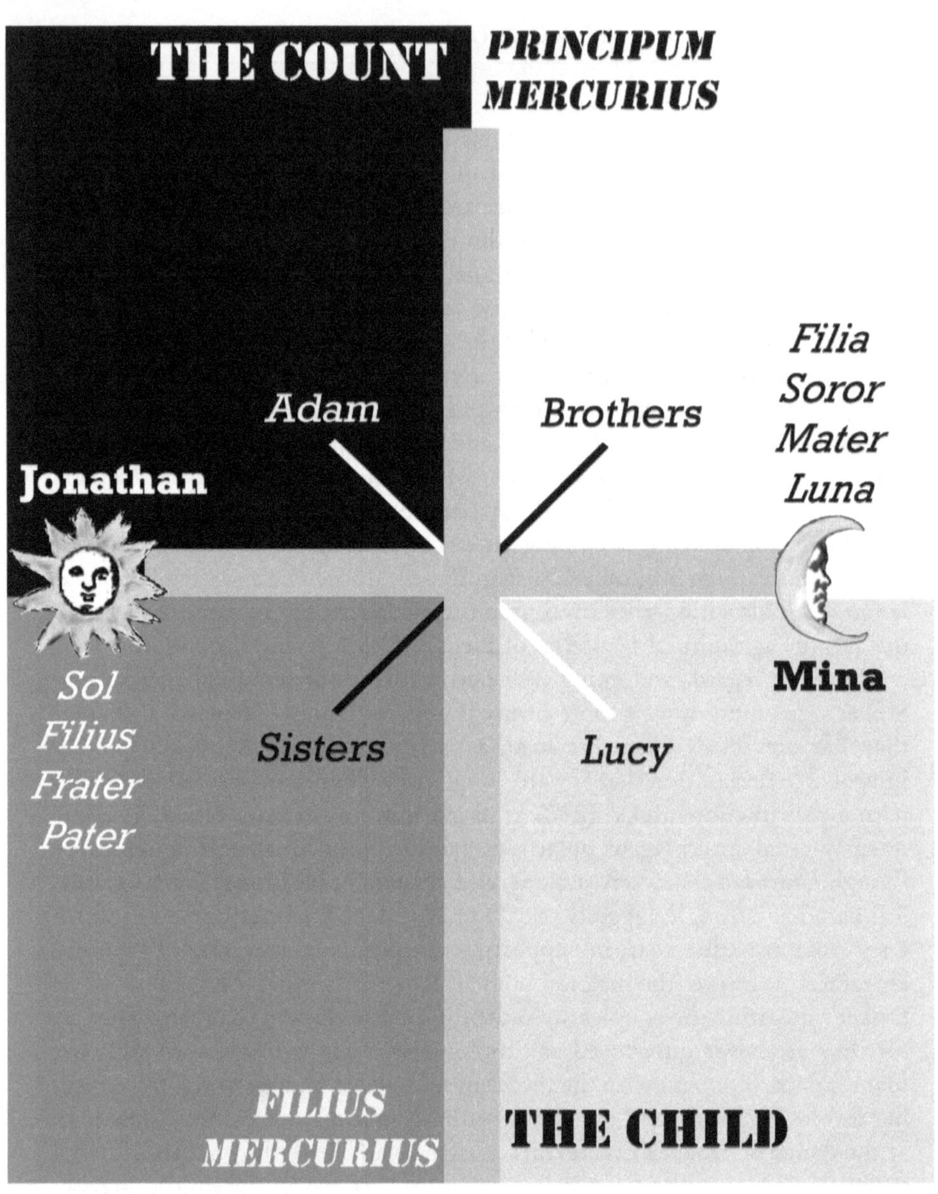

Quaternity based on schematic from Jung (The Personification of the Opposites) and alchemic illustrations. © Rarignac

glass as exemplar of something monolithically and invariably concrete. The watery weakness of this particular example, previously highlighted by repartee concerning the Miracle at Cana, is again pointed out when Lazarus rapidly drains three glasses of wine in succession. Lazarus, familiar with his former employer's wine, cannot believe the vintage he has tasted to be Rozo's, judging it transformed and infinitely improved. His being offered three glasses, a ploy to loosen his tongue on the part of the travelers, is prefatory to his recounting a series of ghost stories about Tormenar. According to Lazarus, the Tormenar family was cursed and subject to a phenomenon of triple deaths. Dumas will offer, in triple triads, an ennead of victims, comprised of Lazarus's tales of two generations of ill-fated brothers of Tormenar, three in each generation (Luis transgenerationally expiating the sins of the instigator of the family curse in his stead), and the *mise-en-scène* of the deaths of three sisters of Tiffauges — vessels filled with blood as *anima*— who are sacrificed to Ruthven.

Alluding to an exchange he had with Charles Nodier that is recounted in *Mes Mémoires* (553), Dumas has Gilbert contest the materialist's thesis through an invocation of the material's microcosm as he discovered it revealed in the eyepiece of a microscope. The innovation of the compound lens made the mid–19th century microscope a powerful and revelatory scientific tool that provided proof of the existence of beings invisible to the naked eye. Dumas has the empirical and invisible lead directly to the spiritual and immaterial, however, for the travelers enthusiastically question Gilbert on his professed belief in supernatural beings. Gilbert brightly explains how every Britton peasant has an elfin assistant to help with the chores, particularly with shoeing horses. He further notes that as an infant he had had a noble water-nixie as a nurse and counselor, even describing her dance and listing the co-residents of the tapestry she inhabited. Hardly gratuitous dialogue, Dumas is beginning to prepare his climax. A few scenes later, Lazarus recounts how, en route to Tiffauges from Nantes, Gilbert's horse threw four shoes at once. Clearly this unlikely occurrence has been orchestrated with the complicity of the prescient elves of Clisson as a meaningful coincidence intended to lead us to Mélusine, the Tapestry Room, and an exercise in alchemy.

In alchemy, which — seeing each existent thing as both itself and a sign of itself within a coextensive unity that permeates a signifying cosmos — functions as much through metaphor, metonymy and symbol as through substantive elemental interaction, the animal body exemplifies the world in microcosm. The complex of the living being, Gilbert's horse, is understood as composed of Empedocles's four elements (air, earth, fire, and water) plus the ethereal life-force. The horse's living-and-signifying four limbs (like the four limbs of the human being) represent the four codependent essential material elements. The fifth, the *quinta essentia*, ethereal quintessence or anima, resides symbolically in what's left — head, trunk, genitalia — but most particularly in the retort of the heart, where the immaterial solar essence, said to burn with greater intensity than the hottest burning coal, is circulated throughout the body via the blood. The horse losing its shoes metaphorically separates out the four elements and isolates the quintessence.

Gilbert's horse also functions as a powerful symbol of the finite limitations of humanity's animal nature. The beast forces Gilbert to stop before reaching Tiffauges, his intended destination. With the loss of the horseshoes, he has been implicated in an alchemistic revelation concerning Ruthven, Hélène, and himself that is already in the midst of execution. As Lazarus recounts to Hélène at Tiffauges the ordeal he underwent in the defile between two hills, Gilbert is being put through his own, similar trial. Upon his unshod steed, he encounters the masked Ruthven and a disguised love interest in the desolate, sylvan gorge between two eminences. The scene is triply reminiscent of Aubrey's misadventures in Polidori's *Vampyre*: first, in the horse whose animal nature forces the solar spiritual hero to stop; second, in the "ambuscade" occurring in the narrow "defile" that must necessarily be traversed; and third, in the unexpected encounter with a woman. In Polidori's mise-en-scène, Aubrey encountered his conductress Ianthe at the humble Telesterion where her material life was being sacrificed. With Dumas, the feminine figure is discovered to be the Ghoul, who, functioning more like a guardian angel than a stalking predator, is present to preserve the solar hero from saturnine Ruthven's assassination attempt. Ziska not only urges Gilbert to flee Ruthven, but later finds a way to instruct him to sleep in the Tapestry Room, where the transformation engaged with the ill-shod horse will continue towards its conclusion through the concourse of the tapestry's fairy forms. She will further her role as conductress by preparing Hélène to receive a revelation.

In the Tapestry Room, Mélusine is presented as being the familiar spirit of Gilles, *le maréchal de* Rais; the inhabitants of the Gothic tapestry provide the elements of his alchemistic undertakings. In the two knights who assist the ancient baron, Dumas undoubtedly seeks to personify the alchemist Antonio Francisco Prelati, and Rais' right-hand man and betrayer, Étienne Corriault. Mélusine states her intention to rekindle yesterday's fires through her quadrille. "This fire, [Paracelsus] says, contains nothing more of the 'Salamandrine Essence or Melusinian Ares,' but is rather a '*retorta distillatio* from the midst of the centre, beyond all coal fire'" (Jung 13: 138), a divine fire imbued with the golden solar nature of the anima. The tapestry chamber itself forms the alchemist's crucible, the "philosophical egg" that is divided and subdivided in all its dimensions by the sign of the cross, in order to be rejoined as *Unus mundus*. This scene seems designed to establish the proof of the success of Gilles de Rais' magnum opus. Orphan siblings Gilbert and Hélène represent the fruit of Rais' chemical wedding of four centuries previous. Through them, Ruthven shall renew himself.

In Dumas' alchemy subtext, Lazarus, recruited from the Bible for his knowledge of death and life, suffering and glory, constitutes and occupies the fiction's middle ground, present to facilitate and enable the protagonists' movements from higher position to lower, lower position to higher, as they transform in their turn. A celebrated dictum of *The Emerald Tablet of Hermes Trismegistus* teaches that which is above is like that which is below; though it fails to explain that what is below is what is above but is inverted and reversed, even should that be the case. Heraclitus, propounding a corollary axiom, insists that the path up and the path down is one and the same. For Dumas, that path is Lazarus. Lazarus takes Ruthven's place at the supper at Tormenar; informs Hélène of her spouse's inhuman nature; opens the door to Gilbert when he rises from the mysterious place in Tiffauges's depths in which Ruthven had confined him; pulls Ruthven as *Rex marinus* out of the Black Sea's depths; takes Gilbert's sword to the cleric for its sanctification leading to the black king's death, surely a prerequisite to his rebirth in a purified state. In serving Gilbert, Lazarus serves Ruthven, and vice versa.

Alchemist Michael Maier views Ruthven's *Rex marinus* as the king fallen from on high "into the darkest depths of matter where he awaits deliverance. But no one will plunge into these depths in order, by his own transformation in the darkness and by the torments of fire, to rescue his king" (Jung 13: 146). Paracelsus's disciple Gerhard Dorn is recalled for theorizing that God requires saving by man, who finds his own salvation through the undertaking. In a near approximation of a Buddhist way of discovery, alchemy's esoteric view is that the king—that is, the divine—can be redeemed through transformation and purification and that purification presumes as its prerequisite condition corruption. This understanding contrasts with the orthodox Christian view and particularly the Cathari view of the satanic black king, *Rex mundi*, as one given over to the material and mired in the evil of his own stony heart. Neither alchemistic nor Cathari, Lazarus's intent in saving Ruthven falls fully within the limits of Christian orthodoxy. Indeed, Lazarus pursues a faithfully Catholic doctrine: He was seeking to overcome his cowardly nature, to perform a good and heroic deed, and to gain favor with heaven, thinking his action will enable him to redeem some of his sins—"*Racheter quelques pêchés*" (521) are his precise words.

It was noted that while Montague Summers approved of Mélusine because of the position Paracelsus attributed to her, he could not envisage Dumas' reason for inserting the Ghoul into plot. As mentioned earlier, Mélusine and the Ghoul appear to be at the very least closely allied beings, if not avatars, of the same force. Yet an additional need for Ziska seems likely in play: She was necessary to balance the masculine and feminine aspects of the supernatural to accommodate the Dumas explicit alchemy subplot. In *Le Journal des Débats* of 7–8 July 1819, Nodier, in one of his earlier critical texts on the Vampire antihero, predicts that the Vampire's deadly love would haunt the fantasies of womankind. Nodier, an expert on Galland's *Mille et Une*

Nuits, also insists that the Vampire is a transformation of the Mesopotamian Ghoul, a notion that Dumas asserts as fact in Gilbert's "last supper" dialogue. Therefore, to call on the feminine Ghoul to complement and counterbalance masculine Ruthven seems not merely natural but obligatory; to amalgamate her with Mélusine makes even more sense.

Dumas ends his drama with the prospective wedding of Gilles and Antonia assured and blessed by celestial sister spirits. By the time the curtain falls on Circassia, Ruthven, seemingly true-dead at last, has made his final appearance of the 19th century. Yet even as Nodier's *Lord Rutwen* inspired Planché's *Bride of the Isle*, Dumas' *Vampire*, traveling incognito as *The Phantom*, quickly made its way across the channel.

Dionysius Boucicault, proponent-in-chief of the "sensation" melodrama that enthralled the English-speaking world of the mid–Victorian period, Dublin-born-and-bred son of a Frenchman, spent several years of economic exile from his London theatrical base at Paris's Porte Saint-Martin Theatre, out of the reach of his creditors. There he met his composer-collaborator, Robert Stoepel. In the early 1850s these two adapted the works of Sardou, Delavigne, and other French playwrights into English, their output including adaptations of Dumas' *Pauline*, *The Corsican Brothers* and *The Vampire*. The French dramas were sufficiently lucrative to afford Boucicault return fare to England. As Planché had once served Samuel Arnold and the English Opera House, Boucicault would serve Charles Kean and his Princess Theatre, becoming house playwright and plying his trade by liberally borrowing from the French melodramatic stage. Of the numerous plots Boucicault imported into a lively English vernacular, nearly all brought Kean success, but when, in 1853, Boucicault handed him *The Phantom*, Kean thought the part of the Vampire beneath his talents or too sharply at odds with his image as an actor. Nonetheless The Princess put on the play—Boucicault taking on the role himself in what is generally, if erroneously, credited as his acting début. The play, which fared poorly, is better remembered for terminating Boucicault's association with Kean and inaugurating Boucicault's influential American career: Boucicault ran off to New York and eloped with Kean's ward, the 19-year-old Agnes Robertson, who had played opposite him as the Vampire's victim.

Kean, a world-touring actor-theater manager celebrated for lavish, meticulously-detailed productions of Shakespearean tragedy thoroughly anticipated the theatrical enterprise of Henry Irving. Kean's death from exhaustion coincided magically with Irving's rise to celebrity in his breakthrough role in *The Bells*. Shortly thereafter, Kean protégée Ellen Terry launched a Kean-like theatrical endeavor, leasing the Lyceum Theatre, formerly the English Opera House, and taking Henry Irving as her creative partner. Irving enticed solicitor

Abraham Stoker to quit his secure government job at Dublin Castle and to join him in London as the Lyceum business manager. Stoker stepped into Kean's organizational shoes as Irving donned his Thespian mantle; Terry, Irving, and Stoker, forming the Lyceum's "unholy trinity," dominated the London theatrical world of the late-19th century. Stoker knew the plays Boucicault adapted for Kean, as Townsend Walsh's biography of Boucicault makes clear: "In after years, Henry Irving, at the instigation of Boucicault, took the role of Louis XI and played it, in Boucicault's opinion, with much more force than Kean; while in *The Corsican Brothers* Kean excelled Irving in the depth of his intensity. But it was all inspired by the French" (Walsh 43). Irving and Kean shared in their contempt for the Vampire.

In adapting Dumas' *Le Vampire* Boucicault consciously sought to emulate Planché, whose adaptation of Nodier's melodrama was still playing to appreciative audiences in the provinces, and, as Planché noted, continuously generating revenue. Boucicault energetically set to work to condense Dumas and Maquet's five-act monument by combining the scenes from Tormenar, Tiffauges, and Circassia and transferring them to Raby Castle, Wales. He discarded Ruthven, putting in his place Sir Alan Raby, a fratricidal Cromwellian Puritan; replaced Juana with a sunny English fiancée named Lucy; and, excising Mélusine, introduced Dr. Rees, a medical doctor whose hobby is research into alchemy. Boucicault's two-act play marries Dumas's Spanish scenes to Planché's last act with the Ruthven-Hélène dialogue of Hélène's final scene incorporated. The play emphasizes Dumas' alchemistic core by making a John Dee tome instead of a sanctified sword the instrument of denouement and the Vampire's destruction. Two lines reveal something of Boucicault's perception of Dumas' alchemy subtext: Davy, a cowardly synthesis of Lazarus and Botaro, exclaims "Oh, mysterious matrimony—as the dying philosopher said, 'Now for the great secret!'" (Act 2, 2) whereas "Yonder is the bridal chamber" (Act 2, 4) is reserved for alchemist Dr. Rees to announce, as he prepares to enter it to interrupt the great dark secret's unveiling.

The fruit of alchemy, which enjoyed a leaden golden age in post–Renaissance Europe, survives primarily as a collection of allegorical texts and iconological woodcuts that purportedly form a repository of great, powerful, and ancient secrets. It is current to say these mysteries are of a spiritual and philosophical nature, but for centuries alchemists were equally focused on the substantial, elemental, and medical—the material and the spiritual being so confounded and interrelated in the alchemists' vision as to be initially indistinguishable. This is, in fact, the transformative heart of the alchemist's project: division and conjunction. The unitary becomes a duality that requires a third to bind them; the trinity yields to the quaternity, and so on, reaching to the ogdoadic through division by the three-dimensional cross before subdividing elements reunify in order to become one renewed, indivisibly whole entity, *Unus mundus*. As things unfold and reunite in inviolable proportions, accordance with Pythagorean principles, and eternal geometric rules — whose quantifiable ratios are made manifest at every level of our heuristic cosmos — alchemy perfectly anticipates the genius of baroque thought and aesthetics. Its grandeur is in its detail; its detail is the mirror of its grandiosity, all with a concentration on ratio as rationality.

Even when anonymous or pseudonymous, these hermetic texts' authors unfailingly represent themselves as devout students of nature humbly seeking to serve God by completing or perfecting His work. The flowering of alchemy concurrent to the Reformation undoubtedly required the indication of theological orthodoxy in Catholic countries; while a conspicuously pious stance may have been adopted to inoculate against the charges of witchcraft and heresy that were leveled against a certain number of alchemists, most writers — not a few of whom were ordained priests — are convincingly devout, a religious faith underlying the enterprise. Although the Platonic component of the alchemists' theoretical teachings and their search to transmute the sacred self retain the interest of contemporary New Age seekers, the elemental recipes the alchemists prescribe seem derisively at odds with current scientific knowledge. Paradoxically, it was precisely as scientific methods of inquiry and production became fundamental to society's economic base that these tracts became more widely known, due, in no small part, to the late-Victorian theosophical spirit. Alchemy's re-evaluation began, however, in France.

The brilliant French chemist Marcellin Berthelot brought the more mystical origins of his discipline to light in the mid–1880s, publishing *Les Origines de l'alchimie* (1885), *Introduction à l'étude de la chimie des anciens et du moyen âge* (1889), as well as translating ancient Greek, Syriac and Arabic treatises on alchemy and chemistry (*Collection des anciens alchimistes grecs*, 1887–1888, and *La Chimie au moyen âge*, 1893). Arthur Edward Waite, using Berthelot's material and translating treatises lodged in British libraries, made a wide variety of alchemistic works available in English across the 1890s. Nearly simultaneous to the *Book of Enoch*'s appearance, Waite brought out two anthologies, the *Collectanea Chemica* (1893), the *Hermetic Museum* (1893); the *Turba Philosophorum* (1896) followed; he also translated Paracelsus from German, beginning with *The Hermetic and Alchemical Writings of Paracelsus* (1894). An early member of the Hermetical Order of the Golden Dawn, eventual factional leader and founder of other mystical orders, Waite worked closely with his contemporaries, translating into English Eliphas Lévi's *Dogme et rituel de la Haute Magie* and other works which were directly influential upon the Golden Dawn and its successors.

Popularly recalled for the pursuit of transmuting lead into gold and for counting among their number colorful charlatans, frauds, and scoundrels, European alchemists of the early modern period are seen as a driven and troubled lot, compulsively and frantically searching out an inexistent grail. The Faustian alchemist survives as modernity's mad scientist, a cultural trope still very much alive in the contemporary imagination, though as a rather clownish, degraded figure. In the 19th century the alchemist was a more troubling and riven character, a mortal trespasser into the divine reservation — Gilbert emerging haggard and wild-eyed from the Tapestry Room is as one affected by alchemy. Yet the studious alchemists were also placid Platonic heirs to Pico della Mirandola, Marsilio Ficino, and the Florentine Academy, and, as Berthelot realized, the substantive and practical forerunners to modern inorganic chemistry, physics, and industrial manufacturing processes.

Paradoxically perhaps, brilliant minds pursuing alchemical thought brought about the rise of scientific materialism. Alchemists, peering into the inner-workings of the universe, leveraging observation with the fulcrum of rationality, exposing truths parabolically by means of analogy, intuited notions of the atomic, the molecular, and of the recombinant properties of the elements, and conceived of a reflexive and fractal universe operating at macrocosmic and microcosmic levels. Their philosopher's stone is, as its name indicates, necessarily an abstraction, yet, in a world defined by Cartesian dualism, alchemistic reasoning maintained that operations that can be performed on the substantive can be carried out on the spiritual and vice versa. The stone, elixir, panacea, arcanum, and solvent are all expressions of a quest for the universal principle of being, begottenness, some more sacred unified field theory that offers insight into the divine through the material. Commenting on its multiple appellations Petrus Bonus Lombardus of Ferrara remarks, "The consequence of this great multiplicity of names is that our stone has no proper name of its own" (150); this is true not only of their stone but of all aspects of their entire enterprise.

Despite inherently fluid notions, deliberate efforts to occult meaning, and constant conceptual and lexical differences that separate alchemists one from another, certain general principles do emerge that are consistently founded on ideas of transformational separation and reunion. Alchemy's great notion weds material synthesis and spiritual transportation, the purification and subsequent enrichment of matter and soul, bringing both closer to a luminous essence and astral light: gold, God, and the good. Bringing binary alchemy in line with the Christian trinity, the matter-soul duality has been bound together by a third, mediating mind-force, thought (spirit), since Paracelsus. The separation of the material into its four constituent elements, two dyadic pairs binding male to female, prepares their recombination, through the "art," into the magical prime matter. Four shared qualities —

moistness, dryness, heat and coldness — characterize these elements to different extents. Four colors — black (*nigredo* or *putrefactio*), white (*albedo*), yellow (*citrinitas*), and red (*rubedo*) — shape or reveal the state of inorganic transformation; which also relate to organic Hippocratic humors. Yielding to the trinitarian ideal, in many post–Paracelsus accounts the processes of yellowing and reddening are combined into a syzygy, thereby reducing a quaternity to a trinity.

The "great work," or *magnum opus*, entails the successful transmutation of base earthly matter into the spiritual structural element from which all things can be built, commonly referred to as "the stone"; analogically this is equivalent to the attainment of a transporting self-knowledge that places the alchemist within the sphere of the divine. Step-by-step processes — seven, ten or 12 depending on the accounting — were enumerated in various grimoires, the number of steps undoubtedly reflecting mystical and numerological considerations. Seven steps illuminate the fact that the seven heavenly bodies of the classical sky — Mercury, Saturn, Jupiter, Luna, Venus, Mars, and Sol — intervene in a process that seeks to join heaven and earth. As the whole snake-enwrapped spherical or ovoid Orphic "egg" is divided into quadrants by the serpent-killing sign of the cross, the steps were grouped into the four-phased, color-coded process that met with general agreement.

The first phase consists of corruption and degradation through fire, decay, and the agencies of Mercury and Saturn. The second, said to be a lunar process of purification, engages Jupiter, Luna, and Venus, and results in a baptismal action. During the operations of burning, charring, extracting, humidification, and distillation, etc., various substances are produced and believed to contain the *sacrae particulae*, the microcosmic essence of *prima materia*. The third phase, solar and masculine in its conjunctive force, centers on hieros gamos and requires the intervention of Mars and Sol. This transportation of the spiritual self entails the destruction of older identities; the former man and former woman, orphaned and sibling or related through blood, must be sacrificed individually and reborn collectively to give life to the new syzygy. The third phase's sacred union of masculine and feminine in *coniunctio oppositorium* yields, through the spilling of blood, the fourth, final phase's productive result: *Mercurius philosophorum*, the prime matter that marks the great work's accomplishment. But *Mercurius philosophorum* is not merely a substance, it is also an expression of an enigmatic being, a dual, living-and-dead force that is killed to be reborn and also goes by the name of Mercurius.

Morpheus-like Mercurius accommodates serpentine, shape-shifting beings such as Mélusine, but stands as a distinct though double personality. Although Mercurius represents the universal Solvent, Arcana, life-force and soul, he is seen as dark and filthy without, associated with excrement and everything repulsive to human senses, yet bearing within an unseen shining radiance. Masculine without, feminine within, requiring purification and resolution, Mercurius exists as alchemy's object, the *magnum opus* being conceived to transform saturnine, soul-killing, material, grandfatherly-though-savage Mercurius *senex*, into the hermetic, glorious, spiritual infant Mercurius *filius macrocosmi*; that is, to transmute lead into gold. This transmutation is more profoundly an act of releasing Mercurius's luminous nature, of liberating the divine from the most basely material. This is achieved through the above-outlined operations whose full sequence is termed the Chemical Wedding, and during which *coniunctio oppositorium*, the joining of opposites, is the principal operation, allowing the syzygy to find its unified expression in *filius*. The infant born through the syzygy and old Mercurius's death is Mercurius inverted and turned inside out.

Christian Rosenkreutz's allegorical account of a regal "*Chymical Wedding*," celebrated over a seven-day period of revelation and transformation, makes clear the linkage between the wedding, the Mosaic account of creation, the Christian account of sacramental Transubstantiation and Resurrection, and alchemistic transmutation. As *Genesis* represents God creatively separating one existential element from another, deconstructive-reconstructive alchemy seeks to tease the material apart, isolating component elements in order to fuse them anew into the magical original matter: the primordial chaos, that formless plasmatic absence of stuff Nodier terms *le néant*, conceptualized as "the Stone," *lapis philosophorum*.

While the alchemists' cryptic texts portray pious Christians striving to perfect the work of God, they simultaneously perpetuate, through the planets of the classical sky, the ancient gods as they reside in myth and matter, their proclivities and properties, ancient relationships and powers, bringing antique arcane knowledge to bear to inform a Christian-influenced view of resurrection. Petrus Bonus declares in *The New Pearl of Great Price*,

> our Stone is cast out into the streets, raised aloft to the clouds, dwells in the air, is nourished in the river, sleeps upon the summits of mountains; its mother is a virgin, its father knows no woman. These ancient Sages also knew that God must become man, because on the last day of our Magistery that which generates, and that which is generated, become absolutely one; then the old man and the child, the father and the son, are indistinguishably united. Hence they concluded that the Creator must also become one with the creature; moreover, they knew that man was, alone of all created beings, made in the image of God [126].

This is what comes to pass at God's seat on Judgment Day.

Dracula's unmistakeable and relentless use of Christian symbols cannot and does not account for the every detail of Stoker's celestial drama, so filled with heavenly personae whose desperate and daring deeds reverberate at diverse discursive levels. Stoker's portrait of Jonathan, "so full of volcanic energy" (202) as Apollonian Sol, and Mina, "pearl among women" (194) as Luna, have been amply commented, but Lucy, though previously characterized as luminous or a western light, is, in her own way, very much presented as an independent heavenly body as well, and, as the Professor's hammer forcefully attests, she is not alone in this.

Lucy rules over Hillingham as Venus in all her complexities, being at once Venus *Celeste* and Venus *vulgare*. Lucy, hair shining like copper, embodies Venus's paradox: virginal and pure, yet sensuous and earthy. Under the Count's influence, her "sweetness was turned to adamantine, heartless cruelty, and the purity to voluptuous wantonness" (187), her sought-after embrace became *mors osculi*— the kiss of death — and her "whole carnal and unspiritual appearance, seeming like a devilish mockery of Lucy's sweet purity" (190) confounded those who loved her. Ironic Quincey, the adamant Texan, "his hand ... as firm as a piece of steel" (285), with his Winchesters and fearsome Bowie knife, is figured as Mars, innately ready to lead the battle. "Quincey Morris had always been the one to arrange the plan of action.... With a swift glance round the room, he at once laid out a plan of attack, and, without speaking a word, with a gesture, placed us each in position" (266). Stoker originally considered the name Brutus Marix (Rosenbach #1 *Notes* 7) for Quincey, "Marix" undoubtedly couching a divine and planetary reference.

Further supporting the template of an alchemical quadrille, the infant whom they will call "Quincey," the Mercurius *filius* of the story, is born not only on the anniversary of Quincey Morris's death but, ambiguously, that of the Count's as well. The Count's "malignant and saturnine" (29) nature troubles the world of the novel and spreads ambiguity with his mists and fogs. That Stoker indeed attributes the adjective *saturnine* to the Count as one of his primary qualities colors the Vampire's identity and, indirectly, helps to explicate the hammer-wielding Professor, seen as Thor-like in his Nordic ways, as he confronts and counters the Count. If the latter is the grim-reaper and castrating god Saturn, then the former is his thundering offspring and nemesis Jupiter (Zeus), the two being sufficiently alike to make the Professor-as-Jupiter the usurping, uncorrupted son of Saturn. As Saturn and Jupiter maintain their opposing roles, the constantly shifting equilibrium between them must be meticulously maintained. The Count, though saturnine, is not purely saturnian; while he leads to a golden age, he only does so indirectly and through a transformative process.

As the Un-dead Dead personification of paradox, the Count is necessarily the most difficult personality to fathom, for he is what he seems and its opposite. He has been accorded a dual and contradictory nature, the engaging, kingly entity waiting at the threshold with an antique lamp, and the cruel, lifeless "Thing — not even beast" (202) — living and thriving in absolute filth and decay. Like Jonathan's coachman, the grizzled, lamp-carrying old man dwelling atop the mountain's peak who disappears with the coming of the dawn is quickly discovered to be, if not what he seems, something more if less. He is both saturnine — gloomy, dark, fearsome, and static — and mercurial — shrewd, eloquent, swift, thievish, changeable. As Jonathan recognizes, "For a man who ... did not evidently do much in the way of business, his knowledge and acumen were wonderful" (37). Saturn, Kronos in his Greek form — a sort of parricide and paragon of agricultural gods — is associated with the soft metal lead and with giving birth to Time, traits Stoker acknowledges through the phrase "The minutes seemed to pass with leaden feet" (261). Given the scythe as his attribute, Saturn first uses it to castrate his father. He is, in turn, usurped by his own thundering son, Zeus, child born to himself and his mother, the Earth. Mercury, Hermes to the Greek, is an intermediary and psychopomp, whose wings, some say, facilitate the communication of Morpheus's dreams to those who sleep. Son of Zeus, Rome's Jupiter, he maintains frontiers and boundaries; master of ruse, associated with wealth, commerce, synonymous with quicksilver (liquid metal), he mediates the eternal. Like Persephone and Lazarus, Hermes frequents both the world living people inhabit and the Hadean underworld.

Taken as an ensemble these personalities — Sol, Luna, Venus, Mars, Mercury, Saturn and Jupiter — render an accounting of the classical heavens. They can be seen as individual entities that function as a unified whole, each influencing as they are influenced, reciprocally engaging themselves, the world of men, and the divine in their constant joining of hands. Theirs is a grandiose cosmic drama that — while concluding in Christian triumph and an engagement with a divinity beyond our mortal realm — plays upon a great store of mythologies, rites, and practices.

Bram Stoker's Notes for "Dracula" fix *Dracula*'s genesis in the simple idea of placing a young man and an old man (Rosenbach #35, 17) in a triangular relationship with girls, the youth — tentatively named William Young — becoming Jonathan Harker, and the old man, the Count. Yet when first confronted by the feminine, the Count, transforming Nodier's "She is mine," possessively claims *Jonathan*, not the girls, as his own. "The man belongs to me" (43), he insists with such reverberating ferocity that it seems as if he were defending some portion of himself, indeed his very virility. Jonathan forces the Count to bring to recollection that, once, he too could love. The simplicity of the scenario's triangular concept, the chronologically organized plot, the emphasis on the geometric and the mystical serve to support the embroidery of an allegoric interpretation modeled after Hermetic texts like Rosenkreutz's

Dracula's celestial clockwork. Clockwise from far left, Jonathan/Sol, Lucy/Venus, the Count/Saturn-Kronus, Quincey/Mars, Mina/Luna, the infant called Quincey /Mercury. Centered along the axis aligning Sol and Luna, Saturn and Mercury is Mittel Land, Earth, where Renfield is confined; above him, and countering Saturn, orbits the professor/Jupiter-Thor. © Rarignac, with public domain images from NASA and the photographic image of night sky of 1886 by an anonymous astronomer.

"*Chymical Wedding.*" In such a scheme, Young Man, *Sol*, and Old Man, *Sol niger*, become, in part, linked, not only through girls, but, like Aubrey and Ruthven, as quasi-identical-since-oppositional figures whose discrepancies flow from the fact that they exist at different phases of a transformational process. *Sol niger*, great dark orb of the sky that opposes the sun, is indeed saturnine and embodied in the planet Saturn, yet, as will be seen, in a unique and complicated way, he conceals another identity. As plot introduces more characters, the geometry of the initial dynamic, while becoming more complex, is reinforced.

Saturn and Mercury join as alchemy's Mercurius, an amalgamating, paradox-binding, enigmatic figure understandably referred to as "Duplex." Mercurius is at once Saturn and, potentially, Saturn's grandson, Mercury. Jupiter, as son and usurper of the first, father of the second, mediates their relationship. For Mercurius *senex* to become Mercurius *filius* requires various ritual acts of fertilization and the participation of surrogates to bind the paradoxical elements: *coniunctio oppositorium*. Alone, Mercurius is sterile.

Dracula dramatizes the ritual sequence of chemical wedding and its *coniunctio oppositorium* through plot. The orphans King Sol and Queen Luna, Jonathan and Mina respectively, are joined as a syzygy through the aggressive conduit of saturnine Mercurius, the Count. This *ménage-à-trois* projects added dimension onto Stoker's phrase "I needn't tell you of number three, need I?" (61). Freshly orphaned, wandering Venus, the brightest light among the stars of the night, and war-like Mars, with his metallic armaments, die to facilitate the ecliptic royal union of Sun and Moon — Sol being transformed and purified through Venus's blood-soul as Luna is through Mars's. Sol and Luna, Venus and Mars: two dyads binding male to female that permit the chemical wedding. The royal mating produces Mercurius *filius*, the cosmic son, who, despite his "his great multiplicity of names," is called by the name of a dead man. This synopsis of the *Chymical Wedding* distils Stoker's plot to its quintessence.

Like the Mysteries of Eleusis, the chemical wedding, unfolding over time, is organised into "lesser" and "greater" works — works feminine and masculine, white and red, circular and square. The lesser includes the phases *nigredo*, corruption and mortification, and *albedo*, the cleansing, baptismal whitening that follows. The greater is comprised of *citrinitas*— entailing the separation of the Sol/Luna syzygy, the sacrifice of the subsidiary spiritual syzygy of Venus and Mars, whose blood permits *illuminatio*, and the Sol/Luna syzygy's reunification, ecliptic merging, and the fertilization of the seed — and *rubedo*, comprising the death of Mercurius *senex* at the hand of Sol and the production of the sacred offspring Mercurius *filius macrocosmi*. It is unclear what correspondence if any these operations may have with Stoker's initial four-book compositional structure, but they mirror plot to a remarkable degree.

Nigredo

This phase begins with the polluting, chthonic dragon, embodied in the Count. The Little Dragon, Dracula, will exert its influence over all actors yet to be introduced.

After a lengthy separation, a degrading initiatory ordeal on Jonathan's part, and a trial of faith on Mina's, word of Jonathan's existence finally reaches Mina at Whitby. Fate has intervened through the appropriately named Sister Agatha, who summons Mina to her intended's side. Mr. Hawkins, who had initially dispatched Jonathan to Transylvania, speeds Mina towards Budapest, urging her to marry Jonathan immediately upon reaching him. Sol, still suffering and diminished, requires Luna to exhibit greater strength in compensation for his weakened condition. Sol is married while reclining as an invalid, "propped up with pillows" (100), Luna taking "his poor weak hands" (101) as her own. Thus a long-intended marriage occurs as an impromptu rite in an alien environment.

Hawkins, Jonathan's "second father" (49), assumes the role of the active agent in this phase. When the newlyweds return to Exeter, he tells them: "I know you both from children, and have, with love and pride, seen you grow up. Now I want you to make your home here with me" (140). This suggests that orphans Sol and Luna were brought up under some form of Hawkins' tutelage, spending their youths together in a brother-sister relationship, and it brings the Harkers into conformity with the classic situation of the sacred wedding, previously encountered with Aubrey and sister, Gilbert and Hélène. Curiously, Hawkins, who claims to have "neither chick nor child" (140), lives in a rookery, its "chattering and gossiping" (140) fledglings reminding Mina of humans. When Hawkins dies, Mina has to admit that for her as for Jonathan it "really seems as though we had lost a father" (143). The dark bird, raven, eagle, hawk, is instrumental in *nigredo*.

Saturnine *Sol niger*, the Count, arrives in England long weeks before Jonathan, already having encountered Mina on the Crescent through Venus-like Lucy. Mina "daubed [her] feet in mud" (89), covering her skin with the black filth of the earth as she returned from seeing him. As Saturn, "the Aud Man" (74) or "old scytheman" (216), begins his harvest immediately upon his mid-summer's landfall.

Venus, wandering light of the night, corrupted by contact with Mercurius *senex*, dies shortly after the return of the royal couple to Exeter. Venus's blood illness, at first suspected to be caused by a safety-pin, instigates the taking of extraordinary medical and metaphysical measures. It is the unusual corruption of Venus that requires the Professor, Jupiter, to be present on the Western Isle, where he first resides in the Great Eastern Hotel (106). "A philosopher and a metaphysician" (106) "with a strongly humorous side" (113), and "so abnormally clever" (182), the metaphysical nature of his patient's condition informs his use of the sacred white Eucharist and the Cross as a shield, and sends him "off to the British Museum looking up some authorities on ancient medicine" (240). The death of Venus leads to the formation of a brotherhood of purity, and her body being placed in a "casing of lead" (176), *the* purely saturnine material. Death and burial of Lucy and those claimed by equinox terminate this phase.

Albedo

In the case of Hawkins, death transforms the dark bird of prey into a ghostly dove, an absent presence seen in "empty chairs" (155) and felt in the Exeter nest by his heirs returning from his interment. Before they can reach home, however, Jonathan believes he sees his nemesis in London. The mere sight of Mercurius causes him to turn ever more pale, distracted, and uncertain. This sighting marks the beginning of the successful process of purification—while earlier attempts had been made to purify and protect Lucy, they were thwarted and to no avail as, in Byron's phrase, it was not yet time. Indeed, the intermittent process of whitening continues until the snows fall on Judgment Day.

To release Venus from her complete corruption, to save Venus *Celeste* from Venus *vulgare*, the Professor, Jupiter, penetrates the saturnine casing—the veil of lead—that is her shroud with "a swift downward stab" (176). Arthur "did not know that there was a leaden coffin, or at any rate, had not thought of it. When he saw the rent in the lead, the blood rushed to his face for an instant, but as quickly fell away again, so that he remained of a ghastly whiteness" (185). The pure white Host, itself taking the form of the full moon, is frequently fragmented and atomized in order to serve as a magically potent *sacrae moleculae*, a kind of philosopher's stone, the most minute particle containing the whole of the sacred principle. Whiteness and the image of baptism complete the section.

The lesser works are recapitulated through a vision-fraught dream that Mina dreamt. "All was dark and silent, the black shadows thrown by the moonlight seeming full of mystery of their own" (226). She felt herself seized by "leaden lethargy" as her chamber was penetrated by a mist that became thick "like smoke" (227) and charged with "white energy" (227) that finally "concentrated into a sort of pillar of cloud" (227). "Things began to whirl" until "through it all came the scriptural words 'a pillar of cloud by day and of fire by night'" (227). "But the pillar was composed of both the day and night" (227). The perceived pillars, beyond Exodus, instruct on the nature of day and night. They are the feminine and masculine principles, Venus and Mars, and between them passes the harrowing narrow defile. The pillar of cloud also personifies Mina herself; the pillar of fire, Jonathan, Sol. In her dream, she watched with horrified fascination as "the fire divided, and seemed to shine on me through the fog like two red eyes, such as Lucy told me of in her momentary mental wandering when, on the cliff, the dying sunlight struck the windows of St Mary's Church the fire divided" in two, as if forming glowing eyes or, indeed, heavenly bodies; then "all became black darkness" (228). Like the pair Dumas formed from the eyes of Petra and Ziska, the two eyes of Mina's vision belong one each to Sol and Sol *niger*. *Nigredo* yields to *albedo*, however, for she soon remarks "A livid white face bending over me out of the mist" (228). Joining above and below, Jonathan notes that when he woke Mina, "for a few seconds she did not recognize me, but looked at me with a sort of blank terror, as one looks who has been waked out of a bad dream" (224); she momentarily found it impossible to distinguish between the whitened black of Sol *niger* and the golden light of Sol. The division of the masculine will be more fully articulated on a succeeding day's night with *coincidencia*, for after having requested Dr. Seward to make up some of the modern Morpheus, and having delivered herself to it, Mina comes to realize her error: "As sleep begins to flirt with me, a new fear comes: that I may have been foolish in thus depriving myself of the power of waking" (228). Having completed the lesser works, she has prepared the way for the greater, the hierogamous *coniunctio oppositorium*.

Citrinitas

In clever wordplay, Stoker asserts the blind permitted sight: "The moonlight was so bright that through the thick yellow blind the room was light enough to see" (246). What the saffron filter allows to be seen is a mystical, trinitarian union dominated by saturnine Mercurius as the self-devouring Ouroboros. His self-consumption is facilitated by looping through the crescent of lunar Madam Mina. Luna, bitten by the serpent, drinks her own blood passed through the filter of the circular, ring-forming serpent. Jonathan, once again supine on his bed during the marriage ceremony, now "flush-faced" (246) rather than pale, is a witless witness to his own *coniunctio oppositorium*; he has nonetheless been joined to the Count through his bride. Mina, whose "white nightdress was smeared with blood" while "a thin stream trickled down from the man's bare breast" (247), is aware but drained of volition by Morpheus. The blood begins moving the prime material towards *Rubedo*. This

Opposing hierophants contained in the Ouraboros-enveloping Above-Below Emblem—"*Le Grand Symbole de Salomon*"—of Eliphas Lévi's Ritual Magic. 1841.

inverted bridal chamber ceremony is central to Stoker's chemical wedding, for the chamber, crucible of the alchemistic operation, *is* the philosopher's egg that must be divided into eight, the cross dividing each of its three dimensions.

The rite initiated by one hierophant, the Count, changes significance and theologies at its midpoint by the intervention of another; the Professor enters brandishing the Holy Eucharist, proclaiming that "all chambers are the same to the doctor; and even were they not they are all as one to me tonight" (246). Indeed, all are as one — *Unus mundus*— that night. The triadic tumbles into the quaternate with the Professor's forming of the Sign of the Cross, and the subsequent division of the egg into four quadrants and four elements even as the quadrille of Mélusine had divided the moving world to reconstitute it transformed. But a second triangular relationship is also constituted. Each of the twin hierophants links the royal couple into a trinity. One from above, one from below. Their union forms the alchemical symbol that is identical to the interlinking Star of David, the Kabbalistic *Magen David*.

Like Lazarus in *Le Vampire*, Renfield enables those from above and below to move from one realm to another. Despite his birdlike spirit, provisionally unable to attain "Himmel" (118), he is confined to earth, meaning very much Earth herself. As one so confined, encaged, he is central, occupying the middle ground in which we all are held captive. Through his offices *Dracula*'s bridal chamber ceremony is conducted, Renfield not only admitting the Count, but also dispatching the Professor. Deprived of the aerial view Seward imagines, Renfield's perspective defines the Earth's central position of the pre–Copernican sky. The place where opposites, high and low, celestial and chthonic, masculine and feminine, active and passive, gold and silver, come together: Mittel Land. Beyond the symbolism of the Ragnarök, Mittel Land constitutes a space where things previously set apart come together once again.

When the Professor gains ritual primacy in the bridal chamber sacrament, he renews Jonathan for a second time: Jonathan "seemed dazed for a few seconds and then full consciousness seemed to burst upon him all at once" (248). Full consciousness is not only brought to Jonathan but, shortly thereafter, to Mina as well; they attain gnosis and can now actively seek resolution through the completion of the alchemistic process. Although their volition is essential, the act of communion that Mina was engaged in brings about transformations — immediate and eventual — of its own that progressively work to challenge the syzygy as they complete the rites of *coniunctio oppositorium*.

Astrology and alchemy associate the Moon with the brain and intellectual force; Mina becomes more man-like in her thinking after *coniunctio*, according to the Professor. Jonathan, on the other hand, becomes more rash, emotional, hysterical, his rational faculties being affected by his part in the ordeal of *coniunctio*; he is dismissively told to "hush." Through the Count, a 19th-century feminine soul becomes apparent in Jonathan as a 19th-century masculine soul is reflected within Mina; this is as it is dictated by the philosophers. The result, however, separates the couple anew — Mina is isolated from Jonathan due to her changed state, and is joined through mind and spirit, to the Count's dead body as he passes over the surface of the waters, even as God hovers above. It is now that volition is required to negotiate the final and most delicate phase of the wedding ceremonies.

Rubedo

Reddening begins concurrent to yellowing with the discovery of Renfield in "a glittering pool of blood" (241) and ends only on a Judgment Day marked by redness, from when "the red of the dawn began to fall through the snow-gloom" (318) to the moment of the miracle at which the "castle of Dracula now stood out against the red sky" (325). As the month-long ordeal unfolded, Mina, despite "the red blotch on [her] forehead" (280), "grew snowy white at times ... and red at others" (268). The ruddy dragon, entwining mercurial serpent, having long dwelt in the filth of the world, now gorged with blood, must be slain to permit the birth of the renewed, spiritually pure Mercurius. His cosmic counterweight, the Professor, cut by a gangrenous knife, was saved by Seward's sucking the venom out of the blood before it could reach the heart; in Mina's case the venom, absolutely immaterial, exists not in her blood, but in the absence of her blood — darkness, *le néant*, the soul-damning *nigredo* of the serpent replacing the world-creating soul-force, *anima mundi*, that was drawn from her. The exchange can only be reversed through the destruction of Mercurius *senex*.

In a kind of Sign of the Cross, the Count is doubly killed: "But, on the instant, came the sweep and flash of Jonathan's great knife. I shrieked as I saw it shear through the throat; whilst at the same moment Mr Morris's bowie knife plunged into the heart" (325). In his beheading, one hierophantic figure is reduced to dust, his corrupted body reduced to its prime matter. In Mars' delivering the fatal blow to the heart — that retort that circulates the precious anima — Luna's soul is restored as pure as 24 carat gold. Mina watched the ambuscade from "a wonderful spot ... with an entrance like a doorway between two boulders," a defile so narrow that the professor remarks, '"if the wolves do come I can meet them one by one"' (321). As Mina looked on, she saw that even as Quincey's right hand brought about the weighing of hearts in heaven, the Count's and her own, "with his left hand he was clutching at his side, and that the blood was spurting through his fingers" (324) on to the earth. In the piercing of the Adamic figure, celestial Mars, Morris's blood flows and spills from the altar onto the Earth, now one with the Count, rendering the Mittel Land fertile through sacrifice as the prelude to rebirth in the new Adam, founder of a new race in Christ.

As Venus saved Luna from fully going through the ordeal of material feminine corruption, Mars, who must be lanced as if "in the side of Him who died for man" (209), spares Sol from the sacrifice *coniunctio* requires of the material masculine figure in dying. Correspondingly, since alchemy believes the male has a feminine soul, and the female a masculine, and that both Man and Woman are supported by the twin pillars of fire and cloud, the sacrifice of Venus makes Sol's soul ready for *coniunctio* as the sacrifice of Mars prepares Luna's. Like Mrs. Westenra, Lucy and Quincey were destined to die. The lengthy attention to Quincey's proposal of marriage to Lucy now becomes justified, explicated, for through their deaths the two are eternally joined in double-harness in the manner of Juana and Luis. As with Melusine's quadrille, the changing of partners allows the joining of opposites and the binding of paradox. While both Sol Jonathan and Luna Mina lose some quantity of blood to Mercurius, the Vampire, Venus-Lucy and Mars-Quincey's sacrifice and the resulting alloy of copper and iron brings about the fertilization and transformation of Mercurius.

Much has been made of the symmetries that *Dracula* displays, of the importance attached to midnight and "the stroke of noon" (108), and of the fact that the narrative's chronological midpoint is marked by the Count's arrival in England. Although what happens on the tale's dark side, from November to May, remains obscure, it can be presumed to reflect the occurrences of the half-year of light in negative image. It seems safe to conclude that the mercurial infant called Quincey was conceived 183 days after the wreck of *The Demeter*, opposing the spiritual infant to the material entity birthed by The Mother, Demeter — Stoker thus illustrating *The Emerald Tablet*'s great maxim: That which is below corresponds to that which is above, and that which is above corresponds to that which is below, to accomplish the miracles of the One Entity. In the cycle of time, a cross has been formed, one axis running from St. George's Day to the antipodal moment of the death of Quincey and the Count, the perpendicular joining the date of *The Demeter*'s dereliction to that of Luna's insemination.

The events transpiring across the luminous half of the annual solar revolution have been seen as being arrayed like a peacock's tail spread in a fan-like semicircular form. Through the device of bilateral symmetry, the work issues an invitation to imagine its form further folded in two, one quadrant mirroring the other and revealing the four-fold's essence through *coniunctio*. In this way, putting the first last and the last first, the plot refigures so that, in reading it, the beginning sections inform the ending and the ending sections

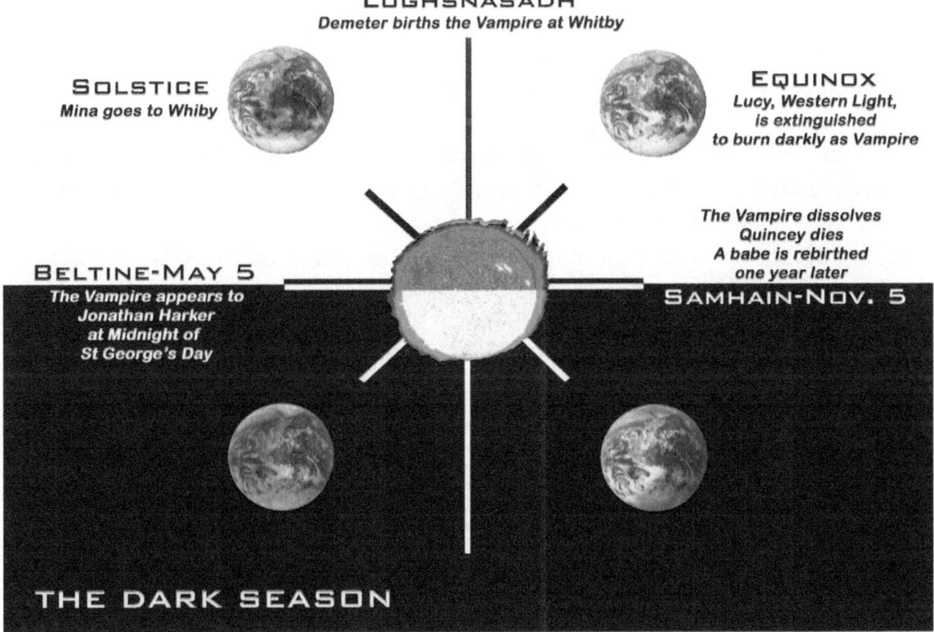

Phases of opposing personalities as a unified celestial body. © Rarignac

the beginning. This is a particularly appropriate operation, since *Dracula*'s cyclic theme is treated in a flat, linear manner; in spatial terms, the plot runs from East to West back to East without ever specifically marking a corresponding passage northward or southward.

In the beginning that is wedded to the ending, Jonathan and Mina would simultaneously be driven towards God's seat by their individual drivers; one would stop to be circled by wolves, the other by fire. The Count would be seen opening his door with an antique lamp in his hand immediately after he dies and turns into dust. Jonathan would escape from the castle as the Count both sets sail from London to return to the castle and departs the castle to go to London. Mina would go to Whitby to see Lucy as she is introduced to the Brotherhood formed in the aftermath of Lucy's death. Tides would be seen washing out even as they came flooding in again. This reflection of ends in beginnings based on the symmetric cross, this *coniunctio oppositorium*, formulation of paradoxes and rendering of "possible impossibilities" (Stoker 172) clarifies the story's essence. The mirror image provides no bauble of vanity but provokes more intently pious humility—it awakens. As Jung remarks:

"One finds in Christian symbolism the same 'circular' Gnostic thinking as in alchemy. In both the sacrificer is the sacrificed, and the sword that kills is the same as that which is killed" (13, 84).

The role of simple gold in *Dracula*, weighed in the scale of Themis, was found to be corrupting; it is dust that matters. The gold that is so important to Stoker is the luminous quality of being that unites the human and the divine: the good. *Coniunctio oppositorium* is designed to bind paradox in an act of purification of cathartic essence. The purpose of this alchemy is purely sacred, the awakening to full consciousness.

Stoker concludes the novel with the appearance of an undated "Note" in which Jonathan initiates a perspectival shift as he distances himself and the reader from the present tense of the events previously related through the insertion of a remove of seven years. He describes the protagonists as purified, saying, "We all went through the flames; and the happiness of some of us since then is, we think, well worth the pain we endured" (326). That all have passed through the flames appears to indicate that they all have been transformed, all been tested or tempered as if steel or some other forged or purified metal. Jonathan then refers to Mina's "secret belief" "that some of our brave friend's spirit" (326), implicitly meaning Quincey, has passed into her son, confiding that the son has been given a "bundle of names" (326) linking "all our little band of men together; but we call him Quincey" (326). This curious phrase reads as if "Quincey" were not the boy's true name at all. Jonathan then accounts for the principal actors and their lives over the intervening years. As Seward and Holmwood have both been incorporated into a syzygy, it is safe to assume that Lucy was never either one's true intended. The Professor has assumed a grandfatherly role in the upbringing of the child. All is right in the heavens.

In The Book of Stoker, transmutation of matter is identical to the transubstantiation of Christ's body and blood, the Host becoming "the sacred emblem" (189). Even as the dead hand at the wheel was termed "emblemship," it is the guiding element and emblem of the sacred discourse that the book promulgates. Its *sacrae particulae* mixed with "some whitish stuff, like dough" (186) allows the Professor to seal bodies hermetically within tombs as if prayers enclosed within bottles. It is the hermetically-sealed grave that becomes the final philosopher's egg. Through the transformational process brought about by King Sol's slaying of Mercurius *senex*, Luna, Madam Mina, is healed, the metaphysical poison drawn out of her by the decimation of Saturn's corrupt material, leaden being; Jung claims, "It is the task of alchemy to root out the original sin, and this is accomplished with the aid of the *balsamum vitae*" (14: 34). No ordinary gold is created in the *magnum opus* of Stoker—quite the opposite.

Jung concedes that

> it must be admitted that the fairytale and alchemy both show Mercurius in a predominantly unfavourable light, which is all the more striking because his positive aspect relates him not only to the Holy Spirit, but, in the form of the lapis, also to Christ and, as a triad, even to the Trinity. It looks as if it were precisely these relationships which led the alchemists to put particular stress on the dark and dubious quality of Mercurius, and this militates strongly against the assumption that by their lapis they really meant Christ [13: 241].

The interest of Mercurius is his potential for enabling transformation, the radiant new Mercurius brings joy and hope after the dark, saturnine dragon has been slain. Mercurius teaches humanity that it is possible to perfect ourselves, to change, to overcome the blacker than black that is within our nature and to find the gold that is surely hidden within as if a deep, bright secret, indeed a bright promise. Stoker's fairytale rejects alchemy as anything more than the armature for supporting the Vampire, refusing any Faustian bargain. When Jonathan declares, "I would sell my soul to do it!" (265), meaning to kill the Count, he is recalled to the service of Christ. Like Mina, he must maintain his soul at all costs.

As he sets off, Jonathan muses, "We saw little towns or castles on the top of steep hills such as we see in old missals" (11); as the Professor arrives at the end of the world he notes, "We were near the top of a steep-rising hill, on summit of which was such a castle as Jonathan tell of in his diary" (316). In the last of Stoker's missal's illustrations, (which so resembles an alchemist's picture book), Mina stands a Marian figure by Mercurius's perched castle, expired serpent at her feet, heavenly objects beginning to appear in the night sky, Mina's face illuminated by a divine light. In the illuminated manuscript of Stoker, suddenly all becomes clear. More than a single Dionysian creature of the night invaded the day when from the "black mass of Kettleness" (75) *The Demeter* washed ashore and ran aground with her dark cargo at Whitby; it was sky of Night herself that appeared at mid–summer to wrest dominion from Day.

Stoker has represented a *coniunctio oppositorium* and great work like no other, and in so doing he has purified earlier renditions of the Tale of the Vampire. Because of him, it is now clear that Nodier's Lovette, the character whose pursuit across the proscenium into the audience's side of the theater so shocked the Parisian critic of two centuries ago, was the goddess Venus herself, due to wed Edgar, the servant from Marsden whose name references Ares' principal attribute, the lance. They underwent their ordeal to permit the orphaned Aubrey brother and sister to renew Mercurius, who dissolves into prime matter no doubt to emerge again. The growls of thunder that sounded in the plays of

Nodier and Dumas were the voice of Jupiter. The out-of-plot death of Ruthven's brother, the Baron of Marsden — that is, Mars himself— was forever essential to enabling the saturnine, Diosyian Vampire to access Aubray's lunar sister, whose "soul concious of a brighter realm" was "never brightened by the smile of joy; but when her brother breathed to her his affection"(278). The cycle has been completed; the ring that Byron's Darvell had Aubrey toss into the Blessed Bay has been recovered. Petrus Bonus observes that "gold being worked up into different shapes is called by different names, such as ring, bracelet, crown, etc., though in substance all these are nothing but gold" (150). Ring, bracelet, and crown may all be of one substance but they are also of one shape, the ovoid of the Ouboros. This is what has been clarified. One shape, one matter, *Unus mundus*. The philosophy that has endured since ancient times and informs the parables of Jesus reads as a missal to instruct the modern era. The marriage and birth viewed in the Telesterion of Eleusis is related to the wedding chamber ceremony of the Gnostics and the *Chymical Wedding* of the alchemists and certain rites of Hermetic orders of our current period, but they also inform and interact with the sacred history of Jesus Christ.

Nearly two decades prior to Marcel Duchamp's introduction of the notion of "readymade" art, Stoker created a masterful example. The *Chymical*

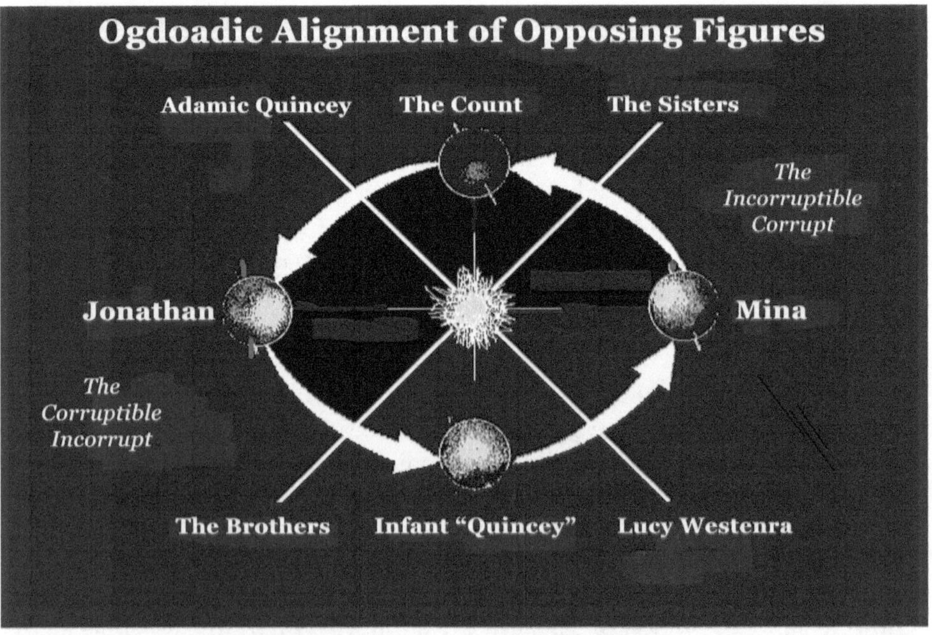

Coniunctio oppositorium. © Rarignac

Wedding contains the essence of *Dracula*'s plot, and perhaps represents the very genesis of Stoker's *magnum opus*. Alchemy reveals that the project was born whole, alive, hermaphroditic, and sacred, albeit with crowning Christian foliage, a Gnostic trunk, and ancient, pre–Christian roots. The baroque tale of *Chymical Wedding, hieros gamos*, and *coniunctio oppositorium*, already present in the Vampire Tale, provided the firm basis for further development beyond the few mornings that Polidori had to dedicate to his summer love. What becomes apparent through Stoker's retelling of the Tale is that the ancient Mysteries, the Gnostic texts, fragments of Cathari creed, and hermetic alchemical allegories, concern the same aspects of humanistic beliefs that embrace with the basic tenets of the teachings of Christ in a pre-schismatic, indeed pre-institutional, form. Michael Maier, reminding one and all to be true Harkers, might have been speaking of Stoker's *Dracula* when in "A Subtle Allegory Concerning the Secrets of Alchemy" he states, "Now, this whole tale ... is addressed to the mind rather than to the ear; it is a mystical narrative, and like the hieroglyphics of the Egyptians, should be mystically (not historically) understood" (*Hermetic Museum* II 219). May the soul of Vlad Tepes find repose! Eternal rest grant unto him, O Lord; and let perpetual light shine upon him. May he rest in peace. Amen.

Bibliography

Anderson, William, and Clive Hicks. *Green Man*. London: Harper Collins, 1990.
Arras, Jean d'. *Le Roman de Mélusine*. Translated by Michèle Perret. Paris: Stock, 1979.
Baring-Gould, Sabin. *Curious Myths of the Middle Ages*. London: Routledge & Sons, 1885.
Bataille, Georges. *Le Procès de Gilles de Rais*. Paris: 10/18, 1974.
Belford, Barbara. *Bram Stoker and the Man Who Was Dracula*. Cambridge, MA: Da Capo, 1996.
Benjamin, Walter. *Illuminations*. Edited by Hannah Arendt. New York: Schocken, 1969.
Berard, Cyprien. *Lord Ruthwen ou Les Vampires, Roman de C. B. ...* (see Charles Nodier). Paris: Ladvocat, 1820.
The Bible. The Holy Bible Translated from the Latin Vulgate. New York: Apostolate, 1955.
Blavatsky, Helena Petrova. *The Secret Doctrine*. Edited by Michael Gomes. New York: Penguin, 2009.
Bleiler, E. F., ed. *Three Gothic Novels*. New York: Dover, 1966.
Bond, John. *Observations on the Incubus, or Night-Mare*. London: Wilson & Durham, 1753.
Bonus, Petrus. *The New Pearl of Great Price*. Translated by Arthur Edward Waite. London: Elliot & Co., 1894.
Boucicault, Dion. *The Phantom: A Drama in Two Acts* (as performed at Wallack's Theatre NYC). New York: Samuel French, 1856.
Brown, Dan. *The DaVinci Code*. London: Bantam Books, 2003.
Budge, E. A. Wallis. *Egyptian Book of the Dead*. Sacred-texts.com, 2000. First published 1895 by Trustees of the British Library.
Burke, Edmund. *A Philosophical Enquiry into the Sublime and Beautiful and other pre-Revolutionary Writings*. Edited by David Womersley. London: Penguin Books, 1998.
Burton, Richard F. trans. *Vikram and the Vampire, or, Tales of Hindu Devilry*. Edited by Isabel Burton. London: 1893.
Butler, E. M. *Byron and Goethe*. London: Bowes & Bowes, 1956.
Byron, George Gordon. "A Fragment of a Novel." In *Three Gothic Novels*, edited by E. F. Bleiler. New York: Dover, 1966.
Calmet, Augustin. *Traité sur les Apparitions des Esprits, et sur les Vampires, ou des Revenans de Hongrie, de Moraavie, etc.* Paris: 1751.
Charles, Robert Henry. *The Book of Enoch*. Mineola, NY: Dover, 2007.
Cicero. *De Natura Deorum*. Translated by H. Rackham. Cambridge, MA: Harvard University Press, 1967.
Collin de Plancy (Collin de Maury), and Jacques Auguste Simon. *Histoire des vampires et des spectres malfaisans*. Paris: Masson, 1820.
Collins, Wilkie. *The Woman in White*. London: Penguin, 1994. First published 1868.
Cubasch, Waldemar. *Der Alp*. Berlin: 1872.
Dabo, La Veuve, ed. *Chef d'oeuvres du répétoire des Mélodrames Joués à Différents Théâtres* (containing Nodier's *Le Vampire*). Vol. 18. Paris: 1824.

Day, William Patrick. *In the Circles of Fear and Desire*. Chicago: Chicago University Press, 1985.

Dee, John. *Monad Hieroglyphica*. Translated by J. W. Hamilton-Jones. London: Watkins, 1947. First published 1564.

Delassus, Jules. *Les Incubes et les Succubes*. Paris: La Société des Médecins de France, 1892.

Donteville, Henri. *La France Mythologique*. Paris: Payot, 2004.

Dumas, Alexandre (père). *Mes Memoires*. Paris: Robert Lafont, 1989. First published 1853.

_____. *The Return of Lord Ruthven*. Frank J. Morlock's adaptation of *Le Vampire*.

_____. *Théâtre Complet, Onzième Série*. Paris: Michel Lévy Frères, 1865. Encino, CA: Black Coat, 2004.

Durkheim, Emile. *The Elementary Forms of the Religious Life*. London: George Allen & Unwin, 1976. First published 1915.

Eliade, Mircea. *Myth and Reality*. Translated by Willard Trask. New York: Harper Colophon Books, 1975.

Ellman, Maud. "Introduction." In *Dracula*, by Bram Stoker, edited by Maud Ellman, vii–xxviii. New York: Oxford University Press, 1996.

Eyries, Jean-Baptiste Benoît. *Fantasmagoriana, ou Recueil d'histoires d'apparitions de spectres, revenans, fantômes, etc*. Vol. 1. Paris: 1812.

Faber, Henri, trans. "Le Vampire, d'après Lord Byron." In *Les Cent Ans de Dracula*, edited by Barbara Sadoul, 17–39. Paris: Librio/Flammarion, 1997.

"Fama Fraternitas (1617)" in *The Real History of the Rosicrucians*, edited by Arthur Edward Waite. Forgotten Books, 2008. First published 1887 by George Redway.

Farson, Daniel. *The Man Who Wrote Dracula: A Biography of Bram Stoker*. Leicester, UK: Thorpe, 1975.

Ficino, Marsilio. *The Book of the Sun*. Translated by Geoffrey Cornelius, Darby Costello, Graeme Tobyn, Angela Voss and Vernon Wells. http://www.users.globalnet.co.uk/~alfar2/ficino.html. First published 1494.

Fideler, David. *Jesus Christ, Sun of God*. Wheaton, IL: Quest Books, 1993.

Frayling, Christopher. *Vampyres: Lord Byron to Count Dracula*. London: Faber and Faber, 1992.

Frazer, James George. *The Golden Bough: A Study in Magic and Religion*. 2nd and 3rd editions, abridged. Edited by Robert Fraser. Oxford: Oxford University Press, 1994.

Freud, Sigmund. (*Die Traumdeutung*) *On the Interpretation of Dreams*. London: Wordsworth, 1997. First published 1899.

Galland, Antoine. *Les Mille et Une Nuits*. With notes on Galland by Ch. Nodier. Paris: Garnier Frères, 1949.

Gerard, Emily. "From *Transylvanian Superstitions*." In *Dracula, A Norton Critical Edition*, edited by Nina Auerbach and David J. Skal, 331–335. New York: Norton, 1997.

Gilbert, R. A. *The Golden Dawn Scrapbook: The Rise and Fall of a Magical Order*. York Beach, ME: Samuel Weiser, 1997.

Gray, Robert. *The Theory of Dreams: An Inquiry into the Powers and Faculty of the Human Mind as Illustrated by the Most Remarkable Dreams Recorded in Sacred and Profane History*. London: Rivington, 1808.

Grimm, Jacob. *Teutonic Mythology*. Vols. 1–4. Translated by J. S. Stallybrass. London: Bell & Sons, 1882–1884.

Hamilton, Edith. *Mythology: Timeless Tales of Gods and Heroes*. Boston: Little Brown, 1969.

Hennelly, Mark M., Jr. "Betwixt Sunset and Sunrise: Liminality in *Dracula*." *Journal of Dracula* Studies 7 (2005).

_____. "Dracula: The Gnostic Quest and Victorian Wasteland." *English Literature in Transition* 20 (1977): 13–26.

_____. "Through Every Door and Passage: A Liminal Reading of *Camilla*." *Le Fanu Studies* (Autumn 2009).

_____."The Victorian Book of the Dead." *Journal of Evolutionary Psychology* XII, XIII, XIV (1992, 1993, 1994).

Heraclitus. "The Verses of Heraclitus of Ephesus." Translated by Malcolm Crowe. *Systemic* 18 (1996): 161–76. http://cis.paisley.ac.uk/crow-ci0/Articles/heraclitus.html, accessed 2009/04/01.

Hesiod. *The Theogony*. Translated by Hugh G. Evelyn-White. This edition first published 1914. http://www.sacred-texts.com/cla/hesiod/theogony.htm.

Hobhouse, John Cam. *A Journey Through Albania and Other Provinces of Turkey*. 2 volumes. London: John Cawthorn, 1813.

Homer. *Homeric Hymns*. Translated by Apostolos Athanassaki. Baltimore: Johns Hopkins University Press, 1976.

Hugo, Victor. *Préface de Cromwell*. Paris: Larousse, Petits Classiques, 2001.

Jones, Ernest. *On the Nightmare*. New York: Grove Press, 1959. First published 1931.

Jung, Carl Gustave. *Alchemical Studies*. Bollinger Series XX, vol. 13. Translated by R. F. C. Hull. Princeton, NJ: Princeton University Press, 1983.

_____. *Mysterium Coniunctionis*. Bollinger Series XX, vol. 14. Translated by R. F. C. Hull. Princeton, NJ: Princeton University Press, 1977.

_____, and Carl Kerényi. *Essays on a Science of Mythology: The Myth of the Divine Child and the Mysteries of Eleusis*. Bollinger Series XXII. Translated by R. F. C. Hull. New York: Pantheon Books, 1949.

Keats, John. "La Belle Dame Sans Merci," and "Ode to a Nightingale." In *John Keats : The Complete Poems*, 3rd edition, edited by John Barnard. London: Penguin Books, 1988.

Keightley, Thomas. *The Fairy Mythology Illustrative of the Romance and Superstition of Various Countries*. 3rd edition. London: 1870. http://camelot.celtictwilight/otherworld/fairy_mythology/France.htm#melusina, accessed 2005/10/21.

Kérenyi, Carl. *Eleusis: Archetypal Image of Mother and Daughter*. Translated by Ralph Manheim. Princeton, NJ: Princeton University Press, 1967.

King, Charles William. *The Gnostics and Their Remains*. Forgotten Books, 2008. First published 1887.

King, Francis. *Ritual Magic of the Golden Dawn*. Rochester, VT: Destiny Books, 1997.

Kirk, G. S. *Heraclitus: The Cosmic Fragments, A Critical Study*. Cambridge, UK: Cambridge University Press, 1954.

Lamb, Caroline. *Glenarvon*. Edited by Frances Wilson. London: Dent, 1995. First published 1816.

Leach, Edmund. *Culture and Communications*. Cambridge, UK: Cambridge University Press, 1976.

Lebois, André. *Un Bréviaire du Compagnonnage: La Fée aux Miettes*. Paris: Minard, 1961.

Lévi, Eliphas. *Dogme et Rituel de la Haute Magie*. Paris: Baillière, 1856.

MacDonald, David Lorne. *Poor Polidori: A Critical Biography of the Author of "The Vampyre."* Toronto, CA: University of Toronto Press, 1991.

Macnish, Robert. *The Philosophy of Sleep*. Glasgow, UK: W. R. McPhun, 1838.

MacPherson, James. *The Poems of Ossian*. Edited by Howard Gaskill. Edinburgh, UK: Edinburgh University Press, 1996.

Maier, Michael. "The Secrets of Alchemy: A Subtle Allegory." In *The Hermetic Museum*, by A. E. Waite. London: Elliot & Co., 1893.

Mann, Nicholas. "The Isle of Avalon." *Druidways@ukonline.co.uk*, accessed 2003/08/01.

Martin-Civat, Pierre. *Le Très Simple Secret de Mélusine*. Poitiers, FR: Impr. P. Oudin, 1969.

Meade, G. R. S., ed. *The Pistis Sophia*. London: Watkins, 1921.

Medwin, Thomas. *Journal of the Conversations of Lord Byron*. London: Henry Colburn, 1824.

Miller, Elizabeth. "*Dracula 2* The Sequel?" Revised conference paper.

_____. "The *Dracula* We Might Have Read: What Stoker Cut from His Manuscript." Presented 21 May 2009, Conference of the International Association of the Fantastic in the Arts, Orlando, FL.

Nodier, Charles. *Lord Ruthwen ou Les Vampires*. Marseilles, FR: Lafitte, 1978. First published 1820.

_____. "Le Vampire ou Lord Rutwen." In *Chef d'oeuvres du Répétoire des Mélodrames Joués à Différents Théâtres*, vol. 18, 327–401. Paris: 1824.

Oliver, A. Richard. *Charles Nodier: Pilot of Romanticism*. Syracuse, NY: Syracuse University Press, 1964.

Otto, Rudolf. *Idea of the Holy*. Translated by John W. Harvey. London: Oxford University Press, 1958.

Otto, Walter F. *Dionysus: Myth and Cult*. Translated by Robert B. Palmer. Bloomington: Indiana University Press, 1965.

Ovid. *The Metamorphoses*. Translated by Sir Samuel Garth and John Dryden. http://classics.mit.edu.

Paracelsus. *The Hermetic and Alchemical Writings of Paracelsus*. Translated by Arthur Edward Waite. Forgotten Books, 2010. First published 1894.

Pausanias. *Guide to Greece To Which the translator has added extensive notes concerning the theological and philosophical significance of Pausanias' descriptions*. Volume I. Translated by Thomas Taylor. (1825 edition). Sturminster Newton, Dorset, UK: The Prometheus Trust, 2006.

_____. *Guide to Greece, Volume I: Central Greece*. Translated by Peter Levi. London: Penguin Books, 1971.

Perrault, Charles. "La Barbe-bleue." In *Les Contes de Fées*. 1865. http://www.gaslight.mtroyal.ab.ca/GASLIGHT/barbleu.htm, accessed 2009/04/07.

Phlegon of Tralles. *Book of Marvels*. Translated by William Hansen. Exeter, UK: University of Exeter Press, 1996.

Planché, James Robert. *Recollections and Reflections of J. R. Planché*. London, 1872.

_____. *The Vampire, or The Bride of the Isles*. In Wischhussen, *The Hour of One: Six Gothic Melodramas*. London: Gordon Frazer Gallery, 1975.

Plato. *Phaedrus*. Translated by Benjamin Jowett. Forgotten Books, 2008.

_____. *The Republic*. Translated and edited by Francis MacDonald Cornford. New York: Oxford University Press, 1959.

Plutarch. *Isis and Osiris*. Cambridge, MA: Loeb Classic Library, 1936.

Polidori, John William. *The Diary of John William Polidori Relating to Byron, Shelley, etc*. Edited by William Michael Rossetti. London: Elkin-Mathews, 1911.

_____. *"The Vampire" and Other Writings*. Edited by Franklin Charles Bishop. Manchester, UK: Carcanet, 2005.

Quincey, Thomas de. *Essays of Thomas de Quincey*. London: Ward, Lock & Co., 1886.

Richardson, N. J. *The Homeric Hymn to Demeter*. Oxford, UK: Clarendon Press, 1974.

Robinson, James M., ed. *Nag Hammadi*. Translated by members of the Coptic Gnostic Library Project, Institute for Antiquity and Christianity, Claremont, California. New York: HarperCollins, 1988.

Rosenkreutz, Christian (as anon.). *Chymical Wedding* (1616). In *The Real History of the Rosicrucians*, edited by Arthur Edward Waite. Forgotten Books, 2008. First published 1887 by George Redway.

Sadoul, Barbara, ed. *Les Cent Ans de Dracula*. Paris: Librio/Flammarion, 1997.

Schenck, Eunice M. *La Part de Charles Nodier dans la Formation des Idées de Victor Hugo jusqu'à la "Préface de Cromwell."* Paris: Campion, 1914.

Schliemann, Heinrich. "Exploration of the Boeotian Orchomenus." *The Journal of Hellenic Studies* 2 (1881): 122–163.

Skal, David J., and Elias Savada. *Dark Carnival: The Secret World of Tod Browning—Hollywood's Master of the Macabre*. New York: Anchor Books, 1995.

Smollet, Tobias. *The Adventures of Ferdinand Count Fathom*. New York: Penguin Classics, 1990. First published 1753.

Snorre. *The Younger Edda (The Prose Edda)*. Translated by Rasmus B. Anderson. Chicago: Griggs & Co., 1879. Gutenberg Project ebook.

Staël, Germaine. *De l'Allemagne*. Paris: Garnier-Flammarian, 1968. First published 1810.

Stoker, Abraham. *Bram Stoker's Notes for* Dracula. Edited by Robert Eighteen-Bisang and Elizabeth Miller. Jefferson, NC: McFarland, 2008.

_____. *Dracula: A Norton Critical Edition*. Edited by Nina Auerbach and David J. Skal. New York: Norton, 1997.

_____. *Dracula or The Un-Dead: A Play in Prologue and Five Acts*. Edited by Sylvia Starshine. Nottingham, UK: Pumpkin Books, 1997.

Summers, Montague. *The Vampire*. New York: Dorset Press, 1991.
Taylor, Thomas. *Eleusian and Bacchic Mysteries: A Dissertation*. Edited by Alexander Wilder. San Diego, CA: Wizards Bookshelf, 1997. First published 1791.
Tournefort, Joseph Pitton de, and Bernard le Bouyer de Fontanelle. *Relation d'un Voyage du Levant Fait par Ordre du Roy*. 2 vols. Paris: 1717.
Twitchell, James B. *Dreadful Pleasures*. New York: Oxford University Press, 1985.
Utterson, Sarah Elizabeth Brown. *Tales of the Dead*. Edited by T.J. Hale. Chislehurst, UK: Gothic Society, 1992. First published 1813.
Varma, Devendra P. *The Gothic Flame*. London: The Scarecrow Press, Inc., 1987.
Villa-Nova, Arnyldus de. *Rosarium Philosophorum*. Jean, NV: Rex Research. http://www.rexresearch.com.
Waite, Arthur Edward, ed. and tr. *Collectanea Chemica*. London: J. Elliot & Co., 1893.
_____. *The Hermetical Museum*. Vols. I and II. London: J. Elliot & Co., 1893.
_____. *The New Pearl of Great Price*. London: J. Elliot & Co., 1894.
_____. *The Turba Philosophorum*. London: George Redway, 1896.
Waller, John. *Treatise on the Incubus or Night-Mare, Disturbed Sleep, Terrific Dreams and Nocturnal Visions*. London: Cox & Son, 1816.
Walsh, Townsend. *The Career of Dion Boucicault*. New York: The Dunlap Society, 1915.
Wischhusen, Stephen. *The Hour of One: Six Gothic Melodramas*. London: Gordon Frazer Gallery, 1975.
Witt, R. E. *Isis in the Graeco-Roman World*. London: Camelot Press, 1971.
Zimmerman, Daniel. *Alexandre Dumas le Grand*. Paris: Juliard, 1993.

Index